D0947180

TYPO
GRAPHY
XXXVII

Typography 37

© 2016 by
the Type Directors Club

All rights reserved. No part
of this book may be used or
reproduced in any manner
whatsoever without written
permission except in the case
of brief quotations embodied
in critical articles and reviews.

First Edition

First published in 2016 by:
Verlag Hermann Schmidt
Gonsenheimer Str. 56
D 55126 Mainz
Germany
Tel: +49 6131 50 60 0
Fax: +49 6131 50 60 80
info@verlag-hermann-schmidt.de
www.typografie.de
www.verlag-hermann-schmidt.de
facebook:
Verlag Hermann Schmidt
twitter: VerlagHSchmidt

verlag hermann schmidt

ISBN: 978-3-87439-890-9

Type Directors Club
Carol Wahler
347 West 36 Street
Suite 603
New York, NY 10018
Tel: 212-633-8943
e: director@tdc.org
w: tdc.org

Printed in China

Acknowledgments

The Type Directors Club
gratefully acknowledges the
following for their support and
contributions to the success
of TDC62 and TDC2016:

BOOK DESIGN
Bobby C. Martin Jr.•
Michael McCaughley
OCD | The Original Champions
of Design
originalchampionsofdesign.com

PRODUCTION
Adam S. Wahler for
A to A Studio Solutions, Ltd.

EDITING
Dave Baker
Super Copy Editors

JUDGING FACILITIES
Pratt Institute, Manhattan
Campus

EXHIBITION FACILITIES
The Cooper Union

CHAIRPERSONS' AND JUDGES'
PHOTOS
Catalina Kulczar-Marin

TDC62 COMPETITION
CALL FOR ENTRIES DESIGN
Bobby C. Martin Jr.•
Michael McCaughley
Matt Kay
OCD | The Original Champions
of Design
originalchampionsofdesign.com

ONLINE SUBMISSION
APPLICATION
AND DEVELOPMENT
adcSTUDIO

The principal typeface used
in Typography 37 is Neue
Haas Unica. This typeface was
designed by Toshi Omagari
and distributed by Monotype
in 2015. It is a revival of Unica,
designed by Team '77 in 1980
for the Haas Type Foundry.

OCD | The Original
Champions of Design thrives
on creating brand identity
systems for companies that
have a lot to lose. Using a
strategic approach grounded
in understanding the essence
of each brand, OCD has been
able to develop beautiful and
distinctive systems that stand
the test of time.

• Signifies TDC member

Z
243
.A2
T9a
v.37

GREENWOOD LIBRARY
LONGWOOD UNIVERSITY
REDFORD & RACE STREET
FARMVILLE, VA 23909

LONGWOOD LIBRARY

1000507594

TDC Medalist
Louise Fili

The Type Directors Club awarded its twenty-eighth medal of excellence to Louise Fili for her outstanding work as a graphic designer whose work, from book jackets to restaurant logos and packaging, has emphasized the beauty and power of letterforms.

For over forty years Louise Fili has created some of the most sumptuous, elegant and rich graphic design in America. Fili started her career as a senior designer for Herb Lubalin, working for the legendary designer from 1976 to 1978. Instead of following Lubalin's love for using type expressively, treating letters as the building blocks of elaborate yet compact textual structures and creating visual puns, Fili took a different tack. In this she was influenced by studio client Harris Lewine, art director at Harcourt Brace Jovanovich, who introduced her to design history.

As art director at Pantheon Books from 1978 to 1989, Fili's book jackets—she designed nearly two thousand of them—were marked by the use of type and lettering that resonated with historical, cultural, and literary allusions. Her book jackets avoided the charges of pastiche and nostalgia with their nimble twists of source material and skillful execution. The success of *The Lover* by Marguerite Duras (1985), a runaway bestseller for Pantheon, validated Fili's design history approach to jacket design. This approach marked an end to The Big Book Look pioneered by Paul Bacon that had dominated American publishing for nearly two decades. Fili's work brought back subtlety and intimacy to book jacket design. Her use of pastels and secondary colors, outmoded typefaces and styles of lettering, and unpredictable typographic layouts (including centering and letterspacing titles) represented a direct challenge to the reigning tenets of Swiss modernist design. Fili helped make complexity and richness in graphic design acceptable again.

Fili's work for Pantheon and other publishers in the 1980s was impressive, but it was only her first act. When she left Pantheon in 1989 to set up Louise Fili Ltd., she moved away from the book world and embraced the fickle but fun restaurant world. Her work for restaurants past and present, such as Picholine, Artisanal, The Mermaid Inn, Txikito, Metrazur, and Bolivar, brought a quietly urbane sensibility to the New York food world. Once she began working for restaurants it was inevitable that Fili quickly added package design to her repertoire. She has applied her trademark elegance and cultivated taste to products from Jean-Georges Vongerichten, Bella Cucina, American Spoon, Sarabeth's, and others.

Fili's work with its distinctive historicist aesthetic has had an enormous impact on American typographic tastes over the past four decades. That impact has been amplified since 1993 by a series of books co-written by Fili with her husband, Steven Heller. The Fili style has been further spread by the work of her alumni, foremost among them Dana Tanamachi and Jessica Hische.

Lost in the emphasis on Fili's luscious aesthetic and her deep plumbing of the typographic past is her role as part of a generation of women in the early 1980s who changed the gender dynamics of the graphic design profession. Since she opened her own practice over a quarter of a century ago she has been a role model for women designers, proof that they can escape the gilded ghetto of publishing and succeed in the broader world of graphic design without the aid of a male partner or the need to don masculine attitudes. Her small studio has nurtured a succession of women designers who have come to the fore as part of a new twenty-first-century century generation of eclectic typographers.

Paul Shaw

Tribute to
Adrian Frutiger

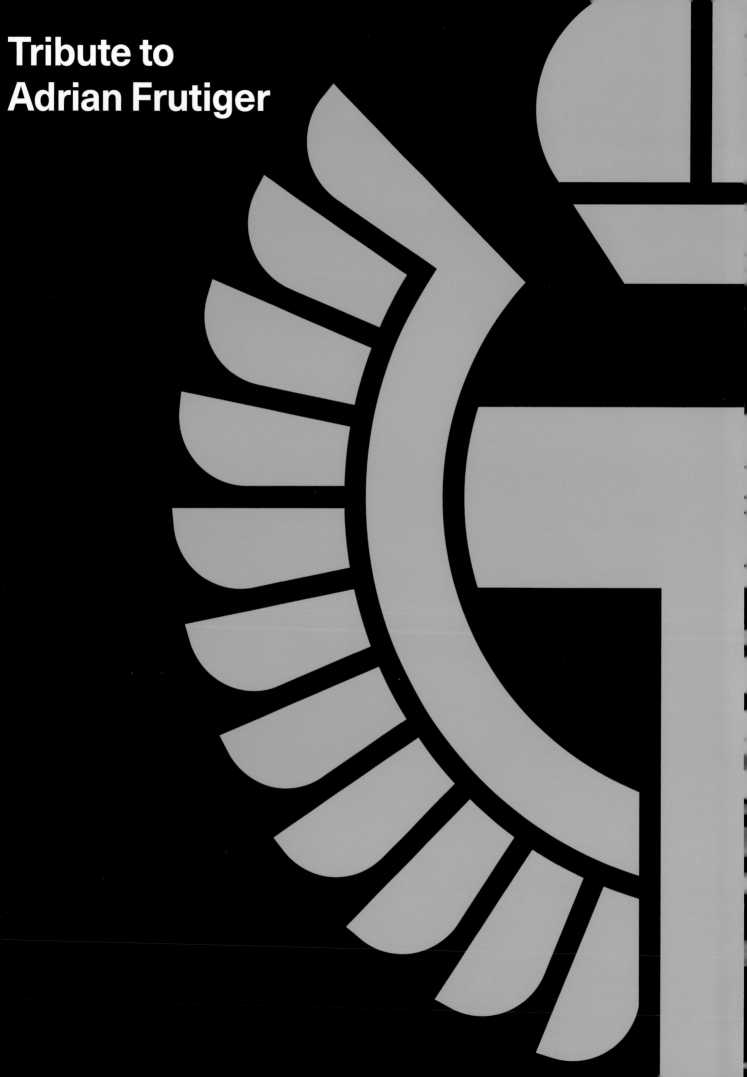

Type designer Adrian Frutiger, who died on September 10, 2015, is best remembered today for the design of the beautiful and popular sans serif typefaces Univers, Frutiger, and Avenir. Of these, Univers is perhaps most famous because of its modernity and large, well-organized family of styles. Typophiles often compare Univers to Helvetica, which was also released in the mid-1950s. Type historian Sebastian Carter describes Univers as "carefully and sweetly drawn," and distinctive because "it eliminated virtually everything but the essential forms of the letters."

The use of the word "sweetly" to describe Frutiger's draftsmanship says something about the depth of feeling and thoughtfulness that Frutiger brought to type design. He was artistic and philosophical, aware of the importance of hand craftsmanship and sensitive to the long history of letterforms. In his designs, the balance of contrast between black and white and positive and negative became almost mystical, evidence of his contemplative observation of the natural world.

France was Frutiger's home for most of his working life, first at the Paris foundry Deberny et Piegnot, then at his own studio near Paris. His typeface designs led to commissions for clients such as the Paris Orly and Charles de Gaulle airports, the Paris Métro, IBM, and the Centre Pompidou. The de Gaulle airport signage alphabet, named Roissy for the village where the airport was built, was later adapted by Linotype and named Frutiger after its designer. The typeface was so effective for signage that the French highway system adopted Frutiger for its roadside signs. Adrian claimed the typeface was his favorite.

Of course, Adrian Frutiger leaves us the legacy of his typefaces and a high standard of excellence in type design, but he and his wife, Simone, a theologian, left a humanitarian legacy as well: the Fondation Adrian et Simone Frutiger, an institution devoted to improving mental health services for young people. Appropriately, the foundation's logo uses Frutiger's poetic symbols of the stages of human life.

To commemorate Frutiger's life and work, the Type Directors Club asked renowned type designer Matthew Carter to speak about his old friend. The TDC is very grateful to Carter for his moving memorial, which took place at the Parsons School of Design on April 26, 2016.

The Type Directors Club awarded its TDC Medal to Adrian Frutiger in 1987. A selection of other awards he received are:

Prix du Département Fédéral de l Intérieur en Suisse (1950), Chevalier des Arts et des Lettres de France (1968), Prix Gutenberg de la Ville de Mayence (RFA) (1986), Officier de l'Ordre des Arts et des Lettres de France (1990), SOTA Typography Award. Boston (2006), Prix Designer, Office fédéral de la Culture à Berne (2007)

Doug Clouse

Alpha BP
Alphabet Algol
Alphabet Brancher
Alphabet EDF-GDF
Alphabet Entreprise Francis
Bouygues
Alphabet Facom
Alphabet Georges Pompidou
Alphabet Orly
Alphabet Métro
Alphabet Roissy
Apollo
Avenir
Breughel
Caracteres Lumitype
Concorde
Delta
Devanagari / Tamil
Documenta
Dolmen
Egyptienne F
Element-Grotesk
Federduktus
Frutiger
Frutiger Arabic
Frutiger (de Gaulle)
Frutiger Capitalis
Frutiger Neonscript
Frutiger Stones
Frutiger Symbols
Gespanate Grotesk
Glypha
Herculanum
Icone
Iridium
Katalog
Linotype Centennial
Linotype Didot
Linotype Univers
Meridien
Nami
OCRB
Ondine
Opéra
Président
Phoebus
Pompeijana
Rusticana
Serifen-Grotesk
Serifa
Shiseido
Tiemann
Univers
Univers IBM Composer
Univers Next
Westside
Vectora
Versailes

Tribute to
Hermann Zapf

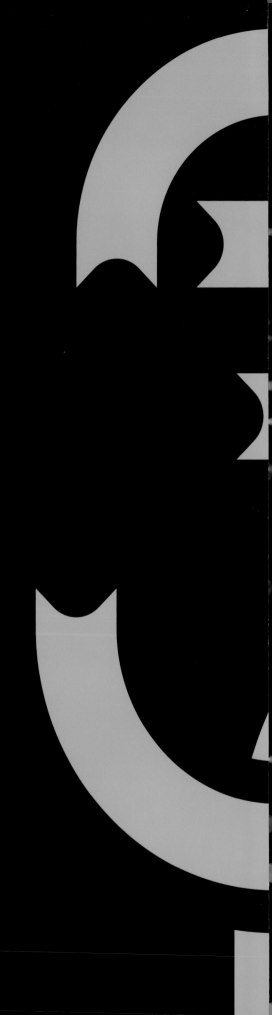

Hermann Zapf, the masterful calligrapher, subtly innovative type designer, and recipient of the very first TDC Medal (in 1967), died in 2015 at the age of ninety-six. Over eight decades, Zapf's long career in type design spanned hot metal composition, phototypesetting, and digital design. He produced more than 200 fonts, including some of the most recognized and widely used typefaces of the twentieth century: Palatino (1948), Melior (1952), Optima (1958), Zapf Dingbats (1978), Zapf Chancery (1979), and Zapfino (1998).

Zapf was born in Nuremberg, Germany, in 1918. His desire to become an electrical engineer stymied, Zapf began an apprenticeship as a photo retoucher in 1934. Soon after, Zapf was inspired by an exhibition devoted to the work of typographer and calligrapher Rudolf Koch (1876–1934). He taught himself calligraphy and studied the work of British penman Edward Johnston. Zapf designed his first typeface in 1938, the ornately calligraphic broken script Gilgengart for D. Stempel AG foundry.

After WWII Zapf created Palatino, which he named after sixteenth century Italian writing master Giambattista Palatino. Based on classical Italian Renaissance forms, the face was created with large, open counters for optimal legibility. It received international exposure when Standard Oil adopted the face in 1956. Among Zapf's numerous designs, Palatino is probably the most well-known. Adapted for digital use, the typeface is incorporated into the Macintosh computer—as are Optima and Zapf Dingbats, the idiosyncratic and beloved proto-emoji symbol face. Zapf produced more than a thousand symbols from which about 360 were chosen by ITC for the final release. In 1994, David Carson, editor of the magazine *Ray Gun*, chose to typeset an interview he disliked entirely in Zapf dingbats, rendering it an illegible cryptogram.

Optima was reported to be Zapf's favorite of his typefaces. A flared sans serif, it is a quietly revolutionary type that bridged the thicks and thins of traditional serifs with sans serif modernity. Optima began

as a few characters sketched hastily onto a thousand-lire note as Zapf admired the carved lettering in the Basilica di Santa Croce in Florence. In 1982, the face was chosen for the Vietnam Veterans Memorial in Washington, D.C., and also appears on the September 11 Memorial in New York.

Zapf's career was informed by a synthesis of history and technology. He was one of the first type designers to embrace the computer. Many of his faces, including Palatino and Optima, were designed for hot metal type, but in the 1960s he also began experimenting, designing, and adapting earlier designs for phototypesetting, the first computer-aided form of typesetting. He later developed Marconi, the first font for digital use, in 1973. In 1976 the Rochester Institute of Technology offered him a professorship in typographic computer programming, the first of its kind in the world. There he collaborated with computer scientists and made contacts at IBM and Xerox. In the early 1990s, Zapf drew on his technological experience to develop typesetting software called Hz-program, which dealt with glyph scaling and optical kerning. The program was acquired by Adobe Systems, and its algorithm later informed Adobe InDesign.

Adapting Zapfino, a dynamic calligraphic font with contextual ligatures and glyph substitutions, was Zapf's last type design project. Working for over two years with Lebanese type designer Dr. Nadine Chahine, they transposed the cursive into Arabic script (2014).

In addition to the faces for which he is best known, Zapf also designed books and postage stamps, as well as typefaces for Hallmark. Writing at the time of a Zapf retrospective exhibition at the Grolier Club in New York (2000), *New York Times* art critic Roberta Smith said of Zapf, "… his career demonstrates the combination of natural (probably prodigious) talent, early achievement and continued growth and innovation that we demand of major artists."

Angela Voulangas

Aldus
Aldus Nova
URW Antiqua
Aurelia
URW Classico
Comenius
Edison
AMS Euler
URW Grotesk
Hunt Roman
Kompakt
URW Latino
Marconi
Medici Script
Melior
Michelangelo
Noris Script
Optima
Optima Nova
Orion
Palatino
Palatino Arabic
Palatino Nova
Palatino Sans
Palatino Sans Informal
URW Palladio
Saphir
Sistina
Vario
Venture Script
Virtuosa Classic
ITC Zapf Book
ITC Zapf Chancery
ITC Zapf Dingbats
Linotype Zapf Essentials
Zapf Humanist
ITC Zapf International
Zapf Renaissance Antiqua
Zapfino
Zapfino Extra

Communication
Design

Chairmen's Statement

It is a privilege to oversee an international competition of this caliber and an honor to be asked. We were surprised to learn that we were the first team to co-chair the TDC Communication Design competition. Looking back, we can't imagine any other way. Our friendship grew and we thoroughly enjoyed the camaraderie. We hope our partnership has started a new tradition. Hats off to the past judges who flew solo. You have our admiration.

Our first charge was to choose a designer for the TDC62 Call for Entries and the Typography 37 annual. Bobby Martin of OCD | The Original Champions of Design took on the daunting task of designing for an audience of designers. From our initial meeting and launch of the TDC62 Call for Entries website through to the book you have in your hands, OCD has been a dream collaborator. They put in countless hours crafting and fine-tuning their dynamic design and met our often demanding deadlines and infuriating social media frenzies with professionalism and conviviality.

Our next assignment was to choose the judges. We were set on getting a mix and balance of diversity, specialty, and location. We were thrilled that everyone we invited accepted and cleared their busy schedules to spend a weekend indoors in New York City looking at over two thousand submissions from forty-nine countries in a multitude of media. This can be fun and thought-provoking, but it can also be perplexing and demanding. Carol and her team made sure we all had plenty of food, conversation, and caffeine to keep us going. There was so much incredible talent in the rooms throughout the weekend. In addition to the designers whose work was on display and the judges there were the many TDC members and board members who graciously volunteered their time, all amazing Creatives in their own rights. A sincere thanks to everyone who made the judging a special occasion.

This year's competition again demonstrates the Type Directors Club's ongoing commitment to excellence and innovation in typography and design. The TDC is the only design organization that we know of that not only sponsors a rigorously judged competition but continues year after year to print an annual and compile a traveling exhibition of the winners. It is worth noting here that Carol Wahler single-handedly manages everything, and we mean every minute detail. She supervises the competition, oversees the publication, and gathers all the 378 winning entries into an exhibition that travels to more than twelve countries throughout the year. Carol, you are simply amazing and a pleasure to work with.

As co-chairs of TDC62, we are both gratified and humbled by the experience. We witnessed the immense magnitude of talent that is at work today and we acquired a deeper appreciation of our complex profession as it rapidly evolves with new technology and global connectivity.

We extend our deepest gratitude to the judges: Darhil Crooks, Sagi Haviv, Robbin Schiff, Jarik van Sluijs, Karen Welman, Forest Young, and Julia Zeltser for their time and expertise; to Lisa Ward, TDC social media director, Chris Andreola, TDC web developer and Catalina Kulczar, photographer. Without them, this competition would not have looked so good or been the success it is. We also want to thank Graham Glifford, TDC Chair, and Matteo Bolgona, TDC President, for their anecdotes, advice, and prodding; to Doug Clouse for sharing his experience of last year's competition; and to Roberto de Vicq de Cumptich. Without Roberto's direction during the judging weekend, there might have been rioting and chaos. We also want to extend our gratitude to Bertram Schmidt-Friderichs for publishing this year's Typography 37 and to Adam Wahler for his production on the annual and printed collateral. Again, we want to thank Carol Wahler, the director of TDC, for her infinite wisdom, love, and guidance. And lastly, to all the TDC members— without your support this competition and annual would not exist.

We hope this book and its content will challenge and inspire the viewer, as we were challenged and inspired.

Abby Goldstein and Karl Heine

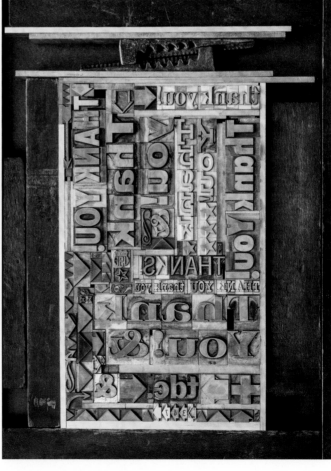

Judges

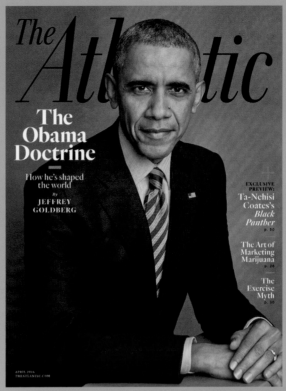

Darhil Crooks

Darhil Crooks is Creative Director of *The Atlantic*. In this role, Crooks oversees the art direction of *The Atlantic* across its platforms: in print, online, and on mobile and tablet devices.

Before joining *The Atlantic*, Crooks worked as Creative Director of *Ebony* magazine, where he oversaw the first cover-to-cover redesign in the title's then sixty-six year history. Working closely with editors, photographers, and illustrators, he helped redefine the magazine's visual identity.

Prior to that, Crooks served as the Art Director of *Esquire* magazine, developing

design concepts and layouts; conceptualizing, commissioning, and directing photo shoots; and editing photography. He also helped develop and design *Esquire*'s iPad app, which was named a finalist for best mobile edition by the American Society of Magazine Editors in 2011. Before joining *Esquire*, Crooks was the Associate Art Director at *Complex* and *Men's Journal*. He began his design career at *The Source*.

Crooks studied Graphic Design at the School of Visual Arts in New York City.

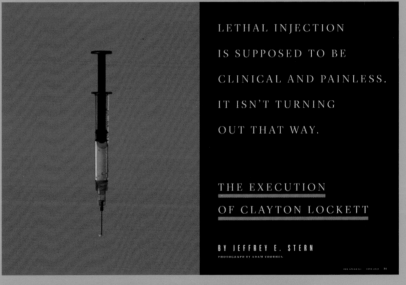

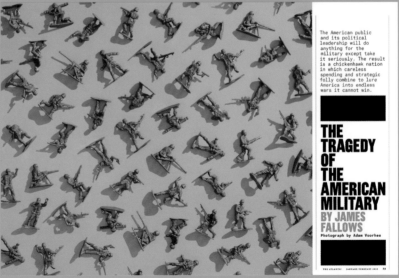

24

Sagi Haviv

Sagi Haviv is a partner and designer at Chermayeff & Geismar & Haviv. Among the more than fifty identity programs he has designed are the logos for the Library of Congress, CFA Institute, Harvard University Press, Conservation International, Women's World Banking, and Armani Exchange.

Sagi designed the award-winning animation "Logomotion," a ten-minute tribute to the firm's famous trademarks that was not only the first animated trademark sequence of such scope, but also introduced a new approach to showcasing a firm's portfolio. Sagi's other motion graphics work includes the opening sequences for PBS documentary series such as *Carrier, Circus, and Half the Sky*.

Sagi joined the firm in 2003 after graduating from The Cooper Union School of Art. He teaches Visual Identity Design at the School of Visual Arts in New York City. A frequent speaker, Sagi has given lectures and conducted workshops at AIGA conferences, the HOW conference, the Onassis Foundation, as well as at design schools and institutions around the world, including an annual workshop at Centro School of Design in Mexico City. In 2014, he served as the chair of the CLIO awards design jury. Sagi is coauthor of *Identify: Basic Principles of Identity Design in the Iconic Trademarks of Chermayeff & Geismar* (Print Publishers, 2011).

Robbin Schiff

A native New Yorker, Robbin
Schiff is VP, Executive Director,
at Random House, where she
has designed and art-directed
award-winning book jackets
for the past twenty-four years.

Jarik van Sluijs

Jarik van Sluijs is co-founder and creative director at PIC Agency, an entertainment and motion design boutique based in Los Angeles, California.

Moving from his native Holland to Los Angeles in 2000, Jarik started his professional career in motion picture advertising as a designer, animator, and editor. In 2001, he earned the Hollywood Reporter Key Art Award for his work on the theatrical teaser for *A.I.* He became a creative director in 2003, and started working on title sequences for feature films like *Van Helsing*, *The Punisher*, and *The Bourne Supremacy*. Since 2005 he's been a founding partner at PIC Agency, and has created more than a hundred feature film title sequences including *The Illusionist*, *The Kingdom*, *Ghostrider*, *Bhutto*, *Sex and the City*, *Cloverfield*, *Twilight*, *Cabin in the Woods*, and *Miss You Already*.

Karen Welman

Karen has always been the curious creative explorer, pushing us beyond what we can see by continually questioning what is possible.

Count on her for the unique, unexpected (and often frank!) viewpoint. She loves working with brave thinkers; those prepared to take a risk are often the ones who create real change. Our Green & Blacks design was a defining moment for her, and she's equally proud of our work for Absolut Vodka.

Innovation and turning great ideas into action has been a lifelong passion of Karen. Her patented inventions include 37°, a range of temperature-regulating baby clothes featuring NASA-developed fabrics that picked up awards all over the world. Karen was also named in the Top 10 Global Female Inventors a few years ago.

Karen is always working on something new and in recent years cofounded private members' gym The Library; it's this diversity and the prospect of venturing head-first into the unknown that keeps her burning as brightly as when she started out more than thirty years ago.

Forest Young

Forest Young is a designer and educator. He is the Executive Creative Director at West, leading design across a portfolio of early stage companies. Prior to joining West, Forest led design at Interbrand's New York City studio, supporting the tech accounts AT&T, YP, Vine, Google, and Microsoft. Forest is also a critic in graphic design at the Yale School of Art and a board member of the AIGA NY. His work has been exhibited at MoMA, the Royal Ontario Museum, the Yerba Buena Center for the Arts, and at international biennials. He is the recipient of design accolades including the Cannes Gold Design Lion and the ADC Black Cube. Forest received his MFA from the Yale School of Art where he was awarded the Mark Whistler Prize.

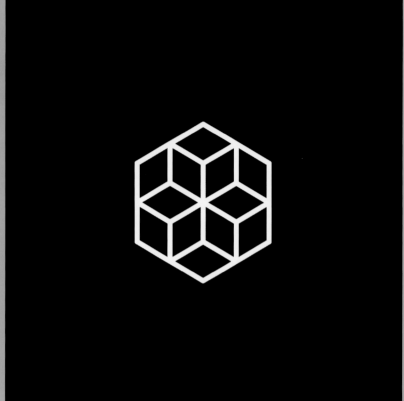

Julia Zeltser

Julia Zeltser is a founding partner and creative director at Hyperakt. With more than fifteen years of design experience in brand development, visualizations, and web, Julia has been instrumental in establishing Hyperakt's creative output.

Julia leads a multidisciplinary team of designers in a wide range of assignments. She has advised clients such as ACLU, Ford Foundation, and UNICEF to extend their brand in print and interactive media.

Julia initiated and leads Lunch Talks at Hyperakt, a monthly event to ignite collaboration and idea-sharing among the design community.

Julia has received accolades from organizations such as Society of Illustrators, *Communication Arts*, Brand New, and *How Magazine* for her design work. She was born in Ukraine and graduated from Parsons The New School for Design in New York. She lives with her husband, Lenny, and her two kids in Park Slope, Brooklyn.

Best in Show

Motion-Unscreen-Experimental

DESIGN AND ANIMATION
Ari Weinkle, Boston
SOUNDTRACK Darkside **URL**
ariweinkle.com **TWITTER**
@ariweinkle **PRINCIPAL TYPE**
Custom **CONCEPT** Feelers
is a typographic experiment
based on the movement of
animal appendages.

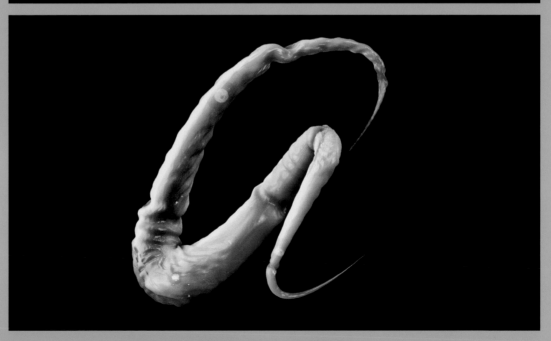

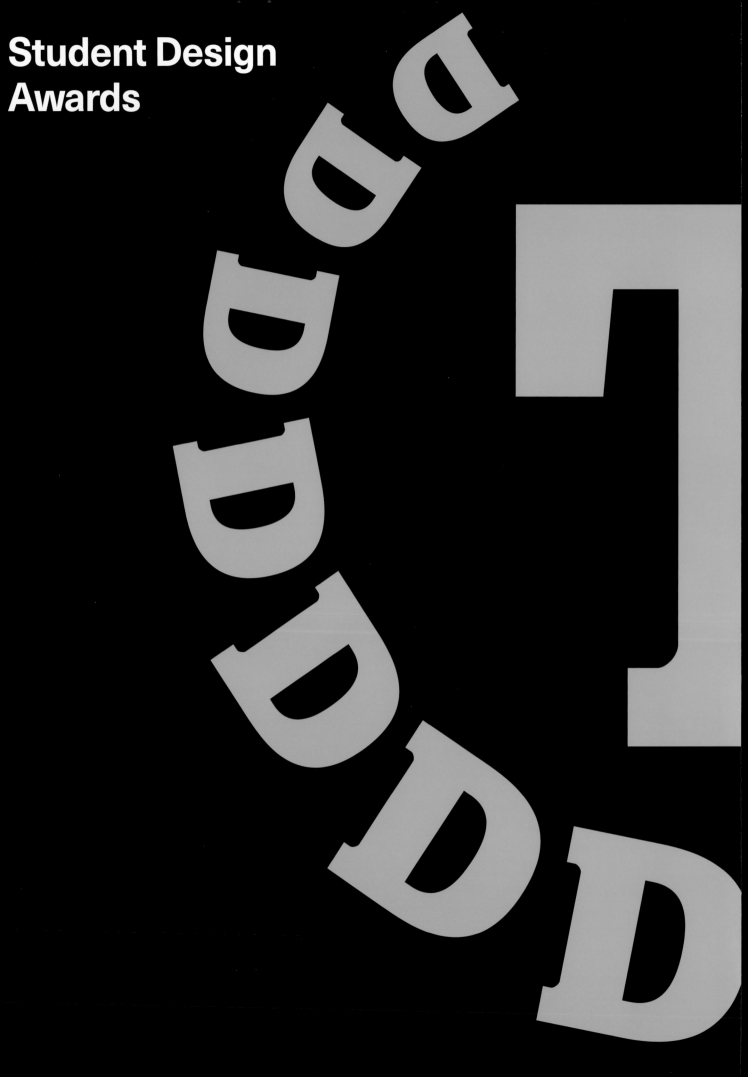

Student Design
Awards

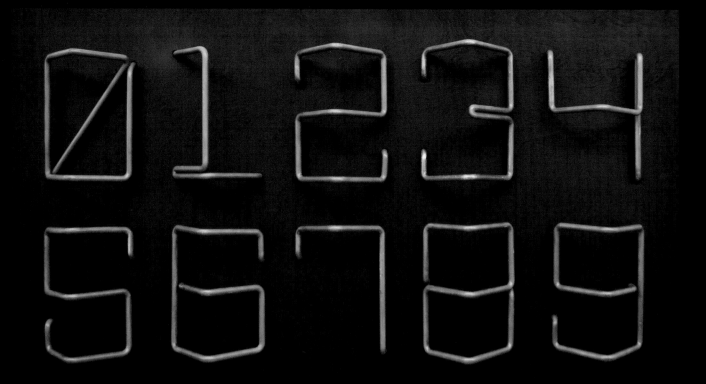

**First Place
Student Work**

DESIGN Elisa Foster, Los Angeles **URL** elisa-foster.com **METALWORKER** Matthew Dumpit **INSTRUCTOR** Andrew Byrom **SCHOOL** California State University, Long Beach **PRINCIPAL TYPE** Bendy Numbers **DIMENSIONS** 8 × 5.5 in. (20.3 × 14 cm)

CONCEPT My objective for this project was to design a system of experimental, physical house numbers. I created numbers using ⅜-inch steel rod bent into continuous lines and inspired by the curves and functionality of handrails. Each crossbar bends forward at ninety degrees, creating dimensionality and shifting angles of perception, depending on the viewer's location. The ends of each number bend backward and mount directly into holes drilled into the substrate, creating a clean, undisrupted look that accentuates the continuous lines of the design.

DESIGN Carmel
Gatchalian, New York **URL**
carmelgatchalian.com
INSTRUCTOR Ori Kleiner
SCHOOL School of Visual
Arts, New York● **PRINCIPAL
TYPE** Audimat **CONCEPT** This
is a self-portrait about my
struggles with procrastination.

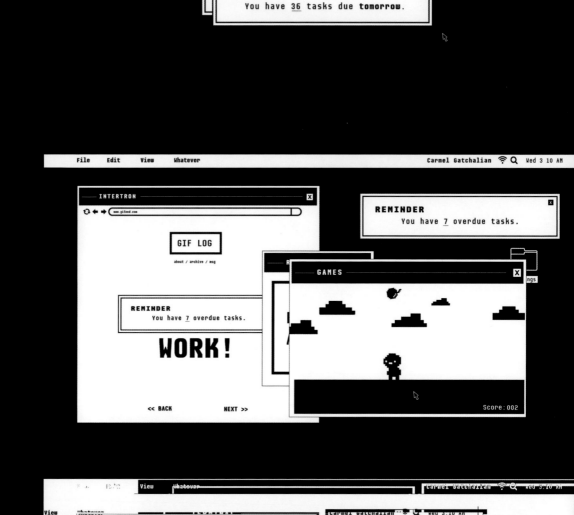

DESIGN Brian Lemus,● Betsy Mei Chun Lin, Henry Nuhn, Kristen Sorace, Zak Tebbal, Olivia Wilson, and Anthony Zukofsky, New York **CREATIVE DIRECTION** Gail Anderson● **PHOTOGRAPHY DIRECTOR** Diana Egnatz **PRODUCTION MANAGER** Gary Montavlo **OPERATIONS AND PROJECT**

MANAGER Ruby Ramirez **PHOTOGRAPHY** Daniel Lopera, Maria Nikolis, Jessica Pettway, and Cooper Winterson **URL** anthonyzukofsky.com, betsylin.com, brianlemus.com, henrynuhn.com, kristensorace. com, oliviamariewilson.com, zaktebbal.com **SCHOOL** School of Visual Arts,

New York● **PRINCIPAL TYPE** Akkurat Mono and Trade Gothic **DIMENSIONS** 5 × 5 × 6 in. (12.7 × 12.7 × 15.2 cm) **CONCEPT** This project is a journey through time in the form of a yearbook for SVA's Class of 2015.

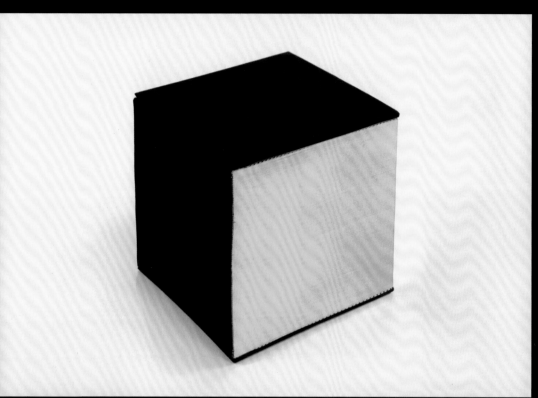

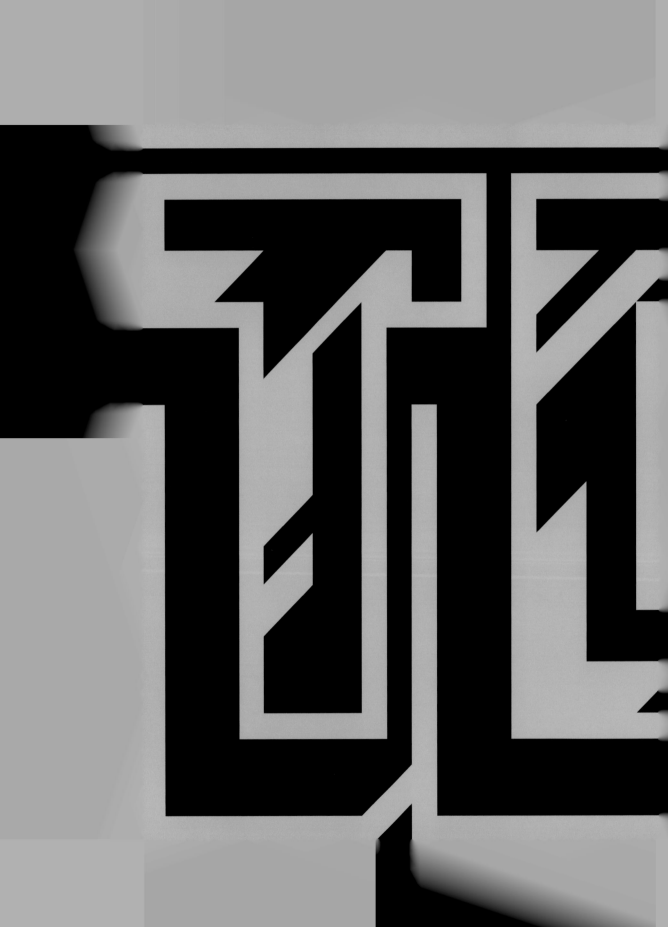

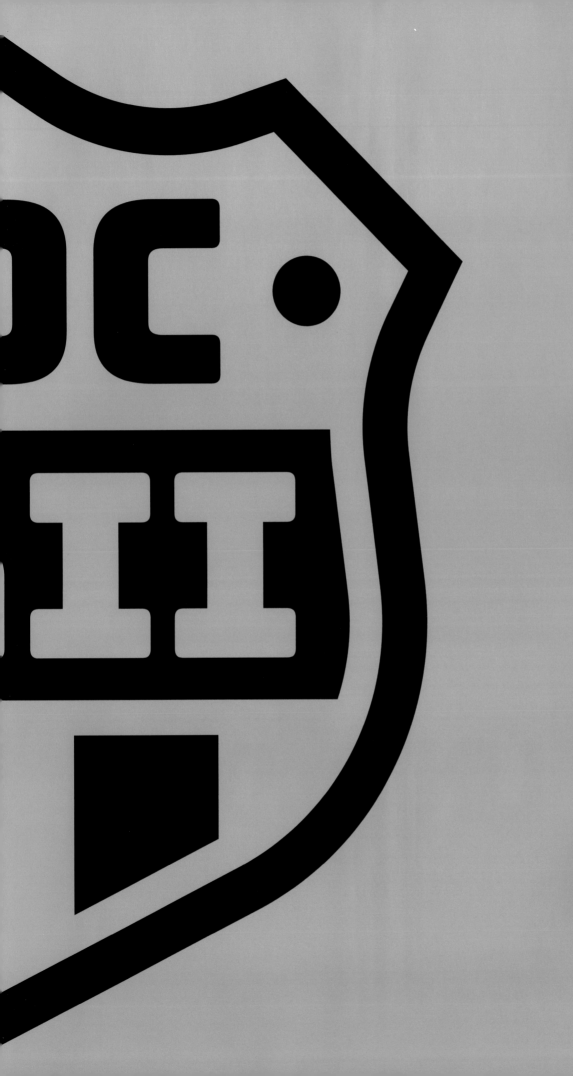

Magazine

DESIGN Nuria Cabrera, Giovanni Cavalleri, Pablo Martín, Rafa Roses, and Astrid Stavro, Palma de Mallorca, Balearic Islands, Spain **ART DIRECTION** Pablo Martín and Astrid Stavro **EDITOR IN CHIEF** Marc Valli **URL** designbyatlas. com **TWITTER** @designbyatlas **DESIGN FIRM** Atlas **CLIENT** Frame Publishers **PRINCIPAL TYPE** Founders Grotesk and Plantin **DIMENSIONS** 8.7 × 11 in. (22 × 28 cm)

CONCEPT Our design for *Elephant* magazine finds the right balance between words and images, creating aesthetically intriguing, thoughtful, and playful layouts that respond to the content without feeling dry or overdesigned. The strong, bold, and confident use of type gives the magazine a unique personality. Changing the main headline typeface in every issue adds an element of surprise and playfulness within the parameters of the branded design. For the "Girl on Girl" issue we used Founders Grotesk Bold in small caps, set in vertical, giving a strong and flavorful presence to the entire Research section.

DARHIL CROOKS As an editorial creative director, I come across something every once in a while that stops me in my tracks. Something that makes me say, "Damn, I wish had done that." Well, maybe more than every once in a while ...

Elephant magazine by Atlas Studio is one of those projects.

It wasn't a hard decision. The only hard part was deciding which issue to pick. Each one balanced confidence, restraint, and excitement at the same time. The mastery of the grid on each page takes the reader from quiet, front-of-the-book type to beautifully kerned, bold letterforms that take up an entire page ... and back again—all of this while doing an amazing job showcasing the best in art culture without distraction.

It's all done with only a handful of fonts and basically in black and white. There's nothing flashy or gimmicky here. From the TOC to the back page, it's editorial design in its purest form.

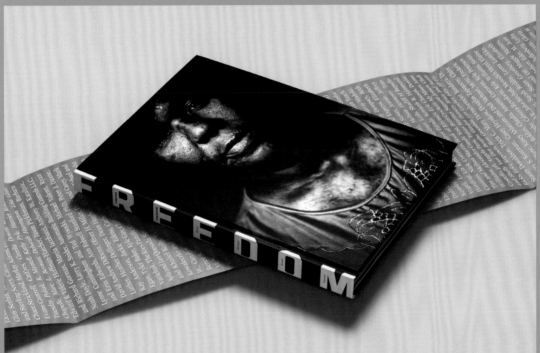

Book and Book Jacket

DESIGN Rob Schelleberg, Chicago **DESIGN DIRECTION** Alisa Wolfson **CREATIVE DIRECTION AND EDITOR** Brandon Crockett **CHIEF CREATIVE OFFICER** Mark Tutssel **EXECUTIVE DIRECTOR OF PRODUCTION** Vincent Geraghty **EXECUTIVE PRODUCER** Juan Woodbury **PRODUCER** Lisa Kunst **PHOTOGRAPHY** Sandro Miller **CREATIVE** Matt Miller **AGENCY** Leo Burnett Chicago **CLIENT** St. Leonard's Ministries **PRINCIPAL TYPE** Founders Grotesk **DIMENSIONS** 9 × 12 in. (22.9 × 30.5 cm) **CONCEPT** Over the past seven years, St. Leonard's Ministries has offered a poetry-writing class to former inmates. The *Finding Freedom* book is a collection of those handwritten poems paired with portraits of the poets. The book's subject matter and content are heavy, so we kept the typography secondary. The minimal layout and design complement the intimate, deeply rich, black-and-white portraiture. Much of the book's raw typography, including the title, was extracted from the handwriting of the poets themselves. The designer chose a grotesk typeface, Founders Grotesk, that pairs nicely with the eclectic styles of handwriting. The breadth of the typeface family allows for a variety of uses, from body copy and titles to transcriptions of the poems in monospace. Moments of thoughtfulness come through in the book's title page, which resembles the prisoner identity board that is used to catalog each prisoner upon entry into the institution. All the design elements, from the color orange to the purposefully cropped dust jacket, come together to tell the enriching and considered story of a personal past that is unfamiliar to most of us.

SAGI HAVIV Often, the most direct and obvious solution is the best one. This is the case with the design for *Finding Freedom*, which features poems of former inmates. Superimposing the handwritten pages on top of beautiful black-and-white portraits creates an interesting and provocative interaction between word and image— a rich expression through simple juxtaposition.

Exhibition

DESIGN AND CREATIVE DIRECTION Cristina Achury and María Silva, Bogotá **CONTENT** National Library of Colombia **PRINT PRODUCTION** Signgraphic **CARPENTRY** William Enrique Cubillos and Emilia Moncada **URL** null. com.co **DESIGN** studio Null. **CLIENT** Ministry of Culture of Colombia **PRINCIPAL TYPE** Bodoni, Bodoni Old Face, and ITC Franklin Gothic Std **DIMENSIONS** 50.2 × 43.2 ft. (15.3 × 13.2 m) **CONCEPT** In
2015, the National Library of Colombia celebrated the sixtieth anniversary of the intellectual magazine *MITO*, published from 1955 to 1968 in Colombia. We created a graphic concept called *Printed Word, a Generation's Memory*. The content in *MITO* explored polemical

and forward-thinking ideals of an intellectual generation, which have become part of our memory as a country. The exhibition's vertical axis features the principal writers involved with the magazine, their names and writings descending through the walls and gathering on the floor to create the floor of content that nurtured the magazine. Here, visitors interact with the word *MITO* and access the magazine's content. Through the horizontal axis, a time line contextualizes the writers. The exhibition re-creates a vital part of one generation's written memory.

ROBBIN SCHIFF As a longtime book jacket designer, familiar with working in historical contexts, I was drawn to the modernist look of the *MITO* exhibit graphics as they appeared on the table as a page-size photo. The document of the exhibit resembles, at first glance, a collage of the red, black-on-cream graphics of a Bauhaus-era poster. A closer look, however, reveals a cohesive design of printed materials interacting with surfaces in all dimensions of the lobby of Colombia's National Library. The content of the exhibit is *MITO*, a publication and intellectual forum for progressive ideas from 1955–1968. The bold execution is almost entirely typographic.

The centerpiece and focal point of the room is a sculptural rendering of the name "MITO," whose individual letterforms act as desk furniture as well as logo and headline for the exhibit. The huge red sans serif sculpture defines the space and creates the scale for the room. This, along with the continuously printed floor and walls, creates the illusion of the viewer having been shrunk to fit inside text.

The painted columns, empty doorways, and gridded windows are all considered and form the architecture as well as the texture of the exhibit. Pages from the magazine's archives, with lists of its contributors, excerpted writings, and timelines of its

history, form a continuous wall and floor of text. The library's banisters, floor moldings, and shelf railings outline and define the planes and serve as rules, panels, and accents to the larger "pages" created by the exhibit's walls and floors of text.

The ambitious concept of the exhibit as an homage to the magazine's forum of ideas is loyal to *MITO*'s mission, and is an elegant tribute to its place in the cultural history of its country. The National Library is the perfect venue.

William Klein
Boris Mikhailov
Guido Guidi
Rosalind Fox Solomon
Bertien van Manen
Bruce Davidson
David Goldblatt
Ishiuchi Miyako
Paolo Gasparini

Magazines

ART DIRECTION AND TYPOGRAPHY Henrik Kubel and Scott Williams London **URL** a2swhk.co.uk and a2-type.co.uk **DESIGN FIRM** A2/SW/HK **CLIENT** *Aperture* **PRINCIPAL TYPE** Aperture Sans and Aperture Serif **DIMENSIONS** 12 × 9.25 in. (30.5 × 23.5 cm) **CONCEPT** For *Aperture*, one of the world's leading magazines dedicated to contemporary photography, we developed a suite of typefaces.

JARIK VAN SLUIJS A couple of years ago, *Aperture* magazine went through a thoughtful and beautiful redesign worthy of its heritage, and the use of outstanding typography was key. I'm obsessed with photography, love typography, and always appreciate a good system, so picking this entry was easy, if not a little biased. For me, every new issue is an instant object of desire.

At the core of the relaunch was a smart and flexible typographic system used to structure the issues into two main sections. The "Words" section uses a serif typeface, and the "Pictures" section a geometric sans serif. The sections use different paper stocks as well, creating differing tactile and visual experiences.

Through consistently strong and disciplined art direction, all issues have maintained the same level of elegance, intelligence, and beauty. The design is both classic and modern, and at first glance, deceptively simple. The oversized pages, modernist grids, and ample use of white space create the perfect conditions to showcase photography. Although these ingredients can easily result in a bland and derivative design, it is the custom typefaces that give a distinctive character to the magazine. This type family doesn't shy away from having a playful and decorative side, which helps to create a unique voice for the publication. And take a look at the cover of the "Interview" issue—a photography magazine with no photo on its cover and relies solely on type. Brilliant.

That said, the typography never gets in the way of the photographic content, and neither does the tastefully small *Aperture* nameplate on the cover.

There are magazines you throw away. This is not that type of magazine.

Baseball Bat

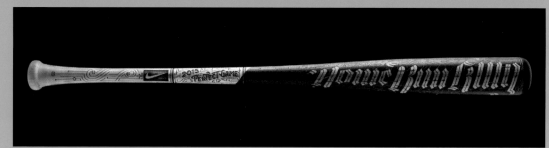

DESIGN AND LETTERING Kevin Cantrell • and Juan Carlos Pagan,• Salt Lake City **ART DIRECTION** Kevin Cantrell **CREATIVE DIRECTION** John Moon (Nike) **PRODUCTION** Big Secret **URL** kevincantrell.com **TWITTER** @kevinrcantrell **DESIGN STUDIO** Kevin Cantrell Studio **CLIENT** Nike **PRINCIPAL TYPE** Custom **DIMENSIONS** 32 × 2.5 × 2.5 in. (81.3 × 6.4 × 6.6 cm) **CONCEPT** Nike: "Can you laser-etch an entire bat?" Kevin: "Of course." Brilliant. Could I? Fabricating a bat was impossible, considering its irregular shape. So I went to etching expert Big Secret and to typographer and friend Juan Carlos Pagan for help creating something as unique as the bat. Carlos came up with the concept of custom italic blacklettering, and we worked back and forth, tag-teaming the work, each designer complementing the others' skill sets. We created a modular design structure to account for the bat's slope and imperceptibly reduce the ornamentation for the viewer. Big Secret hacked its rotary device to spin each piece, engraving in an entirely new way. At the start, the folks at Big Secret confessed they were 80 percent certain the task could be accomplished, to which I said, "Great, because I've already sold Nike on it, so let's go!"

KAREN WELMAN I chose the laser-etched cricket bat, not only because it's an unusual physical object, but also because it's an incredibly clever idea in the context of it being a trophy for Nike.

The cricket bat is already an aesthetically beautiful object, but to add to it the most gorgeous typography and calligraphy to further enhance its beauty is a very simple and elegant solution that makes a statement about sport and winning.

The design has moved typography away from its usual association with paper, books, and screens—and was even etched onto a surface that was supposedly impossible to laser. I love it when a designer breaks the rules, produces something beyond the realms of the expected, and breaks new ground with a successful implementation.

A stunning result.

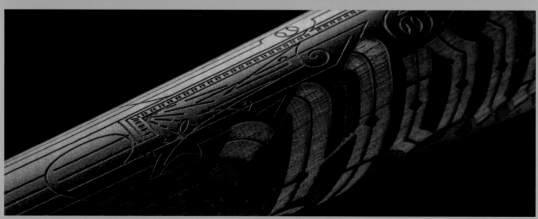

Identity

DESIGN Joseph Han, Jang Hyun Han, Sue Lee, and Maurann Stein, New York **ART DIRECTION** Natasha Jen● **URL** pentagram.com **TWITTER** @pentagram **DESIGN FIRM** Pentagram● **CLIENT** AIA New York **PRINCIPAL TYPE** Herita-Geo **DIMENSIONS** Various **CONCEPT** In October 2015, New York's architects, designers, and other creative professionals came together for the Heritage Ball, the annual black-tie gala that supports the AIA New York chapter and the Center for Architecture. For the event

graphics, we created a playful typographic system based on the idea of the reconfiguration of space, which is similar to the nature of architecture itself. Expanding and contracting, the typography visually echoes the way buildings and structures adapt to fill the available area, especially in cities and urban environments. The custom typeface is composed of letterforms that horizontally scale between the regular and extended widths of the font, which are used all at once.

FOREST YOUNG The invitation to the AIA Heritage Ball 2015 is a viscerally compelling artifact. The memorable soloist here is a bespoke typeface appropriately named Herita-Geo. This piece commanded a Judges' Choice as it was both a sharp concept expressed effortlessly through typographic form, and a confident embodiment of homage, contemporaneity, and experimentation.

The letterforms expand and contract, playfully evoking sentiments of spatial adaptability and flux. The typeface's double line structure mimics the walls in plan and section views from architectural blueprints. The typographic impression carries inflections of geometric sans predecessors like Bayer's Bauhaus letterforms, the concentric striping of Radim Peško's Boymans, and the the elasticity of Experimental Jetset's responsive *W* for the Whitney Museum.

The piece is also surprisingly comedic, echoing contemporary GIF culture and typographic memes. Like Archigram's *A Walking City*, provocation does not need to be exclusively serious. Overall, the invitation eschews telegraphic legibility in favor of narrative. It is refreshing to be reminded that professional design can be a series of playful public experiments.

Poster

DESIGN Stefan Guzy and
Björn Wiede, Berlin **URL**
zwoelf.net/portfolio **STUDIO**
Zwölf **CLIENT** Kunstverein
Harburger Bahnhof, Hamburg
(Kv.H.Bf.) **PRINCIPAL TYPE**
Eesti **DIMENSIONS** 27.5 × 39
in. (70 × 100 cm) **CONCEPT**
We created the poster for an
exhibition at Kv.H.Bf. by artist
Hannah Weinberger called
*As if I Became Upside Down,
Right Side Up*. Taking the title
literally, we screen printed
the design in white and black
on the back side of ordinary
affichen paper.

JULIA ZELTSER As a judge
in a design competition,
I have a split second to
decide whether the work is
award-winning. I have to rely
on instinct, experience, and
design knowledge to make an
instant judgment call. In the
sea of great designs of varying
complexity, the poster "Upside
Down" stood out because
of its clarity.

After reviewing hundreds
of great submissions, I was
struck and inspired by the
poster for an artist exhibition
*As if I Became Upside Down,
Right Side Up*. The designer
chose to represent the work
of the artist with a blank sheet
of paper—an everyday object
that you and I may toss around
our desks, turn and flip, bend,
and write on. The sides of the
folded edges offered just the
necessary information—artist
name, show title, and dates.

The round, geometric,
straightforward characteristics
of Eesti, from Grilli type,
mimicked the simplicity of
the composition. The text
is tilted on an angle, falling,
and bleeding off—illustrating
"upside down, right side up."
Yet, no vital information is lost.
The hard, triangular edges
form a daring composition.
The rest is white space.
Simple, unapologetic,
confident, striking white
space. This basic principle of
design not only cut through
the day-to-day clutter, but also
was a breath of fresh air for
me during the judging.

Bravo! Well done!

Hannah Weinberger „As if I became
upside down, right side up"
Eröffnung 17.4.15, 19:00
18.4. – 26.7.15
Kv.HBf

TDC LXII
Winners

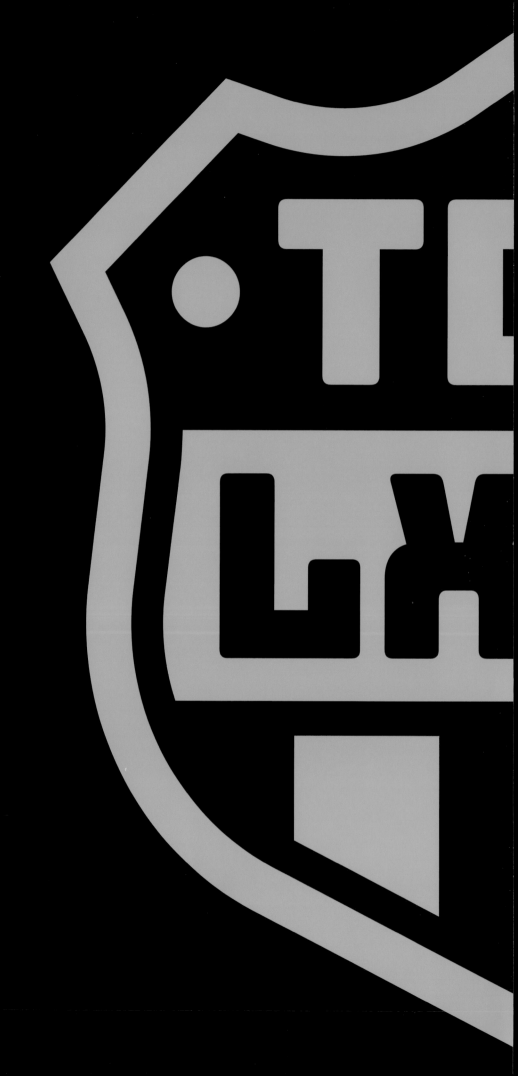

62

Advertising

DESIGN Wendy Xu,● Los
Angeles **ART DIRECTION** Jane
McVey **LETTERING** Wendy Xu
URL petitserif.com **TWITTER**
@petitserif **CLIENT** *Texas
Monthly*, Austin, TX **PRINCIPAL**
TYPE Custom **DIMENSIONS**
5 × 7 in. (12.7 × 17.8 cm)

Book Jacket

DESIGN Oliver Munday, New
York **URL** omunday.tumblr.com
DESIGN FIRM OMG **PUBLISHER**
Pantheon Books **PRINCIPAL**
TYPE Heroic Bold **DIMENSIONS**
6.25 × 9.5 in. (15.9 × 24.1 cm)

19
46

THE MAKING OF THE MODERN WORLD

VICTOR SEBESTYEN

Book Jacket

DESIGN Mitch Goldstein and Anne Jordan, Rochester, New York **ART DIRECTION** Rob Ehle **PHOTOGRAPHY** Mitch Goldstein and Anne Jordan **URL** annatype.com and mitchgoldstein.com **TWITTER** @annatype and @mgoldst **CLIENT** Stanford University Press **PRINCIPAL TYPE** Futura Extra Bold, Gothic Narrow Condensed, Roman X Condensed, Roman X Expanded, and hand-drawn type based on historical artifacts. **DIMENSIONS** 5.5 × 8.5 in (14 × 21.6 cm)

Book Jacket

DESIGN Allison Saltzman, New York **SENIOR ART DIRECTOR** Ecco/HarperCollins **COVER ART** Brooklyn Bridge: Currier & Ives / Library of Congress Decorative Border: Richard Sheaff / Sheaff Ephemera Trapeze Women: Niday Picture Library / Alamy **URL** allisonsaltzman.com **TWITTER AND INSTAGRAM** @al_saltzman **PUBLISHER** Ecco/HarperCollins **PRINCIPAL TYPE** Adonis Oldstyle, Bourbon, Brothers, and Copperplate **DIMENSIONS** 6.1 × 9.25 in. (15.5 × 23.5 cm)

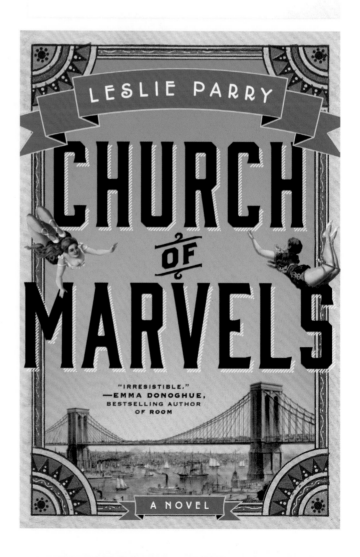

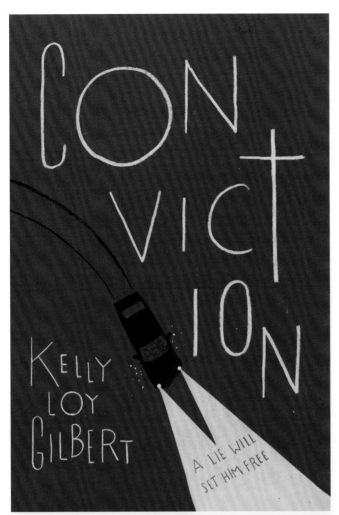

Book Jacket

DESIGN AND ART DIRECTION
Maria Elias **LETTERER** Chris
Silas Neal **ILLUSTRATION**
Chris Silas Neal **AUTHOR** Kelly
Loy Gilbert **EDITOR** Laura
Schreiber **PUBLISHER** Disney
Hyperion **PRINCIPAL TYPE**
Handlettering **DIMENSIONS**
5.75 × 8.5 in. (14.6 × 21.6 cm)

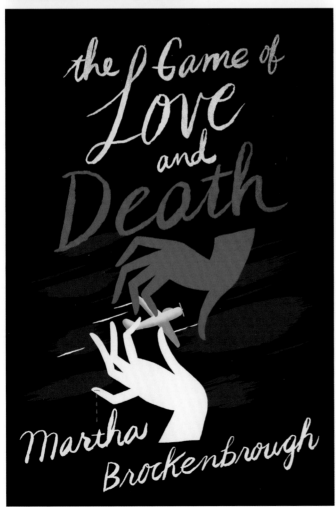

Book Jacket

DESIGN AND ART DIRECTION
Nina Goffi **LETTERING** Chris
Silas Neal, Brooklyn, New York
ART Chris Silas Neal **CLIENT**
Scholastic **DIMENSIONS**
5.75 × 8 in. (14.6 × 20.3 cm)

Book Jacket

DESIGN Hagen Verleger,•
Berlin **ART DIRECTION** Robert
Schumann **URL** hagenverleger.
com **TWITTER** @hagenverleger
STUDIO Buchgut **CLIENT**
Westend Verlag **PRINCIPAL**
TYPE Alternate Gothic No 1
and Alternate Gothic No 2
DIMENSIONS 5.3 × 8.5 in.
(13.5 cm × 21.5 cm)

Book Jacket

DESIGN Utku Lomlu, Istanbul
URL utkulomlu.com **TWITTER**
@utkulomlu **DESIGN FIRM**
Lom Creative **CLIENT** Can
Publishing **PRINCIPAL TYPE**
Avant Garde and Tungsten
Condensed **DIMENSIONS**
4.9 × 7.6 in. (12.5 × 19.5 cm)

59

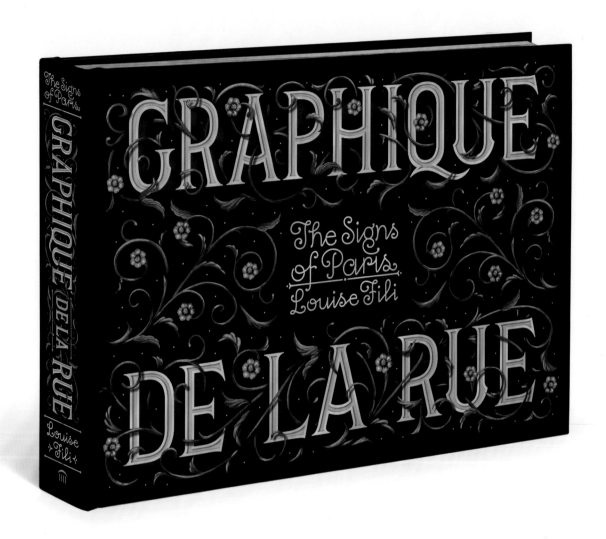

Book Jacket

DESIGN Louise Fili● and
Kelly Thorn, New York **ART
DIRECTION** Louise Fili
LETTERING Kelly Thorn **URL**
louisefili.com **TWITTER**
@louisefili and @jellythorn
STUDIO Louise Fili Ltd
PUBLISHER Princeton

Architectural Press
PRINCIPAL TYPE Handlettering
DIMENSIONS 9.25 × 6.75 in.
(23.5 × 17.1 cm)

Book Jacket

DESIGN Kimberly Glyder,● Philadelphia **ART DIRECTION** Cherlynne Li **URL** kimberlyglyder.com **TWITTER** @kglyder **DESIGN FIRM** Kimberly Glyder Design **CLIENT** Touchstone / Simon & Schuster **PRINCIPAL**

TYPE Alternate Gothic and handlettering **DIMENSIONS** 6.1 × 9.25 in. (15.6 × 23.5 cm)

Book Jacket

SENIOR ART DIRECTOR Allison Saltzman, New York **COVER ART** Lindsey Bunish, Chicago **URL** allisonsaltzman.com and lindseybunish.com **TWITTER** @al_saltzman and @lindseybunish **INSTAGRAM** @al_saltzman **PUBLISHER** Ecco HarperCollins **PRINCIPAL TYPE** Mrs Eaves and found art **DIMENSIONS** 6 × 9 in. (15.2 × 22.9 cm)

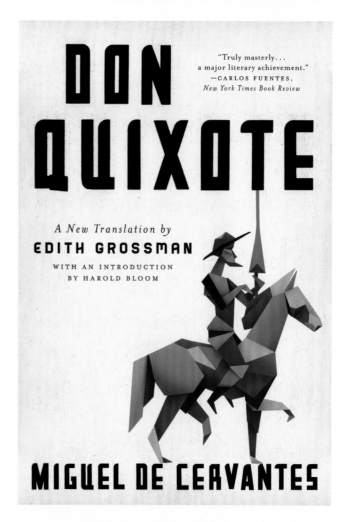

Book Jacket

DESIGN Linda Huang, New York **ART DIRECTION** Megan Wilson **PHOTOGRAPHY** kobps2/Shutterstock **URL** knopfdoubleday.com/imprint/anchor / linda-huang.com **PUBLISHER** Anchor Books / Knopf Doubleday **PRINCIPAL TYPE** FF Elementa and ITC Franklin Gothic **DIMENSIONS** 5.2 × 8 in. (13.2 × 20.3 cm)

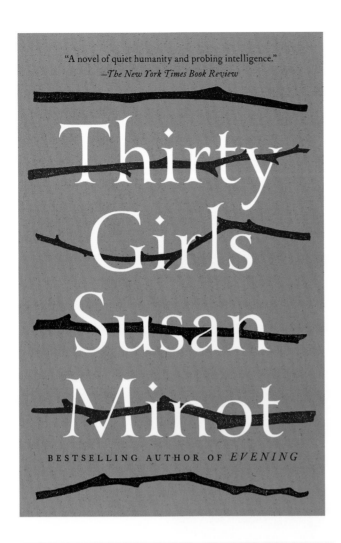

Unpublished

DESIGN Linda Huang, New York **ART DIRECTION** Megan Wilson **URL** knopfdoubleday.com/imprint/vintage **URL** linda-huang.com **PUBLISHER** Vintage Books **PRINCIPAL TYPE** Yana **DIMENSIONS** 5.2 × 8 in. (13.2 × 20.3 cm)

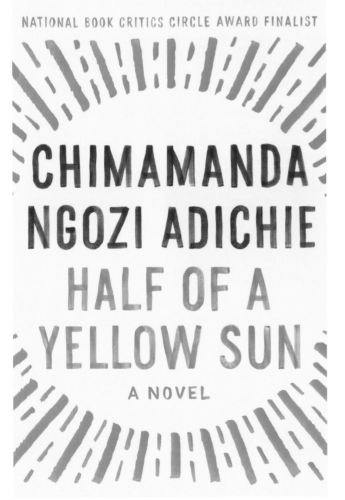

Book Jacket

DESIGN Joan Wong, New York **ART DIRECTION** Megan Wilson **ILLUSTRATION** Joan Wong **URL** joan-wong.com **PUBLISHER** Anchor Books **PRINCIPAL TYPE** Handlettering **DIMENSIONS** 4.4 × 6.25 in. (11.1 × 15.9 cm)

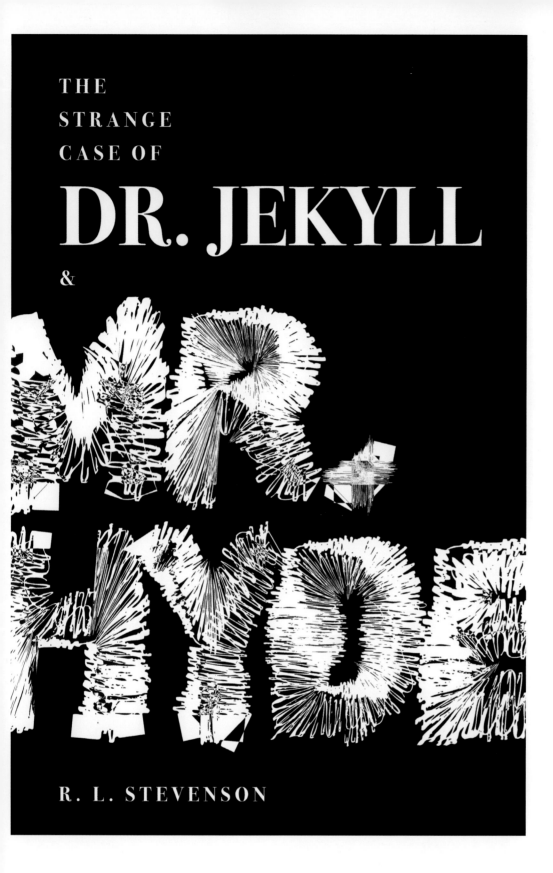

THE
STRANGE
CASE OF
DR. JEKYLL
&
MR.
HYDE

R. L. STEVENSON

27 Book

CREATIVE DIRECTION Jerald
Saddle and Kate Wang, New
York **CLIENT** Maki Fund
PRINCIPAL TYPE Bodoni Bold
and custom **DIMENSIONS**
10 × 15 in. (25.4 × 38.1 cm)

Book Jacket

DESIGN Colin Webber, New
York **ART DIRECTION** Paul
Buckley● and Roseanne
Serra **URL** squareyroute.com
PUBLISHER Penguin Books
/ Penguin Random House
PRINCIPAL TYPE Caslon 3 and
Helvetica **DIMENSIONS**
5.5 × 8.4 in. (14 × 21.4 cm)

the 'ärt

əv 'lan-

gwij

in-'ven

(t)shən

The

Art of

Language

Invention

From Horse-Lords to
Dark Elves, the Words
Behind World-Building

David J.
Peterson

from the author of *Living Language*® *Dothraki*

Book Jacket

DESIGN Oliver Munday, New
York **URL** omunday.tumblr.com
DESIGN FIRM OMG **PUBLISHER**
Alfred A. Knopf **PRINCIPAL**
TYPE Custom **DIMENSIONS**
6.25 × 9.5 in. 5.9 × 24.1 cm)

Book Jacket

DESIGN Oliver Munday, New
York **URL** omunday.tumblr.com
DESIGN FIRM OMG **PUBLISHER**
Alfred A. Knopf **PRINCIPAL**
TYPE Custom **DIMENSIONS**
6.25 × 9.5 in. (5.9 × 24.1 cm)

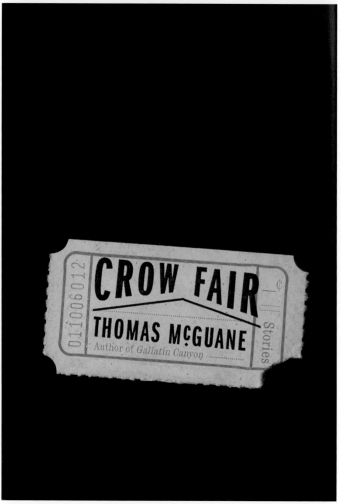

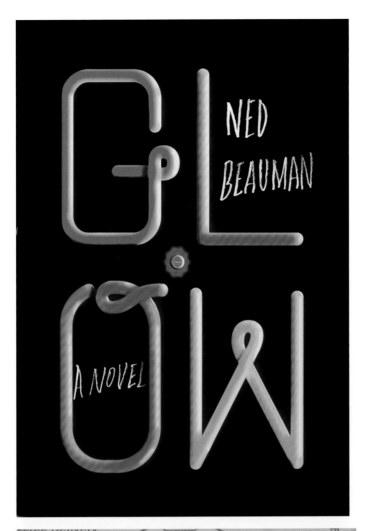

Book Jacket

DESIGN Oliver Munday, New York **URL** omunday.tumblr.com **DESIGN FIRM** OMG **PUBLISHER** Alfred A. Knopf **PRINCIPAL TYPE** Custom **DIMENSIONS** 6.25 × 9.5 in. (5.9 × 24.1 cm)

Book Jacket

DESIGN Oliver Munday, New York **URL** omunday.tumblr.com **DESIGN FIRM** OMG **PUBLISHER** Alfred A. Knopf **PRINCIPAL TYPE** ITC Grouch **DIMENSIONS** 5.25 × 8.1 in. (13.3 × 20.6 cm)

Book

DESIGN Utku Lomlu, Istanbul
URL utkulomlu.com **TWITTER**
@utkulomlu **DESIGN FIRM**
Lom Creative **CLIENT** Hera
Buyuktasciyan **PRINCIPAL**
TYPE Sylfaen and Zine Slab
Display **DIMENSIONS**
6.5 × 8.8 in. (16 × 22 cm)

Book

DESIGN Wendy Xu,• Los
Angeles **ART DIRECTION** Kat
Millerick **LETTERING AND**
ILLUSTRATION Wendy Xu **URL**
petitserif.com **TWITTER**
@petitserif **CLIENT** Workman
Publishing **PRINCIPAL TYPE**
Custom **DIMENSIONS** 6 × 6 in.
(15.2 × 15.2 cm)

Book Jacket

DESIGN Utku Lomlu,
Istanbul **URL** utkulomlu.com
TWITTER @utkulomlu **DESIGN**
FIRM Lom Creative **CLIENT**
Can Publishing **PRINCIPAL**
TYPE Frutiger, Minion, and
DTL Nobel **DIMENSIONS**
4.9 × 7.6 in. (12.5 × 19.5 cm)

Book

DESIGN AND ART DIRECTION
Haruyuki Suzuki, Tokyo **URL**
haruyukisuzuki.com **TWITTER**
@SH8G **STUDIO/AGENCY**
Toppan Printing Company
CLIENT SHP Books **PRINCIPAL**
TYPE Helvetica **DIMENSIONS**
5.4 × 7.5 in. (13.8 × 19.0 cm)

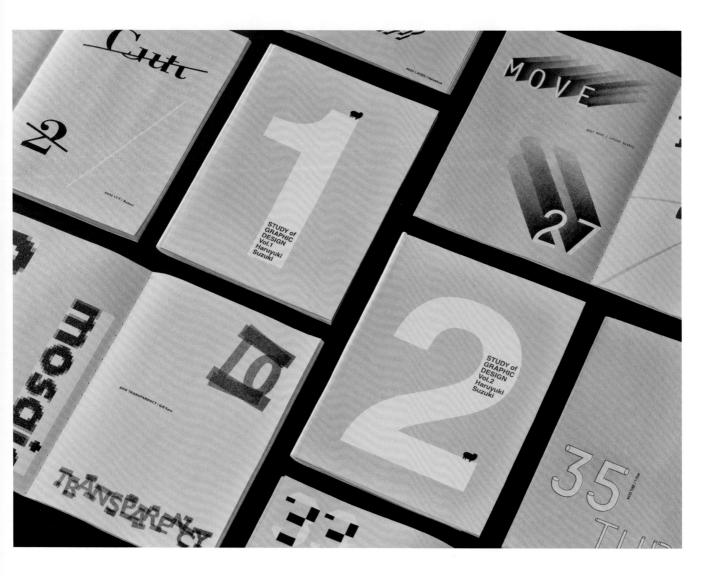

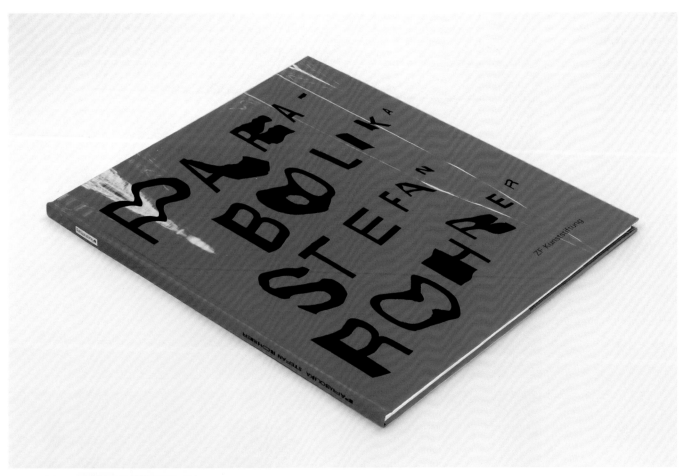

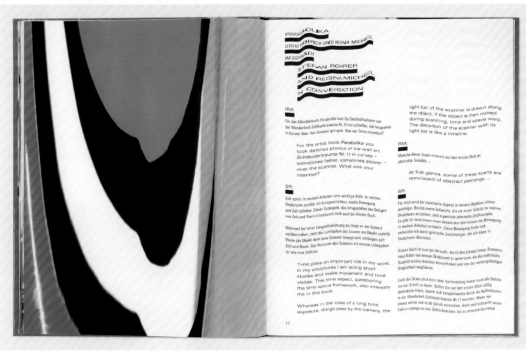

Book

DESIGN Sebastian Fischer and Philipp Hubert, New York and Berlin **URL** hubertfischer. com **DESIGN FIRM** Hubert & Fischer **CLIENT** ZF Art Foundation **PRINCIPAL TYPE** ZF Sans Expanded and ZF Sans Condensed (modified) **DIMENSIONS** 9 × 11 in. (23 × 28 cm)

Book

DESIGN Laura Asmus,
Luzia Hein, Marion Schreiber,
and Svenja Wamser, Hamburg
URL edition-umbruch.de
SCHOOL Hamburg University
of Applied Sciences,
Department of Design Master
Design Project **PRINCIPAL
TYPE** Beirut, Schola, and TeX
Gyre **DIMENSIONS**
9.4 × 6.6 in. (24 × 16.8 cm)

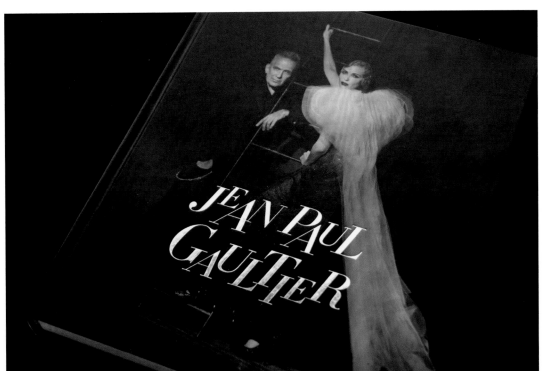

Book

DESIGN AND ART DIRECTION
René Clément, Montréal
CREATIVE DIRECTION Louis
Gagnon● **DIRECTION** Thierry-
Maxime Loriot **URL** paprika.
com **AGENCY** Paprika **CLIENT**
Montréal Museum of Fine
Arts **PRINCIPAL TYPE** Didot
HTF and Helvetica Neue
DIMENSIONS 9.9 × 11.62 in.
(25 × 29.5 cm)

Book Jacket

DESIGN Mitch Goldstein and Anne Jordan, Rochester, New York **ART DIRECTION** Rob Ehle **PHOTOGRAPHY** Mitch Goldstein and Anne Jordan **URL** mitchgoldstein.com and annatype.com **TWITTER** @mgoldst and @annatype **CLIENT** Stanford University Press **PRINCIPAL TYPE** Futura Book **DIMENSIONS** 5.6 × 8.75 in (14.3 × 22.3 cm)

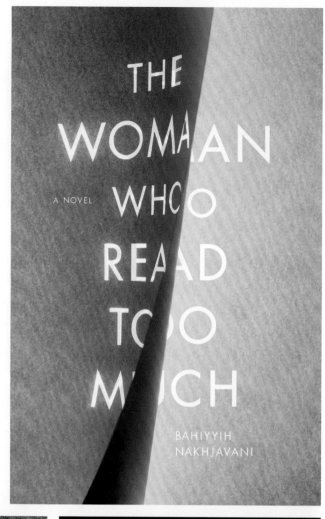

Exhibition

DESIGN Sam Divers, Ariane Forster, Philipp Lüthi, and Andrea Noti, Bern, Switzerland **DESIGN STUDIO** Heyday **URL** heyday.ch **CLIENT** Swiss Agency for Development and Cooperation, Global Programme Migration and Development **PRINCIPAL TYPE** GT Pressura Regular **DIMENSIONS** Various

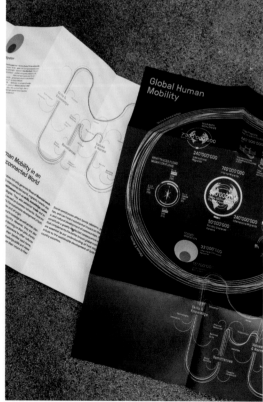

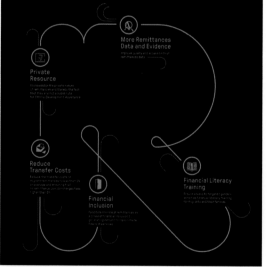

Advertising

ART DIRECTION Mario Cintra and Henrique Del Lama **CREATIVE DIRECTION** Philippe Degen and Eduardo Martins **VICE PRESIDENT CREATIVE** João Livi **CALLIGRAPHY AND LETTERING** Jackson Alves,● Curitiba, Brazil **URL** jacksonalves.com **CLIENT** Talent Comunicação e Planejamento S/A for Cervejaria Kaiser Brasil S/A São Paulo, Brazil **DIMENSIONS** 27.5 × 44 in. (70 × 110 cm)

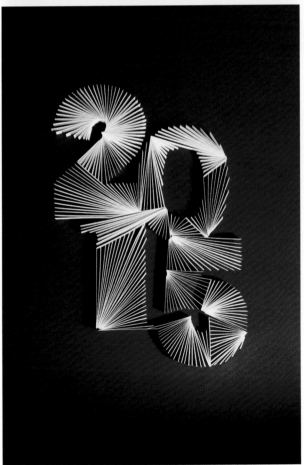

Newspaper Cover

DESIGN Jerome Corgier, Paris, Represented in the United States by the Marlena Agency (marlenaagency. com) **ART DIRECTION** Kelly Doe **PHOTOGRAPHY** Jerome Corgier **URL** jeromecorgier. com and pariri.com **TWITTER** @jeromecorgier **TUMBLR** jeromecorgier.tumblr.com **CLIENT** *The International New York Times / Turning Point* nytimes.com/2014/12/04/ opinion/turning-points-editors-letter.html?_r=0 **PRINCIPAL TYPE** Custom **DIMENSIONS** 5.9 × 7.9 in. (15 × 20 cm)

Magazine

DESIGN AND ART DIRECTION Tobias Dahl, Patrick Martin, Paul Stolle, and Robin Weissenborn, Leipzig, Germany **URL** happy-little-accidents.de **FACEBOOK** facebook.com/happylittlegraphic **INSTAGRAM** @happylittlegraphic **DESIGN STUDIO** Happy Little Accidents **CLIENT** Initiative Horizonte, Bauhaus University Weimar **PRINCIPAL TYPE** Atlas Grotesk and Proto Grotesk Bold **DIMENSIONS** 6.5 × 9 in. (16.5 × 23 cm)

Magazine

CREATIVE DIRECTION Robert Vargas,● New York **DEPUTY CREATIVE DIRECTOR** Tracy Ma **DIRECTOR OF PHOTOGRAPHY** Clinton Cargill **ILLLUSTRATOR** Nejc Prah **PUBLICATION** *Bloomberg Businessweek* **PRINCIPAL TYPE** Heidelbe **DIMENSIONS** 7.9 × 10.5 in. (20 × 26.7 cm)

Bloomberg Businessweek

Read This, Feel Better

The Good Business Issue

p55

$5.99US $6.99CAN

50>

0 74470 02008 0

Advertising

DESIGN Luca Ionescu,•
Sydney **TYPOGRAPHER AND**
3D DESIGN Luca Ionescu
URL likemindedstudio.com
TWITTER @The_Likes_of_Us
FIRM Like Minded Studio
PRINCIPAL TYPE Custom
DIMENSIONS Various

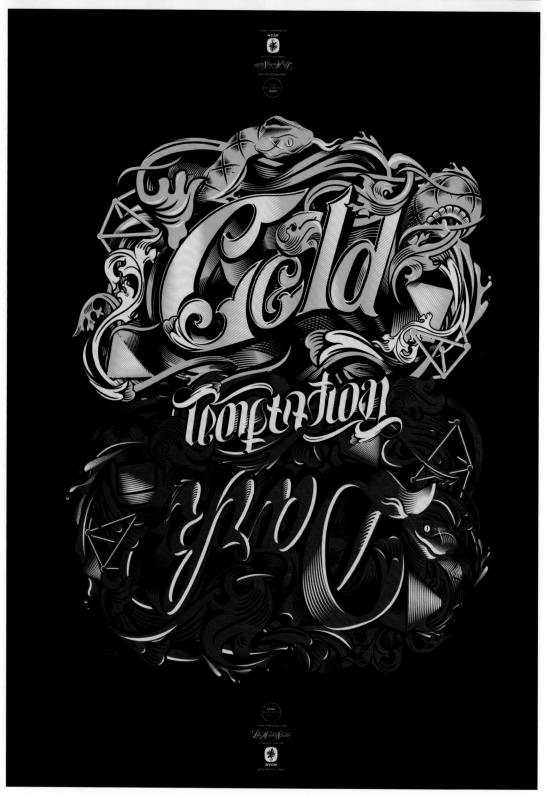

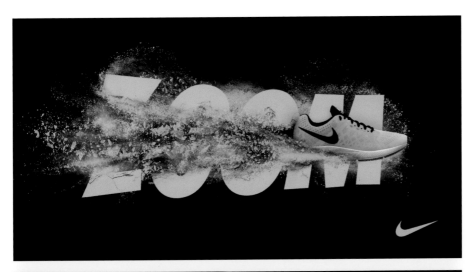

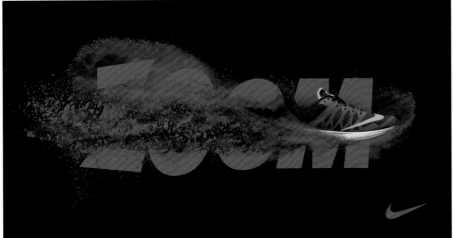

Advertising

DESIGN Ben Oosterkerk, London **CREATIVE PRODUCER** Eve Steben **PHOTOGRAPHY AND TYPOGRAPHY** Sean Freeman **ART BUYER** Cornelie De Kroes **URL** thereis.co.uk **DESIGN FIRM** THERE IS **CLIENT** NIKE Europe **PRINCIPAL TYPE** Futura Extra Bold Condensed Oblique

Advertisement

DESIGN Ben Oosterkerk, London **ART DIRECTION** Lee Owens **CREATIVE PRODUCER** Eve Steben **PHOTOGRAPHY AND TYPOGRAPHY** Sean Freeman **ART BUYERS** Cornelie De Kroes and Marlous Niehot **URL** thereis.co.uk **DESIGN FIRM** THERE IS **CLIENT** NIKE Europe **PRINCIPAL TYPE** Futura Extra Bold Condensed Oblique

Book Jacket

**DESIGN AND CREATIVE
DIRECTION** Jennifer Rider,
Los Angeles **URL**
jenniferrider.com **CLIENT**
Las Cienegas Projects
PRINCIPAL TYPE Folio
DIMENSIONS 6.75 × 8.9 in.
(17 × 22.5 cm)

Identity

DESIGN AND DIRECTION
Daniel Triendl, Vienna **URL**
danieltriendl.com **TWITTER**
@DanielTriendl **CLIENT**
B.Visible **PRINCIPAL TYPE**
Various **DIMENSIONS** Various

Identity

CREATIVE DIRECTION Marie-Élaine Benoit, Montréal
ARTISTIC DIRECTION Nadine Brunet **TYPEFACE DESIGNER** Olivier Valiquette **ILLUSTRATION** Julien Poisson **ACCOUNT DIRECTOR** Cindy Loridon **ACCOUNT COORDINATOR** Jennifer Jackson **URL** sidlee.com **AGENCY** Sid Lee **CLIENT** CRU Oyster Bar **PRINCIPAL TYPE** CRU Regular **DIMENSIONS** Various

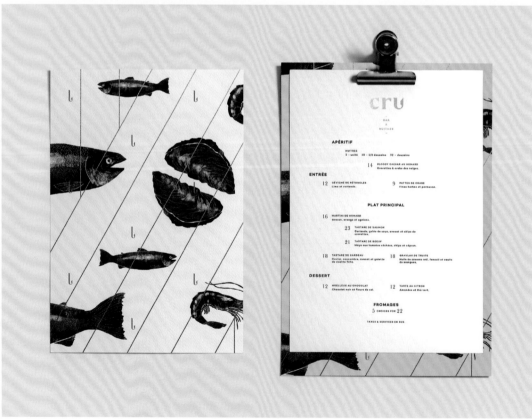

Identity

DESIGN Ivan Khmelevsky,
Moscow **URL**
madebythebakery.com
TWITTER @TheBakeryRocks
STUDIO The Bakery Design
Studio **CLIENT** DJ Trade
PRINCIPAL TYPE GT Walsheim
Latin and GT Walsheim Cyrillic
DIMENSIONS Various

Identity

**DESIGN AND CREATIVE
DIRECTION** Justin Colt and
Jose Fresneda, New York
URL thecollectedworks.xxx
TWITTER @collectedworks
DESIGN STUDIO The Collected
Works **CLIENT** See Through
Lab **PRINCIPAL TYPE** Aperçu
Mono and Kamerik 105 Heavy
DIMENSIONS Various

Identity

DESIGN David Minh Nguyen, San Francisco **URL** davidminhnguyen.com **DESIGN FIRM** Airbnb **PRINCIPAL TYPE** LL Circular Air Pro **DIMENSIONS** Various

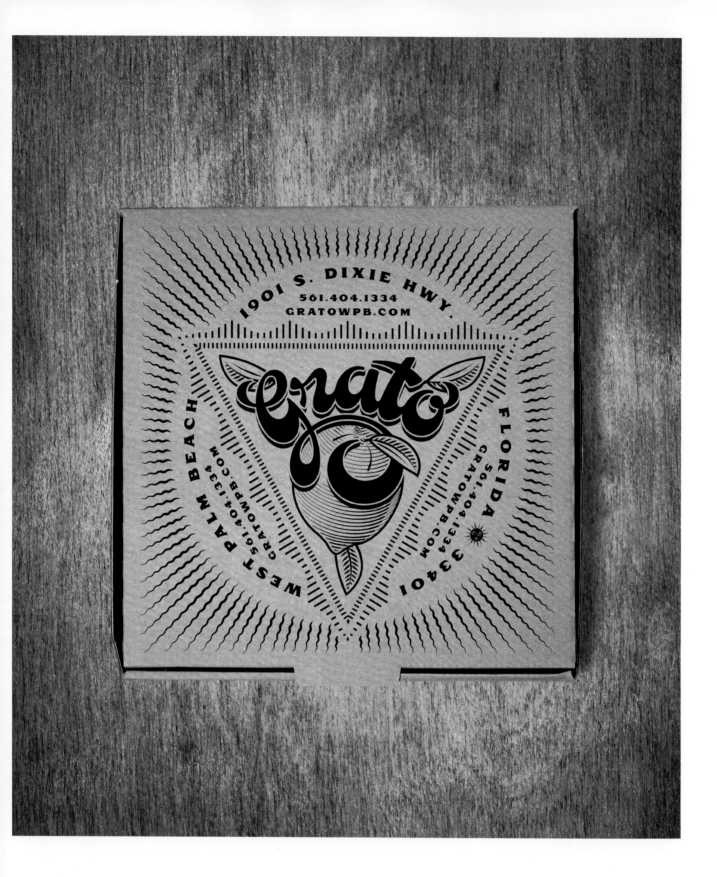

Identity

DESIGN Roberto de Vicq de
Cumptich,• New York **URL**
devicq.com/grato.html **DESIGN
FIRM** de Vicq design **CLIENT**
Clay Conley **PRINCIPAL TYPE**
Taroca, Wonderhand, Zocalo
Text, and handlettering
DIMENSIONS Various

Identity

CREATIVE DIRECTION
Luca Ionescu,• Sydney
TYPOGRAPHER AND 3D DESIGN
Luca Ionescu **CUMMINS**
& PARTNERS CREATIVES
Chris Ellis and Aaron Lipson
PRODUCER Steven Tortosa
URL likemindedstudio.com

FIRM Like Minded Studio
AD AGENCY Cummins &
Partners **CLIENT** Tennis
Australia **PRINCIPAL TYPE**
Custom **DIMENSIONS** Various

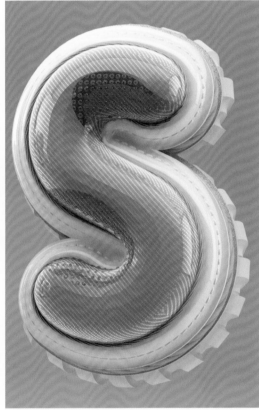

Identity

CREATIVE Jesper Bange and Milla Selkimäki, Helsinki
CREATIVE DIRECTION Jesper Bange **PRODUCTION** Marina Kelahaara **URL** bond-agency. com **DESIGN FIRM** Bond
CLIENT Flow Festival
PRINCIPAL TYPE Flow
DIMENSIONS Various

Identity

DESIGN Marko Salonen, Helsinki **STRATEGIST** Arttu Salovaara **PRODUCER** Piia Suhonen **COPYWRITER** Mira Olsson **PHOTOGRAPHY** Marko Rantanen **URL** bond-agency.com **DESIGN FIRM** Bond

CLIENT Helsinki Philharmonic Orchestra **PRINCIPAL TYPE** Calibre, Founders Grotesk, and Typonine Stencil **DIMENSIONS** Various

HELSINKI PHILHARMONIC ORCHESTRA

Identity

DESIGN Koyuki Inagaki, Tokyo
ART DIRECTION AND LOGO
DESIGN Shun Kawakami
URL artless.co.jp **DESIGN**
FIRM artless Inc. **CLIENT**
Atrium Company and Green
Hospitality Management
Company **PRINCIPAL TYPE**
Brandon Grotesque, FF Mark,
and Risveglio **DIMENSIONS**
Various

Identity

DESIGN Studio Dumbar,
Rotterdam **URL** studiodumbar.
com **TWITTER** @studiodumbar
DESIGN FIRM Studio Dumbar
CLIENT VolkerWessels
Boskalis Marine Solutions
PRINCIPAL TYPE Union
DIMENSIONS Various

Brochure

DESIGN AND ART DIRECTION
David Blumberg, Birmingham,
Alabama **CREATIVE
DIRECTION** Roy Burns III **URL**
lewiscommunications.com
TWITTER @lewisideas **AGENCY**
Lewis Communications
CLIENT Design Week
Birmingham **PRINCIPAL
TYPE** NB Grotesk and NB
International Pro **DIMENSIONS**
8.5 × 11 in. (21.6 × 27.9 cm)

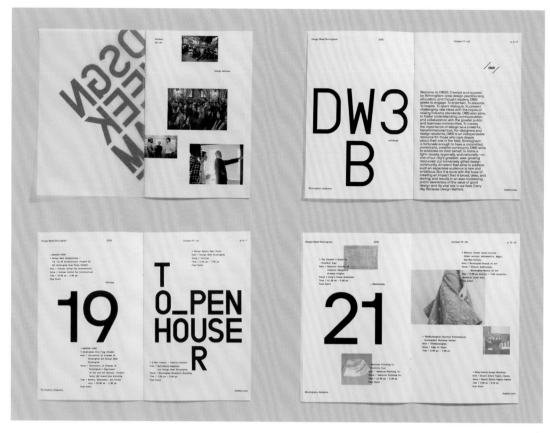

Identity

DESIGN AND ART DIRECTION
Tom Crosby and Anthony
De Leo, Adelaide, Australia
CREATIVE DIRECTION Tom
Crosby and Anthony De Leo
INTERIOR DESIGNER Georgie
Shepherd **TYPOGRAPHER**
Tom Crosby **FINISH ARTIST**
Tom Crosby **PHOTOGRAPHY**
Jonathan VDK **SIGNAGE
MANUFACTURERS** East End
Studios and Iguana Signs **URL**
voicedesign.net **TWITTER**
@voice_of_design **INSTAGRAM**
@voice_of_design **DESIGN
FIRM** Voice **CLIENT** Raw+Real
PRINCIPAL TYPE LL Circular
and custom **DIMENSIONS**
Various

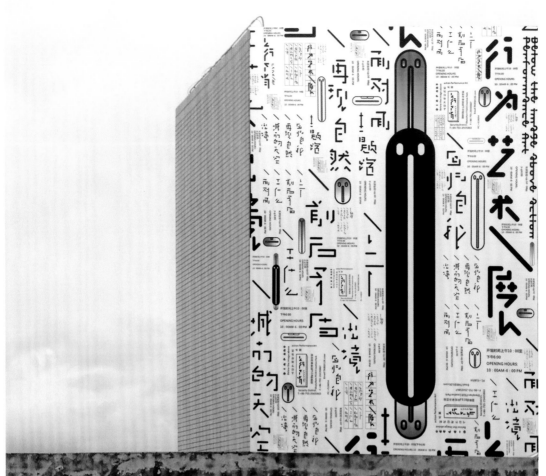

Identity

DESIGN AND LETTERING
Zhang WeiMin, Shenzhen,
China **URL** blog.sina.com.cn/
well197338 **DESIGN FIRM**
WESUN Brand Consultant
CLIENT F518 Creative Park
PRINCIPAL TYPE Handlettering
DIMENSIONS 19.7 × 29.5 in.
(50 × 75 cm)

Identity

DESIGN AND LETTERING
Zhang WeiMin, Shenzhen,
China **URL** blog.sina.com.cn/
well197338 **DESIGN FIRM**
WESUN Brand Consultant
CLIENT MOYU Tea Houses
PRINCIPAL TYPE Handlettering
DIMENSIONS 19.7 × 29.5 in.
(50 × 75 cm)

Identity

ART DIRECTION Mélanie Boucher and Silvan Reste, Montréal **CREATIVE DIRECTION** Yann Mooney **WRITER** Sarah-Maude Beauchesne **ACCOUNT DIRECTOR** Olivier Barreau **ACCOUNT MANAGER** Katherine Letellier **ACCOUNT COORDINATOR** Sarah Lebel-Viens **RETOUCHER** Graphiques M&H **PRINT PRODUCTION** Graphiques M&H **URL** sidlee.com **AGENCY** Sid Lee **CLIENT** SAQ (Québec Alcohol Corporation) **PRINCIPAL TYPE** Brandon, Fresco, and Uomo Piccolo **DIMENSIONS** Various

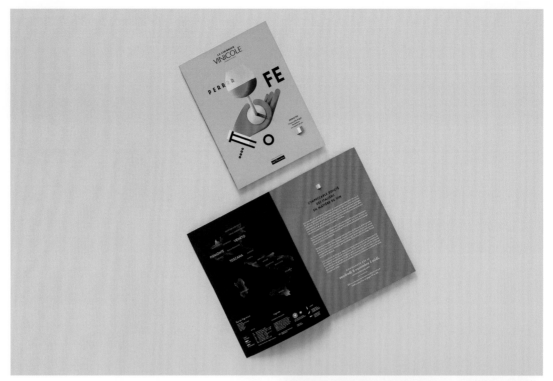

Catalog

DESIGN FIRM Raffinerie
AG für Gestaltung, Zürich
PHOTOGRAPHY Peter Hauser
URL raffinerie.com **CLIENT**
Reseda **PRINCIPAL TYPE**
Mercury Text and
Neuzeit S LT **DIMENSIONS**
5 × 7.4 in. (12.6 × 18.9 cm)

Catalog

DESIGN Ian Crowther, Debra Ohayon and Carl Williamson, New York **URL** familiar-studio. com **TWITTER** @FamiliarStudio **DESIGN FIRM** Familiar **CLIENT** New Museum **PRINCIPAL TYPE** Founders Grotesk, Founders Grotesk Mono, and Tungsten **DIMENSIONS** 9 × 12 in. (22.9 × 27.9 cm)

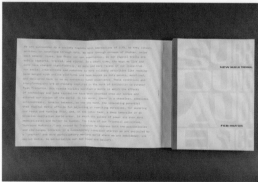

Catalog

DESIGNERS Philip Glenn, Rebecca Leffell-Koren, Lisa Maione, Gabriel Melcher, Scarlett Meng, and Emily Scherer, Providence, Rhode Island **CREATIVE DIRECTION** Lisa Maione and Gabriel Melcher **URL** risd.gd **TWITTER** @risdgd **ADVISOR AND PROFESSOR** Benjamin Shaykin **SCHOOL** Rhode Island School of Design, Graphic Design Department **PRINCIPAL TYPE** Atlas Grotesk, Ivrea, PL Poster, and PL Sans **DIMENSIONS** Various

Calendar

DESIGN DIRECTION Bob
Mytton, Bath, England
CREATIVE DIRECTOR Ed Robin
STUDIO Remote **CREATIVE
DIRECTION** Adam Rodgers
DEVELOPER Tomomitsu
Kanai **JAZZ PIANIST AND
COMPOSER** Tom Berge **URL**
myttonwilliams.co.uk and
studioremote.net **BRAND
AND DESIGN AGENCY** Mytton
Williams **PRINCIPAL TYPE** For
the dates, an individual 3D
rendering for each date that
changes in response to music
and the season; supported
by Univers

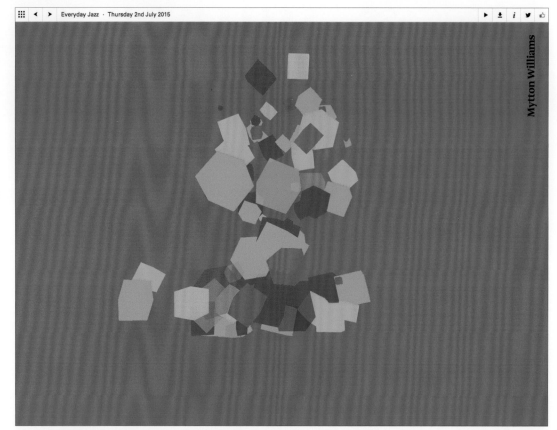

Everyday Jazz · Thursday 2nd July 2015

Mytton Williams

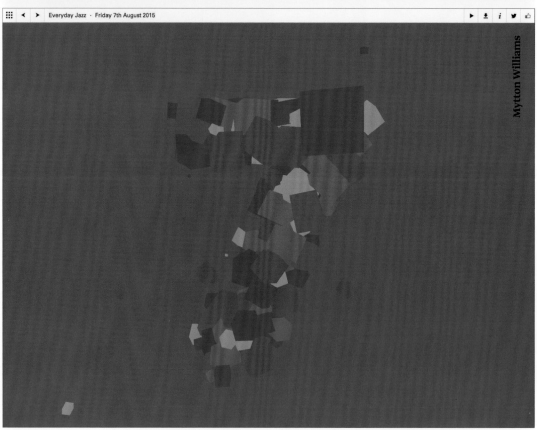

Everyday Jazz · Friday 7th August 2015

Mytton Williams

Brochure

DESIGN Aggie Toppins, Chattanooga, Tennessee **DESIGN FIRM** The Official Studio **URL** theofficialstudio. com **PRINCIPAL TYPE** LL Brown and custom lettering **DIMENSIONS** 11 × 14 in. (28.9 × 38 cm)

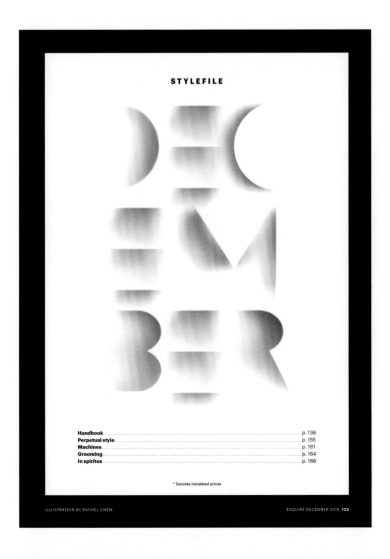

Magazine Section Opener

DESIGN AND LETTERING Rachel Chew, Melbourne, Australia **URL** rachelchew.co **CLIENT** *Esquire* (Malaysia) **PRINCIPAL TYPE** Handlettering **DIMENSIONS** 7.7 × 10.8 in. (19.8 × 27.5 cm)

Magazine Spread

DESIGN Griffin Funk, New York **DESIGN DIRECTOR** Fred Woodward● **PUBLICATION** *GQ* **PRINCIPAL TYPE** Custom **DIMENSIONS** 16 × 10.75 in. (40.6 × 27.3 cm)

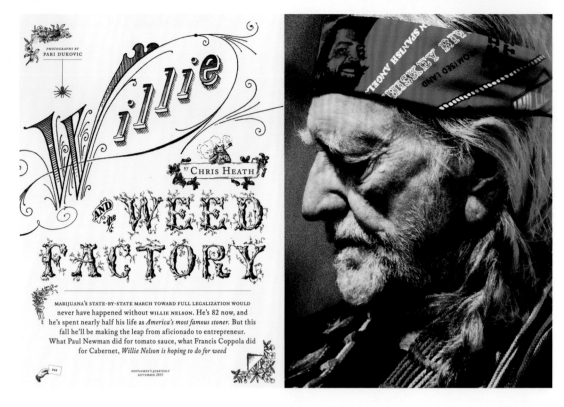

Magazine Spread

DESIGN Kristie Bailey, New York **DESIGN DIRECTOR** Fred Woodward● **PUBLICATION** *GQ* **PRINCIPAL TYPE** Custom **DIMENSIONS** 16 × 10.75 in. (40.6 × 27.3 cm)

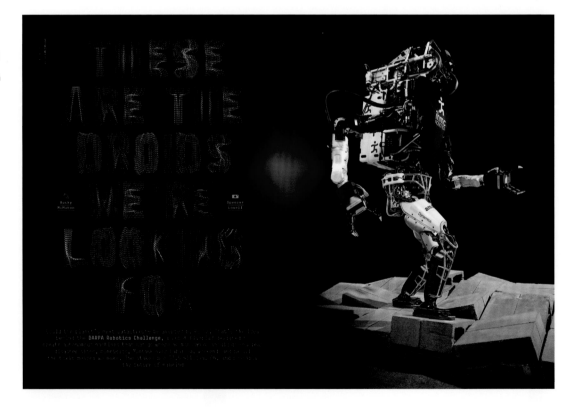

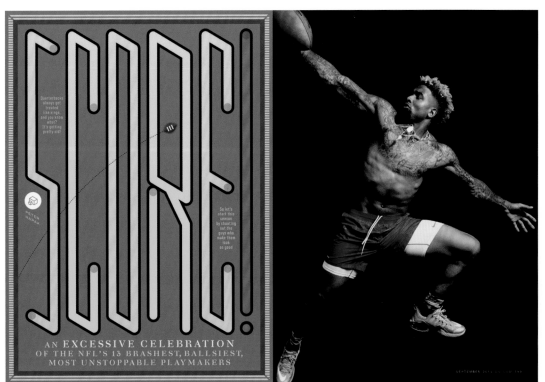

Magazine Spread

DESIGN Martin Salazar, New York **DESIGN DIRECTOR** Fred Woodward● **PUBLICATION** *GQ* **PRINCIPAL TYPE** Custom **DIMENSIONS** 16 × 10.75 in. (40.6 × 27.3 cm)

Magazine Spread

DESIGN John Muñoz, New York **DESIGN DIRECTOR** Fred Woodward● **PUBLICATION** *GQ* **PRINCIPAL TYPE** Custom **DIMENSIONS** 16 × 10.75 in. (40.6 × 27.3 cm)

Magazine Spread

ART DIRECTION Alaina Sullivan, New York **PHOTOGRAPHY** Ted Cavanaugh **LETTERING** Nim Ben-Reuven **URL** nimbenreuven.com **CLIENT** *Bon Appétit* **PRINCIPAL TYPE** Handlettering **DIMENSIONS** 15.5 × 21.5 in. (39.4 × 54.6 cm)

Magazine Spread

ART DIRECTION Raul Aguila, London **CREATIVE PRODUCER** Eve Steben **PHOTOGRAPHY AND LETTERING** Sean Freeman **URL** thereis.co.uk **DESIGN FIRM** THERE IS **CLIENT** *WIRED* **PRINCIPAL TYPE** Handlettering

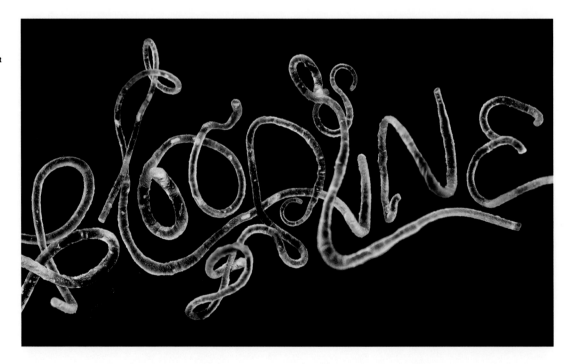

TAY-TANIC

WEREN'T
WE TOLD
THEY DON'T
MAKE
POP STARS
THIS BIG
ANYMORE?

NOBODY
BOTHERED
TO TELL
TAYLOR
SWIFT.

CHUCK
KLOSTERMAN
INTERROGATES
THE MOST
POPULAR
HUMAN
ALIVE

PHOTO-
GRAPHS
BY
MICHAEL
THOMPSON

Magazine Spread

DESIGN Andre Jointé, New York DESIGN DIRECTOR Fred Woodward• PUBLICATION *GQ* PRINCIPAL TYPE Custom DIMENSIONS 16 × 10.75 in. (40.6 × 27.3 cm)

One night in 2012, ROBERT BALES—*a soldier who joined the Army right after 9/11—gunned down 16 men, women, and children in their homes in rural Afghanistan.*

AMERICAN MONSTER

It was the most notorious American wartime atrocity in decades, a tragedy about which he has never spoken. Now, for the first time, Bales explains how he could do something so unimaginable—and how that one long night was actually ten violent years in the making
— BY BRENDAN VAUGHAN

Magazine Spread

DESIGN Martin Salazar, New York DESIGN DIRECTOR Fred Woodward• PUBLICATION *GQ* PRINCIPAL TYPE Custom DIMENSIONS 16 × 10.75 in. (40.6 × 27.3 cm)

Magazine Spread

DESIGN AND ART DIRECTION
Mariela Hsu, Washington, D.C.
CREATIVE DIRECTION Jake
Lefebure and Pum Lefebure●
URL designarmy.com **TWITTER**
@DesignArmy **AGENCY** Design
Army **CLIENT** Washington
Ballet **PRINCIPAL TYPE** LL
Brown, Glosa, High Times,
Sybarite Huge, and custom
DIMENSIONS 10 × 12 in.
(25.5 × 30.5 cm)

Magazine Spread

DESIGN AND ART DIRECTION
Sucha Becky, Washington,
D.C. **CREATIVE DIRECTION** Jake
Lefebure and Pum Lefebure●
URL designarmy.com **TWITTER**
@DesignArmy **AGENCY** Design
Army **CLIENT** *Washingtonian
Bride & Groom* **PRINCIPAL
TYPE** Bebas Neue and Noe
Display **DIMENSIONS**
9 × 11 in. (22.8 × 27.8 cm)

Magazine Spread

DESIGN AND ART DIRECTION
Mariela Hsu, Washington,
D.C. **CREATIVE DIRECTION**
Jake Lefebure and Pum
Lefebure• **URL** designarmy.
com **TWITTER** @DesignArmy
AGENCY Design Army **CLIENT**
Washingtonian Bride & Groom
PRINCIPAL TYPE Austin Fat,
Euclid Flex, Generika Mono,
Sybarite Huge, and custom
DIMENSIONS 9 × 11 in.
(22.8 × 27.8 cm)

Magazine Spread

DESIGN Mariela Hsu,
Washington, D.C. **ART
DIRECTION** Sucha Becky
CREATIVE DIRECTION Jake
Lefebure and Pum Lefebure•
URL designarmy.com **TWITTER**
@DesignArmy **AGENCY** Design
Army **CLIENT** *Washingtonian
Bride & Groom* **PRINCIPAL
TYPE** Custom **DIMENSIONS**
9 × 11 in. (22.8 × 27.8 cm)

Magazine Spread

DESIGN Gabriela Hernandez, Washington, D.C. **ART DIRECTION** Mariela Hsu **CREATIVE DIRECTION** Jake Lefebure and Pum Lefebure● **URL** designarmy.com **TWITTER** @DesignArmy **AGENCY** Design Army **CLIENT** *Washingtonian Bride & Groom* **DIMENSIONS** 9 × 11 in. (22.8 × 27.8 cm) **PRINCIPAL TYPE** Delisia, Fort, Publico, RamaGothic, and custom **DIMENSIONS** 9 × 11 in. (22.8 × 27.8 cm)

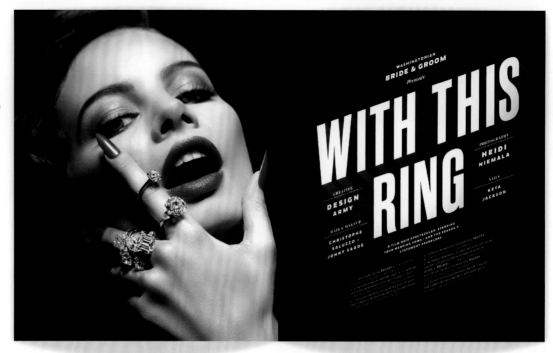

Magazine Spread

ART DIRECTION Sucha Becky **CREATIVE DIRECTION** Jake Lefebure and Pum Lefebure● **URL** designarmy.com **TWITTER** @DesignArmy **AGENCY** Design Army **CLIENT** *Washingtonian Bride & Groom* **PRINCIPAL TYPE** Custom **DIMENSIONS** 9 × 11 in. (22.8 × 27.8 cm)

In the Heart of

FEAST TEXAS

Photographs by
Peden & Munk

In a tribute to his hometown, San Antonio, the chef Quealy Watson cooks a
Tex-Mex barbecue with Asian flavors and gathers friends to celebrate the season.

By Sam Sifton

52

Magazine Spread

DESIGN Matt Willey, New
York **DESIGN DIRECTOR** Gail
Bichler **ART DIRECTOR** Matt
Willey **DEPUTY ART DIRECTOR**
Jason Sfetko **DIRECTOR OF
PHOTOGRAPHY** Kathy Ryan
PHOTOGRAPHY Peden + Munk
PHOTO EDITOR Christine Walsh
PUBLICATION *The New York
Times Magazine* **PRINCIPAL
TYPE** Custom **DIMENSIONS**
11 × 17 in. (27.9 × 43.2 cm)

ROAD WAR- RIORS

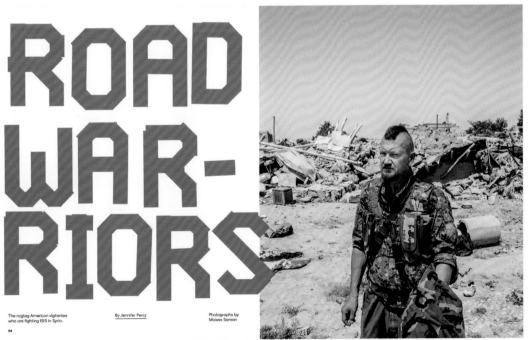

The ragtag American vigilantes
who are fighting ISIS in Syria.

By Jennifer Percy

Photographs by
Moises Saman

54

Magazine Spread

DESIGN Ben Grandgenett, New
York **DESIGN DIRECTOR** Gail
Bichler **ART DIRECTOR** Matt
Willey **DEPUTY ART DIRECTOR**
Jason Sfetko **DIRECTOR OF
PHOTOGRAPHY** Kathy Ryan
PHOTOGRAPHY Moises Saman
PHOTO EDITOR Stacey Baker
PUBLICATION *The New York
Times Magazine* **PRINCIPAL
TYPE** Custom **DIMENSIONS**
11 × 17 in. (27.9 × 43.2 cm)

Magazine Spread

DESIGN Jason Sfetko, New York **DESIGN DIRECTOR** Gail Bichler **ART DIRECTOR** Matt Willey **DEPUTY ART DIRECTOR** Jason Sfetko **DIRECTOR OF PHOTOGRAPHY** Kathy Ryan **PHOTOGRAPHY** Luca Locatelli **PHOTO EDITOR** Stacey Baker **PUBLICATION** *The New York Times Magazine* **PRINCIPAL TYPE** Custom **DIMENSIONS** 11 × 17 in. (27.9 × 43.2 cm)

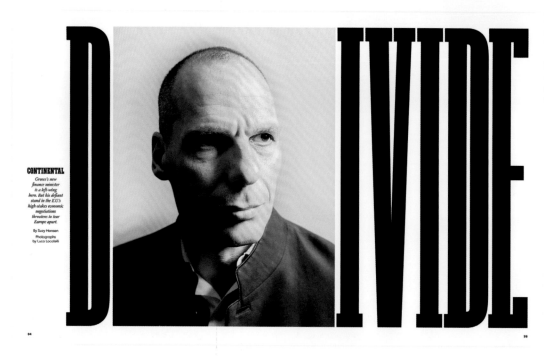

Magazine

DESIGN Rob Gonzalez and Jonathan Quainton, London **URL** Andrew Diprose **DEPUTY CREATIVE DIRECTOR** Ben Fraser **URL** madebysawdust.co.uk **TWITTER** @SawdustStudio **DESIGN FIRM** Sawdust **CLIENT** *WIRED* (United Kingdom) **PRINCIPAL TYPE** Bespoke **DIMENSIONS** 7.1 × 9.25 in. (18 × 23.5 cm)

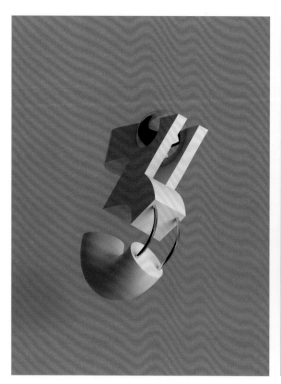

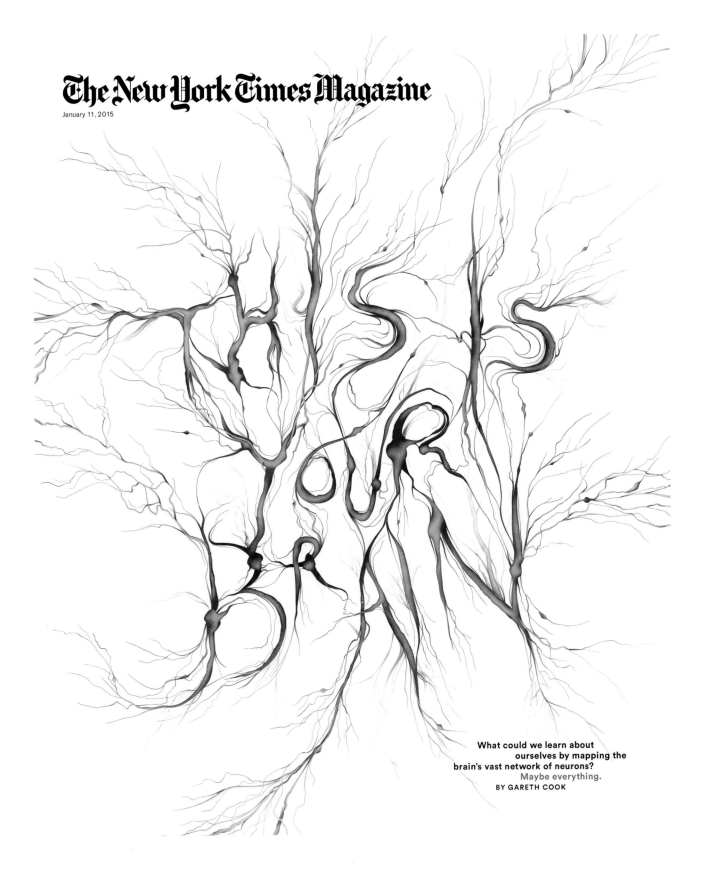

Magazine Cover

DESIGN Rob Gonzalez and
Jonathan Quainton, London
ART DIRECTION Gail Bichler
and Jason Sfetko, New York
URL madebysawdust.co.uk
TWITTER @SawdustStudio
DESIGN FIRM Sawdust
CLIENT *The New York Times*

Magazine **PRINCIPAL TYPE**
Bespoke **DIMENSIONS**
8.9 × 10.9 in. (22.7 × 27.6 cm)

Magazine Cover

DESIGN Matt Willey, New York
DESIGN DIRECTOR Gail Bichler
ART DIRECTOR Matt Willey
DEPUTY ART DIRECTOR Jason
Sfetko **ILLUSTRATOR** Sean
Freeman **PUBLICATION** *The
New York Times Magazine*
DIMENSIONS 8.5 × 11 in.
(21.6 × 27.9 cm)

The New York Times Magazine

December 20, 2015

Has Europe reached the breaking point? By Jim Yardley

DESIGN Anton Ioukhnovets, New York **DESIGN DIRECTOR** Gail Bichler **ART DIRECTOR** Matt Willey **DEPUTY ART DIRECTOR** Jason Sfetko **DIRECTOR OF PHOTOGRAPHY** Kathy Ryan **PHOTO EDITOR** Amy Kellner **PUBLICATION** *The New York Times Magazine*

PRINCIPAL TYPE Helmut
DIMENSIONS 8.5 × 11 in. (21.6 × 27.9 cm)

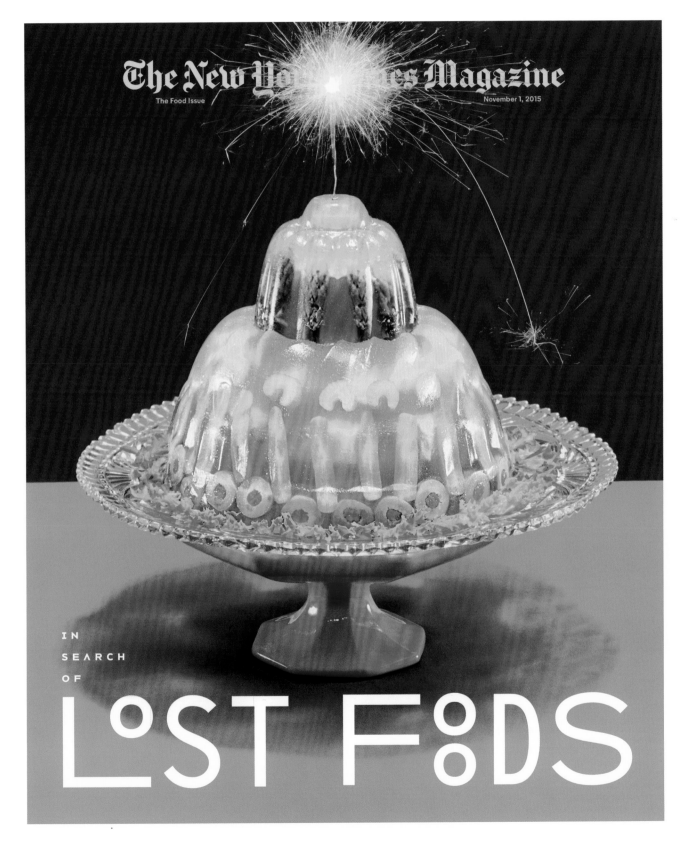

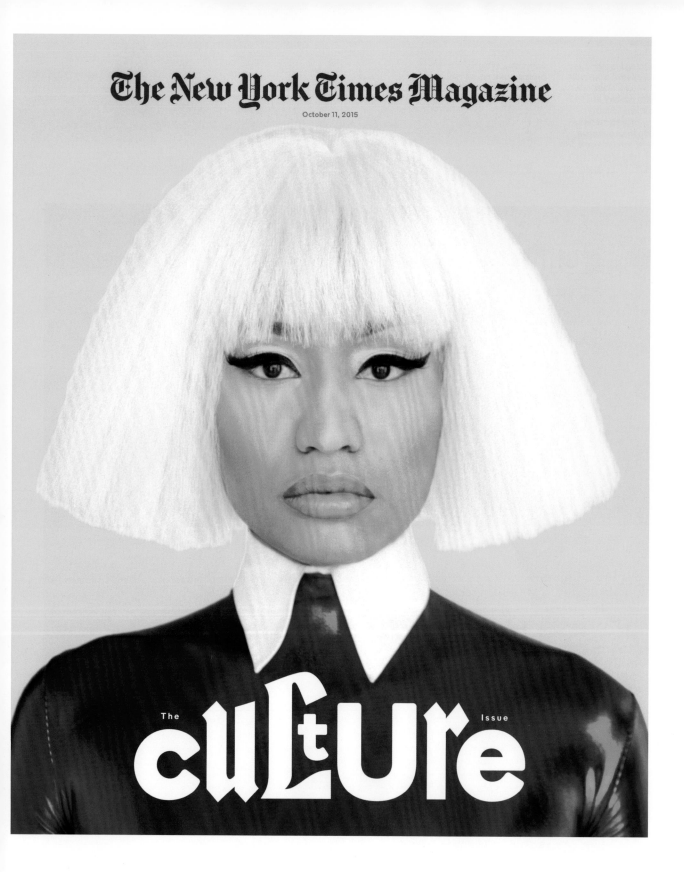

Magazine

DESIGN Anton Ioukhnovets, New York **DESIGN DIRECTOR** Gail Bichler **ART DIRECTOR** Matt Willey **DEPUTY ART DIRECTOR** Jason Sfetko **DIRECTOR OF PHOTOGRAPHY** Kathy Ryan **PUBLICATION** *The New York Times Magazine*

PRINCIPAL TYPE Boing and Bradley-Pro **DIMENSIONS** 8.5 × 11 in. (21.6 × 27.9 cm)

Goodbye,
imaginary friends.
Hello, A.I. dolls.

By James Vlahos

Now I Have A Brain!

Magazine Story

DESIGN Matt Willey, New
York **DESIGN DIRECTOR** Gail
Bichler **ART DIRECTOR** Matt
Willey **DEPUTY ART DIRECTOR**
Jason Sfetko **DIRECTOR OF
PHOTOGRAPHY** Kathy Ryan
PHOTO EDITOR Amy Kellner
ILLUSTRATOR Luke Lucas

PUBLICATION *The New York
Times Magazine* **DIMENSIONS**
8.5 × 11 in. (21.6 × 27.9 cm)

Invitation

DESIGN Nathan Durrant, San Francisco **ART DIRECTION** Jennifer Jerde **URL** elixirdesign.com **TWITTER** @elxrdsgn **DESIGN FIRM** Elixir Design **CLIENT** Tipping Point Community **PRINCIPAL TYPE** Adelle Sans and Knockout **DIMENSIONS** Envelope: 7.1 × 5.75 in. (19 × 14.5 cm) Accordion-fold invitation: 6 × 34.75 in. (15.25 × 88.25 cm)

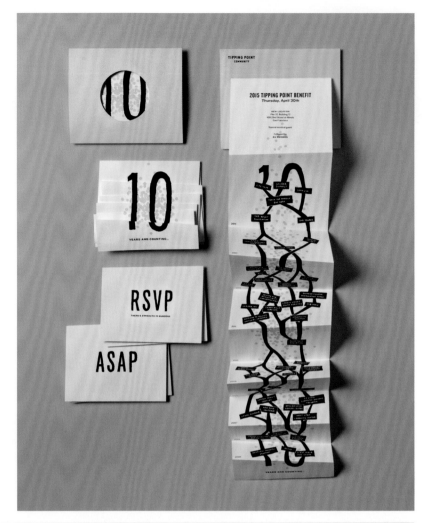

Garbage Bag

DESIGN Christoph Amrhein and Heinz Anderhalden, Sarnen, Switzerland **URL** A-A.ch **DESIGN FIRM** Amrhein Anderhalden **CLIENT** Entsorgungszweckverband Obwalden **PRINCIPAL TYPE** Soin Sans Pro and custom **DIMENSIONS** 22.4 × 23.2 in. (57 × 59 cm)

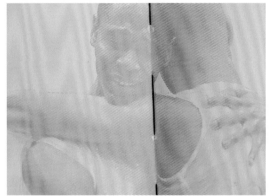

Program

DESIGN Daniel Arenas and Juan Miguel Marin, New York **ART DIRECTION** Juan Miguel Marin **CREATIVE DIRECTION** David Byrne **PRODUCERS** Catalina Kulczar, Adam Rosenblum, and LeeAnn Rossi **COLLAGES** Juan Miguel

Marin **PHOTOGRAPHY** Catalina Kulczar **URL** lamoutique.com **DESIGN FIRM** La Moutique **CLIENT** David Byrne and Todomundo **PRINCIPAL TYPE** Brandon Grotesque, Adobe Caslon Pro, and Minion Pro **DIMENSIONS** Book: 9 × 12 in.

(22.9 × 30.5 cm) Poster: 35 × 23.5 in. (88.9 × 59.7 cm)

Book

DESIGN Fons Hickmann● and Sven Lindhorst-Emme,● Berlin **ART DIRECTION** Fons Hickmann **ILLUSTRATION** Lizzy Onck **AUTHORS** K. Eitner, K. Leesch, and K. Morgenthaler **URL** m23.de **TWITTER** @FonsHickmannM23

STUDIO Fons Hickmann m23 **CLIENT** Greenpeace **PRINCIPAL TYPE** Schulbuch Bayern and Walbaum **DIMENSIONS** 5.9 × 7.9 in. (15 × 20 cm)

Book Jacket

DESIGN Marta Cerdà Alimbau,● Barcelona **URL** martacerda.com **TWITTER** @MartaCerdaAlimb **CLIENT** Atelier / Visual Art, Design and Life **PRINCIPAL TYPE** Pradell Roman **DIMENSIONS** 6.7 × 6.7 in. (17 × 17 cm)

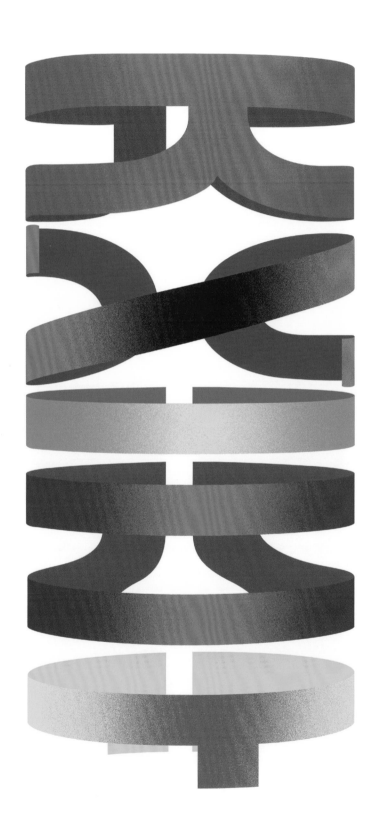

_Goin' Wild

Campaign

DESIGN Olivia King and Jason Little,• Sydney **CREATIVE DIRECTION** Jason Little **WRITERS** Olivia King, Jason Little, Sam Mcguinness, and Ben Walker **ANIMATION** Ben Walker **WEB DESIGN** Zann St Pierre **URL** forthepeople. agency **TWITTER** @forthepeopleau **DESIGN FIRM** For The People **CLIENT** BJ Ball Papers and Mohawk Paper **PRINCIPAL TYPE** Karla and Gt Pressura **DIMENSIONS** Various

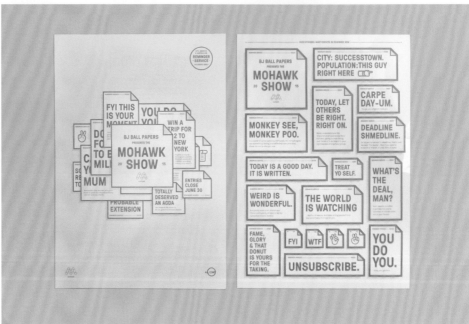

Identity

DESIGN Jeff Canham and
Peter Nowell, San Francisco
URL pnowell.com **TWITTER**
@pnowelldesign **DESIGN FIRM**
Peter Nowell Design **CLIENT**
Juice Shop **PRINCIPAL TYPE**
Egyptian Unified and Livory
DIMENSIONS
21 × 16.5 in. (53 × 42 cm)

Book

DESIGN Anja Delbello and
Aljaž Vesel, Ljubljana, Slovenia
EDITOR Špela Gazvoda
CO-EDITOR Anja Delbello
ILLUSTRATOR Tanja Semion
PHOTOGRAPHY Andraž Šapec
URL weareaa.com **STUDIO**
AA **CLIENT** R-tisk print house
PRINCIPAL TYPE Founders
Grotesk, Founders Grotesk
Mono, Founders Grotesk Text,
and Macula **DIMENSIONS**
5.7 × 9.1 in. (14.5 × 23 cm)

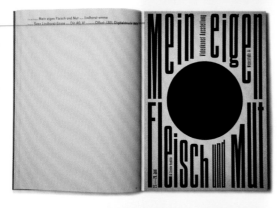

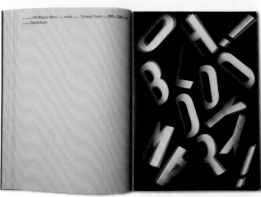

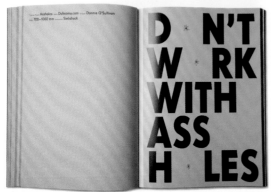

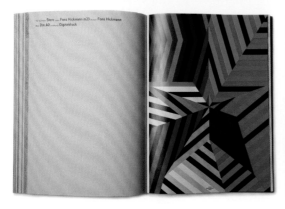

Exhibition and Collateral

DESIGN Loana Boppart, Fons Hickmann,● and Sven Lindhorst-Emme,● Berlin **PRINTER** Gallery Print **URL** fonshickmann.com and lindhorst-emme.de **STUDIOS** Fons Hickmann and Sven Lindhorst-Emme **CLIENTS** seltmann+söhne publisher and weltformat **PRINCIPAL TYPE** FF Cst Berlin West Original **DIMENSIONS** Various

Design · *Never Just a Garnish*

Strategy · *Parses through the Data*

Account Management · *Sage Counsel*

Production · *Always on Thyme*

Self-Promotion

DESIGN Hee Je Wi, New York
SENIOR DESIGN Lingxiao Tan
CHIEF CREATIVE OFFICER
Stewart Devlin● **ASSOCIATE**
CREATIVE DIRECTOR Rafael
Medina **STRATEGIST**
Madeleine Kronovet **URL**
redpeakgroup.com **DESIGN**

FIRM Red Peak **PRINCIPAL**
TYPE Chronicle Text Grade 1
Italic and Chronicle Text Grade
1 Roman **DIMENSIONS**
4.25 × 5.75 in. (11 × 14.5 cm)

Invitation

DESIGN Bob Aufuldish,•
San Anselmo, California **URL**
aufwar.com **DESIGN FIRM**
Aufuldish & Warinner **CLIENT**
California College of the Arts
PRINCIPAL TYPE Libertad,
Onyx, and Poster Bodoni
DIMENSIONS 15.75 × 23.6 in.
(40 × 60 cm)

BLACK
IS THE NEW
BLACK

CCA GALA
ALUMNI FASHION SHOW
MARCH 25, 2015

CCa

California College of the Arts President Stephen Beal and
co-chairs CCA trustee Kay Kimpton Walker, Leigh Sherwood Matthes,
and Cathy Podell invite you to

BLACK IS THE NEW **BLACK**
CCA GALA ALUMNI FASHION SHOW

**FEATURING EMERGING LEADERS
IN THE FASHION INDUSTRY**

**BENEFITTING THE
CCA SCHOLARSHIP PROGRAM**

WEDNESDAY, MARCH 25, 2015

CALIFORNIA COLLEGE OF THE ARTS
1111 Eighth Street, San Francisco

6:00 PM COCKTAILS
7:15 PM DINNER
8:15 PM FASHION SHOW
AFTER-PARTY

Attire: Black ...what else?
Décor by Stanlee Gatti
Catering by Taste
Complimentary valet parking

Please respond by returning the enclosed card or contacting
Kelly Dawson at 510.594.3776 or kdawson2@cca.edu.

HONORARY COMMITTEE

Richard Beard
Gretchen & John Berggruen
Frances Bowes
Sabrina Buell & Yves Béhar
Heidi Castelein
Roselyn Chroman Swig
Chris Columbus & Monica Devereux
Douglas Durkin
Carla Emil & Rich Silverstein
Andrew Fisher (BFA 1978) & Jeffry Weisman
Stanlee Gatti
Lauren Goodman
Jane Griffin Gruber
Kate Harbin & Adam Clammer
Brenda & George Jewett (BArch 1996)
Pam & Dick Kramlich
Leslie & Michael Krasny
Mayor Ed Lee
Mary Lester

Michele & Chris Meany
Tony & Celeste Meier
Eileen & Peter Michael
Lisa & John Miller
Yurie & Carl Pascarella
Nick & Leslie Podell
Becca Prowda & Daniel Lurie
Victoria & Phillip Raiser
Jeanne & Sanford Robertson
Annie Robinson Woods &
   F. Montgomery Woods
O.J. & Gary Shansby
Ali Speer
Norah & Norman Stone
Laura & Joe Sweeney
Susan Swig
Summer Tompkins Walker
Anne Waterman Bassin & Bass Bassin

CALIFORNIA COLLEGE OF THE ARTS
BOARD OF TRUSTEES

C. Diane Christensen, Chair

Simon J. Blattner | Lorna F. Meyer
Tecoah P. Bruce (MA/BD 1978) | Ann Morhauser (BFA Glass 1979)
Catherine Courage | Timothy Mott
Susan M. Cummins | Steven H. Oliver
Patricia W. Fitzpatrick | F. Noel Perry
Nancy S. Forster | Nathan E. (Gene) Savin
M. Arthur Gensler Jr., FAIA | Alan L. Stein
Maria Giudice | Judith P. Timken
Emma J. Goltz | John S. (Jack) Wadsworth, Jr.
Ann M. Hatch | Asher Waldfogel
Nancy Howes (BFA Metal Arts 2005) | Vinitha J. Watson (DMBA 2010)
George F. Jewett (BArch 1996) | Calvin B. Wheeler, MD
Kay Kimpton Walker | Carlie Wilmans
Byron D. Kuth, FAIA | Ronald C. Wornick
Joyce B. Linker | Mary L. Zlot

CALIFORNIA COLLEGE OF THE ARTS
IS PLEASED TO THANK
THE EVENING'S SPONSORS

HAUTE COUTURE | C. Diane Christensen & Jean M. Pierret
 | F. Noel Perry
 | Cathy & Mike Podell

NOUVELLE COUTURE | Patricia W. Fitzpatrick
 | Brenda & George Jewett
 | Lorna Meyer Calas & Dennis Calas
 | Leigh Sherwood Matthes & Bill Matthes
 | Sharon Simpson
 | Judy & Bill Timken

AVANT-GARDE | Gretchen & John Berggruen
 | City National Bank
 | Nancy & Pat Forster
 | Nancy & Timothy Howes
 | Kay Kimpton Walker & Sandy Walker
 | Potasa Foundation
 | Ruth & Alan Stein
 | Anita & Ronald C. Wornick
 | Mary & Harold Zlot

PRÊT-À-PORTER | First Republic Bank, Hawkins Delafield & Wood LLP,
 | and Stern Brothers & Co.
 | GZ Insurance
 | Michele & Chris Meany
 | Tim Mott
 | Panoramic Interests
 | Nick & Leslie Podell
 | PCH
 | Richard Beard Architects
 | Vartain Law Group

FEATURING FASHION DESIGN ALUMNI

AMBER CLISURA (BFA 2005)
OWNER & DESIGNER, **SALT**

HANNAH GALLAGHER (BFA 2006)
DIRECTOR OF PRODUCTION, **BIBHU MOHAPATRA**

ERICK LOPEZ (BFA 2014)
7×7 MAGAZINE'S EMERGING DESIGNER OF THE YEAR AWARD WINNER (2014)
ASSISTANT DESIGNER, **ABERCROMBIE & FITCH**

LES SCHWEIKERT (BFA 2006)
SENIOR DESIGNER OF COUTURE AND BRIDAL, **BADGLEY MISCHKA**

PALOMA VON BROADLEY (BFA 2009)
MANAGER, **D&H SUSTAINABLE JEWELERS**

PIN YUN (SINDIA) LIN (BFA 2014)
FASHION DESIGNER, **SIMPLY**

YOUR GIFT MATTERS TO CCA STUDENTS

SAHARA JOHNSON (TEXTILES 2015)

I knew CCA was where I wanted to study, and thanks to my scholarship that dream
was attainable. CCA challenges me to question assumptions and aspire to make a
profound difference. Now I plan to share all I've learned with children through youth
education programs.

BENJAMIN WASSERMAN (GRAPHIC DESIGN 2015)

It means a great deal to know there are generous people like you willing to support young
designers and artists. Without a scholarship, I never would have been able to attend a
school as inspirational and influential as CCA. My education is transforming me into the
designer I hoped to be, helping people make things look and work better.

PLEASE ALSO JOIN US FOR THE ANNUAL
SENIOR FASHION SHOW MAY 15, 2015

Book

DESIGN AND ART DIRECTION
Ariane Spanier, Berlin **URL**
arianespanier.com **DESIGN**
FIRM Ariane Spanier Design
CLIENT Punkt ø / Momentum
Biennial for Contemporary
Art, Norway **PRINCIPAL TYPE**
Larsseit **DIMENSIONS**
5.9 × 8.7 in. (15 × 22 cm)

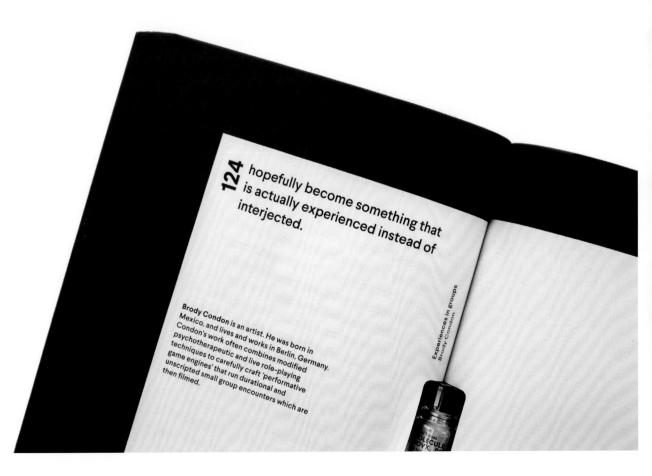

Calendar

DESIGN AND ART DIRECTION
Anton Huber and Elisa Huber,
Munich **DESIGN STUDIO**
etcorporate – creative brand
design **CLIENT** Fedrigoni
Deutschland **PRINCIPAL TYPE**
Avenir, Minion, and custom
lettering **DIMENSIONS**
5.9 × 8.5 in. (15 × 21.5 cm)

Book

CREATIVE DIRECTION Kimoon
Kim, Seoul URL mykc.kr
STUDIO CMYK Books, an
imprint of mykc graphic design
studio PRINCIPAL TYPE Neue
Haas Grotesk and Sandol Neo
Gothic DIMENSIONS
6.5 × 9.6 in. (16.5 × 24.4 cm)

Identity

DESIGN Jolin Masson, Montréal **URL** jolinmasson.com **CLIENT** Association des galeries d'art contemporain **PRINCIPAL TYPE** Mercury Text and Open Sans **DIMENSIONS** Various

Packaging

DESIGN Lucas Campoi, Flora de Carvalho, Dominique Kronemberger, and Rodrigo Saiani, Rio de Janeiro **URL** Rodrigo Saiani **URL** plau.co **TWITTER** @PlauStudio **DESIGN FIRM** Plau **PRINCIPAL TYPE** Freight Text, Knockout 28, and Moccato **DIMENSIONS** Box: 4 × 6.1 × 1.7 in. (6 × 15.5 × 4.3 cm) Shipping Box: 8 × 6.5 × 2 in. (20.2 × 16.5 × 5 cm)

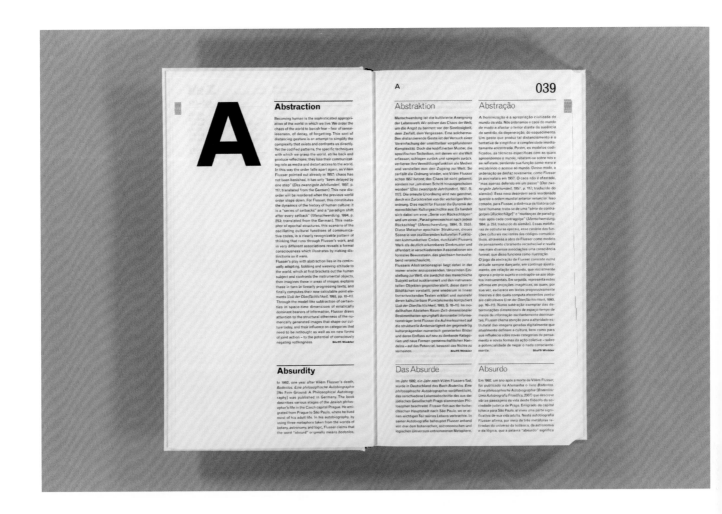

Book

DESIGN Sascha Fronczek and 2xGoldstein, Rheinstetten, Germany **DESIGN FIRM** 2xGoldstein+Fronczek **CLIENT** ZKM | Center for Art and Media Karlsruhe, Vilém Flusser Archiv, UNIVOCAL **PRINCIPAL TYPE** Monotype Grotesque **DIMENSIONS** 6.3 × 11.4 in. (16 × 29 cm)

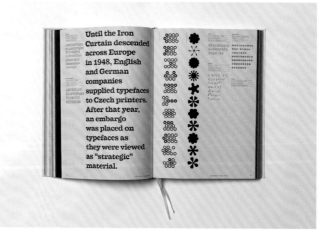

Book

DESIGN Zuzana Lednicka and
Radek Sidun, Prague **AUTHORS**
Tomas Brousil and Petra
Docekalova **URL** typo9010.cz/
en **TWITTER** @BriefcaseType,
@docekalovapetra,
@RadekSidun, @SCTF
CLIENT Suitcase and Briefcase

Type Foundry **PRINCIPAL
TYPE** Urban Grotesk 9010
DIMENSIONS 8.7 × 11.8 in.
(22 × 30 cm)

Book

DESIGN Ludovic Balland and
Thomas Petit, Basel **ART
DIRECTION** Ludovic Balland
DESIGN FIRM Ludovic Balland
Typography Cabinet **CLIENT**
Centre culturel suisse Paris
PRINCIPAL TYPE NEXT
Book and NEXT Poster
Regular, Medium, and Italic
DIMENSIONS 11.7 × 9 in.
(30 × 23 cm)

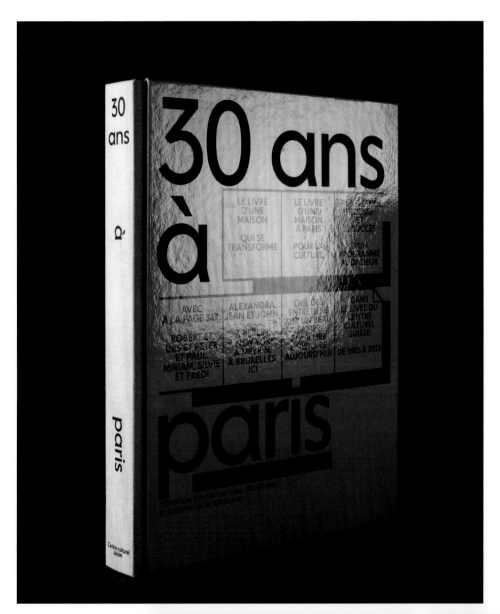

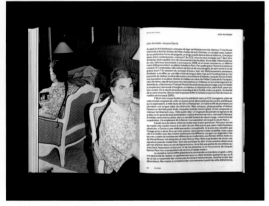

Book

DESIGN Cameron Duncalfe and Shirley Riordon, Oakville, Canada **URL** riordondesign. com **TWITTER** @riordondesign **DESIGN FIRM** Riordon Design **PRINCIPAL TYPE** Fairfield LH 45 Light, Fairfield LH 46 Light Italic, Nudista Light, Nudista Medium, and Nudista SemiBold **DIMENSIONS** 10 × 13.75 in. (25.4 × 34.9 cm)

Poster

DESIGN Brett Ramsay, Toronto **URL** brettramsay.com **TWITTER** @BrettRamsay **CLIENT** Xpace Cultural Centre **PRINCIPAL TYPE** Neutral **DIMENSIONS** 11 × 17 in. (27.9 × 43.2 cm)

Saturday
MAR.
7
from 1–4

TAX WORK -SHOP
for Artists, Designers & Creatives

HOW TO WRITE OFF YOUR PROFESSIONAL PRACTICE

SPEAKER — **BRIAN BORTS, Chartered Accountant**
(specializing in the arts & entertainment industry)

TOPICS —
Harmonized Sales Tax (HST)
Registered Retirement Savings Plan (RRSP's)
Legal Entities
Employment vs. Self-Employment
Self-Employment Expenses
Filing Requirements
Record Keeping

XPACE CULTURAL CENTRE
303 Lansdowne Ave, Unit 2 / between Dundas & College

The workshop is **FREE** but please RSVP to brette@xpace.info as space is limited

Book

URL Nour S. Kanafani,● Beirut
GRAPHIC DESIGN Maya Akel
EDITING Leila Musfy **ARABIC**
TYPESETTING Lara Captan
URL cd-sal.com **DESIGN FIRM**
Communication Design SAL
CLIENT American University
of Beirut **PRINCIPAL TYPE**
Arabic fonts: DT Emiri, DT
Naskh, and DT Nastaliq; Latin
fonts: Univers 67 Condensed
Bold, Univers 65 Bold, and
Univers 47 Condensed Light
DIMENSIONS 9.1 × 11.8 in.
(23 × 30 cm)

Book

DESIGN Emanuel Cohen and Catherine Plouffe, Montréal **PHOTOGRAPHY** Virginie Gosselin **AUTHOR** Marie-Pier Gosselin **URL** 26lettres.com **CLIENT** Fromagerie Au Gré des Champs **PRINCIPAL TYPE** Maison Neue and New Fournier **DIMENSIONS** 8 × 10.5 in. (20.3 × 26.7 cm)

Experimental

DESIGN Jason Heuer,[•] Astoria,
New York **URL** jasonheuer.
com **PRINCIPAL TYPE** Trade
Gothic Bold Condensed No. 20
DIMENSIONS 8 × 10 × 1.5 in.
(20 × 25 × 4 cm)

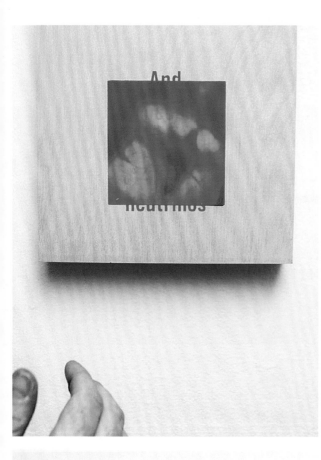

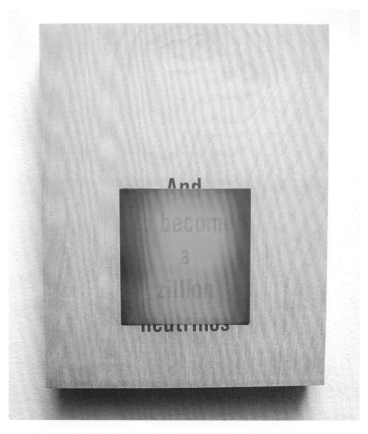

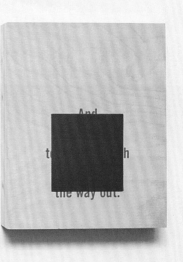

Identity

DESIGN Fidel Peña, Toronto
CREATIVE DIRECTION Claire
Dawson and Fidel Peña **URL**
underlinestudio.com **TWITTER**
@underlineinc **DESIGN FIRM**
Underline Studio **CLIENT**

Advertising and Design Club
of Canada **PRINCIPAL TYPE**
Suisse BP Int'l **DIMENSIONS**
Smaller posters: 15.75 × 19.7
in. (40 × 50 cm) Larger posters:
19.7 × 27.5 in. (50 × 70 cm)

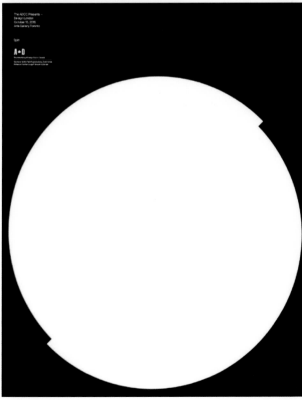

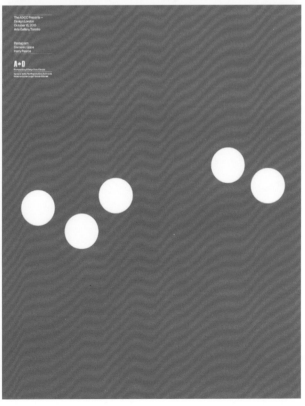

Book

DESIGN Qing Zhao, NanJing,
China **CLIENT** Li Jin and Jin
Weihong **PRINCIPAL TYPE** Bell
MT and SimSun **DIMENSIONS**
11.7 × 7.5 in. (29.8 × 19 cm)

Identity

DESIGN Michael Bierut●
and Britt Cobb, New York
ART DIRECTION Michael
Bierut **ASSOCIATE** Britt Cobb
ANIMATION Anthony Zukofsky
URL pentagram.com **TWITTER**
@pentagram **DESIGN FIRM**
Pentagram● **CLIENT** The

Architectural League of New
York **PRINCIPAL TYPE** Helvetica
Neue Bold **DIMENSIONS**
Various

Identity

DESIGN Luis A. Díaz-Alejandro
and Luis A. Vázquez O'Neill,
San Juan **DIRECTOR** Luis A.
Díaz-Alejandro **URL** dd-diseno.
com **DESIGN FIRM** DD–Diseño
CLIENT Institute of Puerto
Rican Culture **PRINCIPAL**
TYPE Proxima Nova
DIMENSIONS Various

Brochure

DESIGN AND LETTERING
Jeff Rogers,• New York
BOOK Bradford Louryk
PHOTOGRAPHY Zack DeZon
URL HowdyJeff.com **TWITTER**
@frogers **CLIENT** Playwrights
Horizons **PRINCIPAL TYPE**
Bodoni Egyptian Pro, Brandon
Grotesque, and custom
DIMENSIONS 10.5 × 12 in.
(26.7 × 30.5 cm)

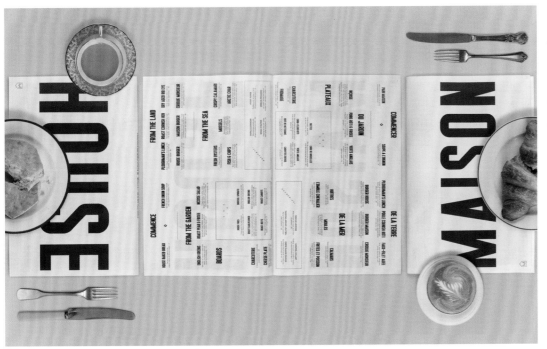

Menu

DESIGN Ryan Crouchman,
Toronto **ART DIRECTION**
Ryan Crouchman and
Lisa Greenberg **CREATIVE
DIRECTION** Lisa Greenberg
and Judy John **CHIEF
CREATIVE OFFICER** Judy John
COPYWRITER Steve Persico
STYLISTS Ryan Crouchman
and Lisa Greenberg
PHOTOGRAPHY
Rob Fiocca and Arash
Moallemi **PRINTING HOUSE**
Somerset Graphics and
Webnews Printing **URL**
leoburnett.ca **TWITTER**
@LeoBurnettTor **AGENCY**
Leo Burnett Toronto **CLIENT**
House-Maison **PRINCIPAL
TYPE** Futwora and Kane
dimensions 11.5 × 17 in.
(29.2 × 43.2 cm)

Catalog

CREATIVE DIRECTOR Regina
Jaeger, Überlingen, Germany
URL jaegerundjaeger.de
DESIGN AGENCY jäger &
jäger **CLIENT** Nils Holger
Moormann GmbH **PRINCIPAL
TYPE** ITC Franklin Gothic Std
DIMENSIONS 11.4 × 8.9 in.
(29 × 22.5 cm)

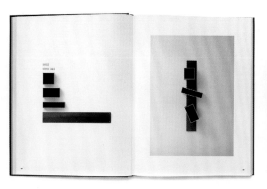

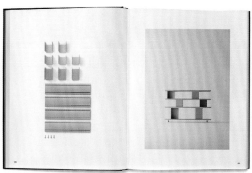

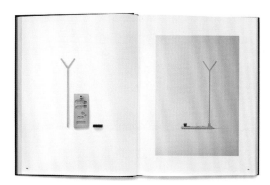

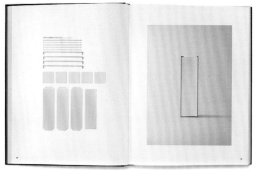

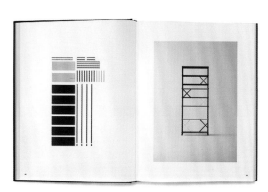

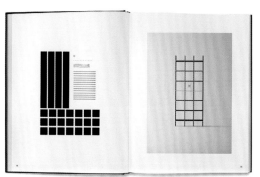

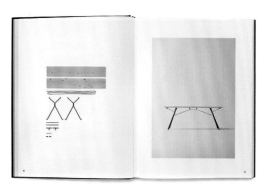

一緒なら、どんな未来も創っていける。

Co-innovating tomorrow

Co-innovating tomorrow
このコーポレート・ブランド・スローガンは、
次代をひらくイノベーションをお客様とともに、という
私たちの次の100年に向けた約束です。
この約束を果たしていくために、私たちは、
計測・制御・情報を組み合わせたソリューションで、
業界や国境を超えて「モノ」をつなぎ、
これまでにない「コト」や価値を創り出していきます。
こうした挑戦の積み重ねによって、
明日という未来はより確かなものになるでしょう。
世界中のお客様と、「夢」をかなえる歩みをともに。
イノベーションのパートナーはYOKOGAWAです。

Co-innovating tomorrow™

YOKOGAWA ◆ | 100th ANNIVERSARY 1915-2015

おかげさまで、横河電機株式会社は
本日創立100周年を迎えることができました。

www.yokogawa.co.jp 横河電機株式会社

Advertising

DESIGN AND ART DIRECTION
Hiroyuki Nakamura and
Masayasu Saito, Tokyo
CREATIVE DIRECTION Kiyohiko
Tozawa **COPYWRITER** Takeshi
Wakabayashi **PHOTOGRAPHY**
Tetsuro Ikejima **RETOUCHER**
NEVE producers Masanobu
Chiba, Yuji Goto, and Hiroshi
Oyamada **URL** nks.co.jp
DESIGN FIRM Nikkeisha
Creative Center **CLIENT**
Yokogawa Electric Corporation
PRINCIPAL TYPE Custom
DIMENSIONS 15 × 20.2 in.
(38 × 51.25 cm)

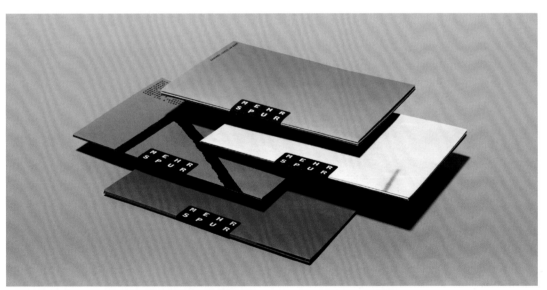

Programs

DESIGN Benjamin Burger
and Adrien Moreillon, Zürich
URL dernieretage.ch **DESIGN
FIRM** Dernier Étage **CLIENT**
Mehrspur **PRINCIPAL TYPE**
Founders Grotesk and
Founders Grotesk Mono
DIMENSIONS Folded:
7.5 × 5.2 in. (19 × 13.3 cm)
Unfolded: 31.5 × 22.5 in.
(80 × 57 cm)

Catalog

CONCEPT AND DESIGN
Johannes Bissinger, Munich
PHOTOGRAPHY Conny Mirbach
SUPPORT Kurt Eckert, Zürich
STUDIO Studio Johannes
Bissinger **CLIENT** Stiftung
Buchkunst **PRINCIPAL TYPE**
Favorit Italic and Favorit
Regular **DIMENSIONS**
8.5 × 12 in. (21.5 × 30.5 cm)

Catalog

DESIGN Stefanie Ackermann,
Ina Bauer, and Sascha
Lobe,● Stuttgart **URL**
L2M3.com **STUDIO** L2M3
Kommunikationsdesign GmbH
CLIENT Stadttheater Ingolstadt
PRINCIPAL TYPE LL Brauer
Neue **DIMENSIONS** 6.3 × 8.7 in.
(16 × 22 cm)

Packaging

DESIGN AND ART DIRECTION
Jeff Watkins, Toronto **CREATIVE**
DIRECTION Lisa Greenberg
CHIEF CREATIVE OFFICER
Judy John **GROUP CREATIVE**
DIRECTOR Ryan Crouchman
COPYWRITER Marty Hoefkes
PHOTOGRAPHY Arash

Moallemi, Fuze Reps **PRINTER**
Flash Reproductions **URL**
leoburnett.ca **TWITTER**
@LeoBurnettTor **AGENCY** Leo
Burnett Toronto **CLIENT** Fuze
Reps **PRINCIPAL TYPE** Neue
Haas Grotesk **DIMENSIONS**
9.75 × 3.75 in. (4.8 × 9.5 cm)

Brochure

MANAGING DIRECTOR
Professor Ruediger Goetz,
Düsseldorf **CREATIVE**
DIRECTION Juergen Adolph
SENIOR ART DIRECTOR
Sabine Schoenhaar **SENIOR**
COPYWRITER Anja Stough
MANAGING DIRECTOR Michael
Rewald **ACCOUNT EXECUTIVE**
Laura Kallenbach **URL**
kw43.de **AGENCY AND**
STUDIO Grey Germany /
Grey Düsseldorf and KW43
BRANDDESIGN **CLIENT** Grey
Germany, TNS Infratest,
Markenverband e.V., and
Deutscher Marketing Verband
e.V. **PRINCIPAL TYPE** FF Din
Condensed Bold and Georgia
Regular **DIMENSIONS**
7.9 × 10.5 in. (20 × 26.6 cm)

Catalog

DESIGN Simon Brenner and
Sascha Lobe,● Stuttgart **URL**
L2M3.com **STUDIO** L2M3
Kommunikationsdesign
GmbH **CLIENT** Stiftung
Kunstsammlung Nordrhein-
Westfalen **PRINCIPAL TYPE**
Berthold Akzidenz Grotesk
DIMENSIONS 9 × 13.7 in.
(23 × 35 cm)

Direct Mail

DESIGN Paul Dunbar, Lillian Ling, and Erin Scarena, Washington, D.C. **ART DIRECTION** Sucha Becky **CREATIVE DIRECTION** Jake Lefebure and Pum Lefebure● **URL** designarmy.com **TWITTER** @DesignArmy **AGENCY** Design Army **CLIENT** Neenah Paper **PRINCIPAL TYPE** Replica **DIMENSIONS** 8 × 10.5 in. (20.5 × 26.5 cm)

Identity

DESIGN Cameron McKague, Toronto **CREATIVE DIRECTION** Claire Dawson and Fidel Peña **PHOTOGRAPHY** Daniel Ehrenworth **URL** underlinestudio.com **TWITTER** @underlineinc **DESIGN FIRM** Underline Studio

CLIENT Daniel Ehrenworth Photography **PRINCIPAL TYPE** Cooper and ITC Serif Gothic **DIMENSIONS** Various

Posters

DESIGN Konstantin Eremenko **URL** eremenko-vis.com **CLIENT** FHNW HGK Visual Communication Institute, The Basel School of Design **PRINCIPAL TYPE** Berthold Akzidenz Grotesk Bold **DIMENSIONS** 23.4 × 33.1 in. (59.4 × 84.1 cm)

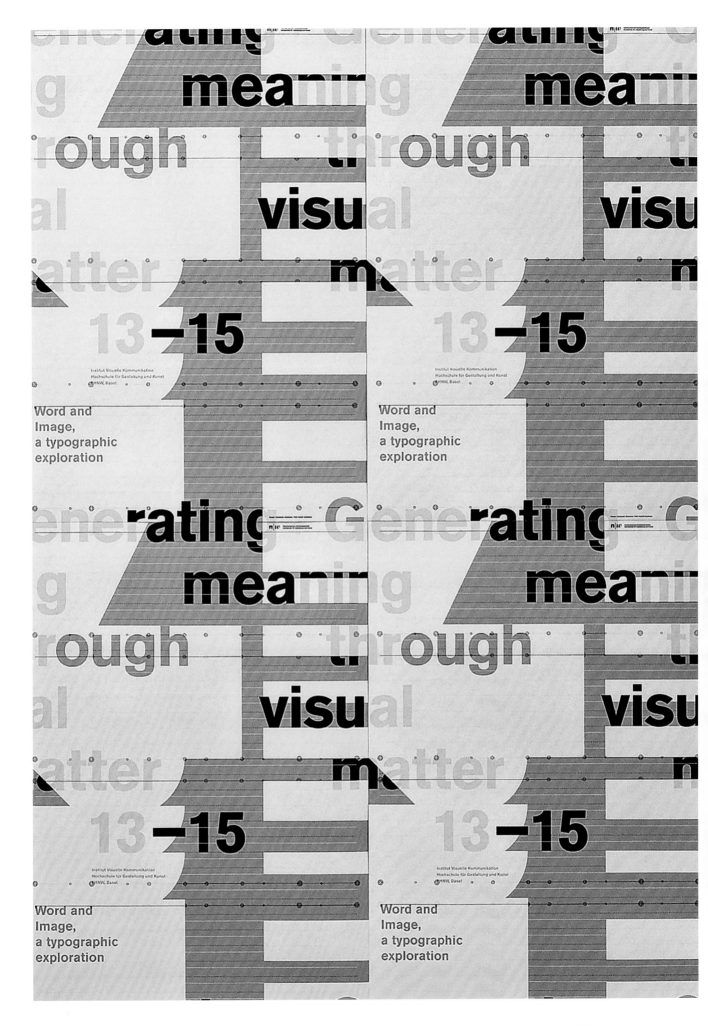

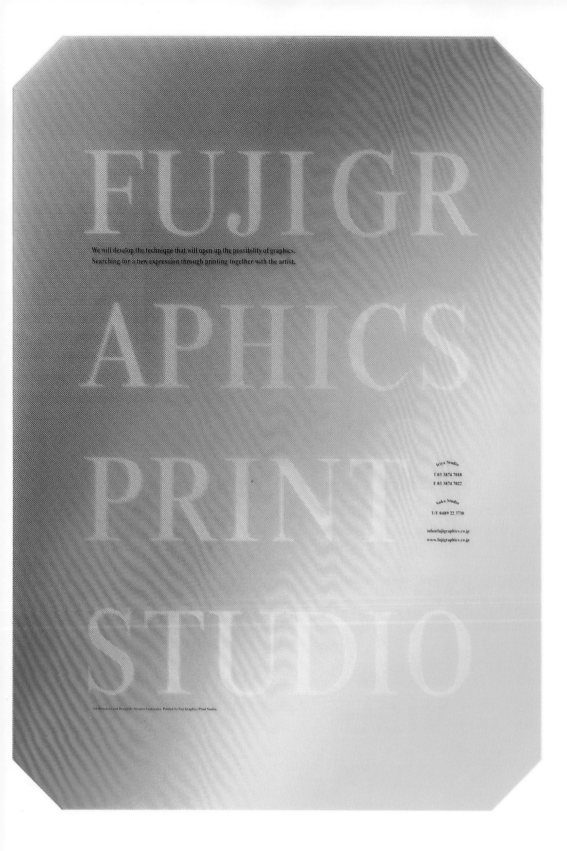

Poster

DESIGN Melchior Imboden,
Buochs, Switzerland **CLIENT**
Weltformat, International
Poster Festival, Lucerne,
Switzerland **PRINCIPAL TYPE**
Custom **DIMENSIONS**
35.6 × 50.4 in. (90.5 × 128 cm)

Poster

DESIGN AND ART DIRECTION
Shunryo Yamanaka, Tokyo
PRINTING DIRECTOR Fuji
Graphics Print Studio **URL**
shunryo.wix.com/portfolio
CLIENT Fuji Graphics Print
Studio **PRINCIPAL TYPE**
Custom **DIMENSIONS**
20.3 × 28.7 in. (51.5 × 72.8 cm)

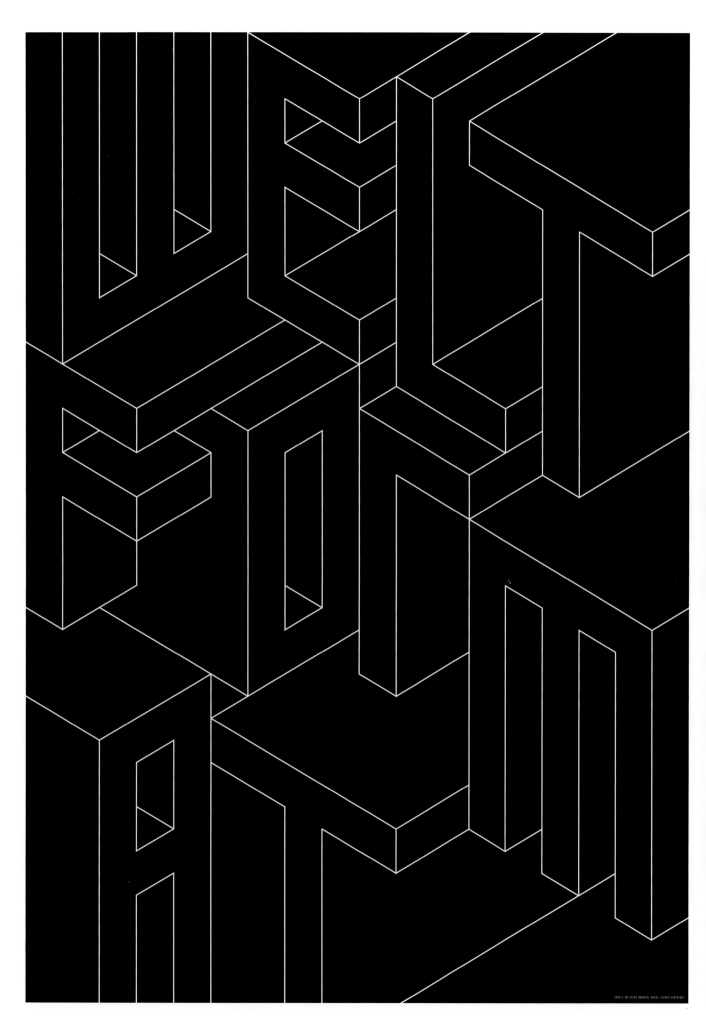

GRAFIK. MELCHIOR IMBODEN DRUCK GISSLER GRAPHICS

Packaging

DESIGN AND ART DIRECTION
Chad Michael, Dallas
ILLUSTRATOR Marija Tiurina
URL chadmichaelstudio.com
TWITTER @ChadMStudio
STUDIO Chad Michael Studio
CLIENT Distillerie du St.
Laurent **PRINCIPAL TYPE**
Various **DIMENSIONS**
4 × 9 in. (10.2 × 22.9 cm)

Packaging

DESIGN AND ART DIRECTION Chad Michael, Dallas
PHOTOGRAPHY Rusty Hill
URL chadmichaelstudio.com
TWITTER @ChadMStudio
STUDIO Chad Michael Studio
CLIENT Old Town Distilling Co.
PRINCIPAL TYPE Freight Text, Old London, Stratum, and Trade Gothic **DIMENSIONS** 3.5 × 9 in. (8.9 × 22.9 cm)

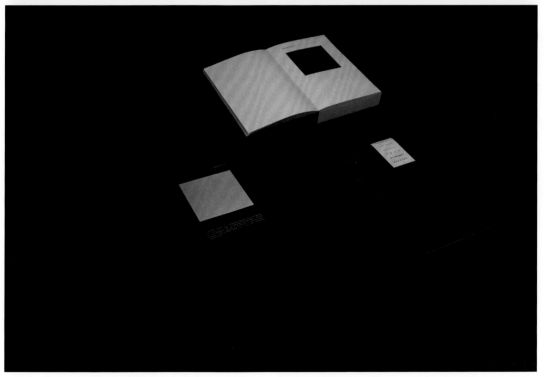

Book

DESIGN Weiwei Zhou, Nanjing, China **STUDIO** Tenmilliontimes Design **CLIENT** Nanjing University Press **DIMENSIONS** 5.7 × 8.3 in. (14.5 × 21 cm)

Book

DESIGN Konstantin Eremenko,
Basel **URL** eremenko-vis.com
CLIENT FHNW HGK Visual
Communication Institute,
The Basel School of Design
PRINCIPAL TYPE Univers 45
Light, Univers 55 Medium, and
Univers 65 Bold **DIMENSIONS**
4.3 × 7.5 in. (11 × 19 cm)

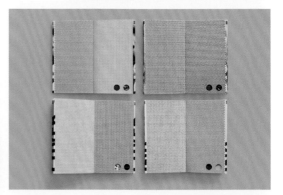

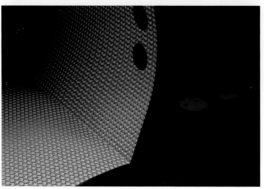

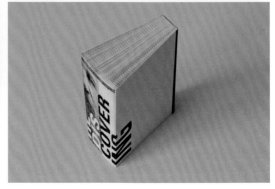

Packaging

DESIGN Paul Belford, Martin Brown, Bethan Jones, and Luke Robertson, London **URL** paulbelford.com **TWITTER** @Belford_Paul **DESIGN FIRM** Paul Belford Ltd. **CLIENT** The Soap Co. **PRINCIPAL TYPE** Founders Grotesk **DIMENSIONS** Various

153

Catalog

DESIGN Cameron McKague, Toronto **CREATIVE DIRECTION** Claire Dawson and Fidel Peña **URL** underlinestudio. com **TWITTER** @underlineinc **DESIGN FIRM** Underline Studio **CLIENT** Derek Sullivan and Oakville Galleries **PRINCIPAL**

TYPE Fleischmann, Neue Haas Grotesk, and Romana **DIMENSIONS** 6 × 9 in. (15.5 × 23 cm)

Identity

DESIGN Léo Breton-Allaire,
Ugo Varin Lachapelle,
and Samuel Larocque,
Montréal **ART DIRECTION** Léo
Breton-Allaire and Ugo Varin
Lachapelle **URL** studiocaserne.
ca **DESIGN FIRM** Caserne **TYPE
DESIGN** Coppers and Brasses
PRINT Atelier BangBang
PRINCIPAL TYPE Custom
DIMENSIONS Various

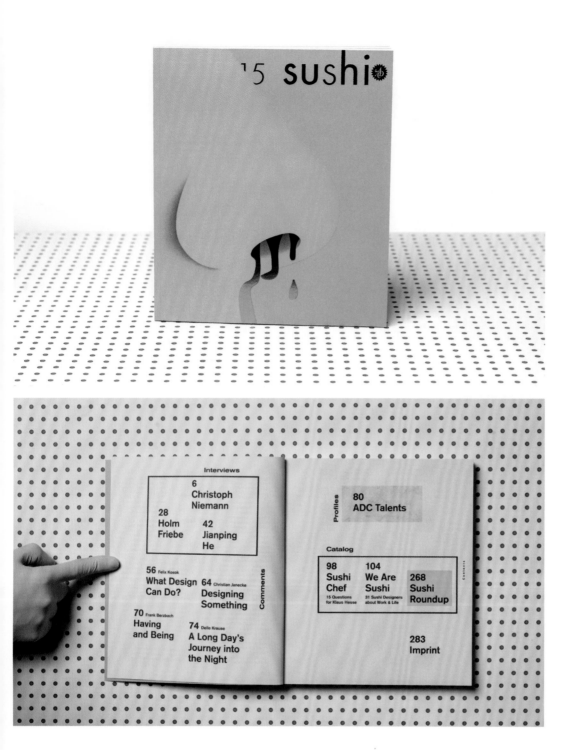

Book

ART DIRECTION Felix Kosok,
Karin Rekowski, and Yuan
Wang, Offenbach, Germany
ILLUSTRATION Jan Buchczik,
Xinyue Deng, Xi Lou, Christoph
Niemann, and Benedikt Rugar
URL www.hfg-offenbach.de
PROFESSOR Klaus Hesse•

SCHOOL Hochschule für
Gestaltung Offenbach
PRINCIPAL TYPE Akzidenz-
Grotesk and King's Caslon
DIMENSIONS 9 × 10.2 in.
(23 × 26 cm)

Self-Promotion

DESIGN AND ART DIRECTION
Jon Robbins,• Brooklyn, New
York **COPYWRITER** Maddison
Bradley **URL** Typeworth.com
ORGANIZATION Typeworth
PRINCIPAL TYPE Various
DIMENSIONS 18 × 24 in.
(45.7 × 61 cm)

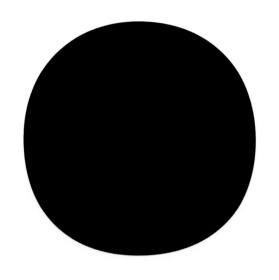

W

Typeface: Barnard Century Modern

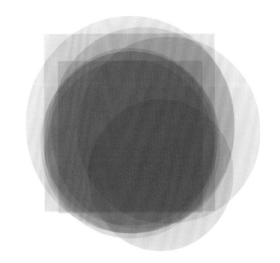

W

Typeface: ITC Tiffany, Drophos
Optima, Times New Roman, Marvel,
Cottonwood, Helvetica Neue, Gill Sans
Poplar Text & Barnard Century Modern

W

Typeface: left weights top to bottom:
Poplar, Stymie, Times New Roman,
Helvetica Neue, Century Expanse,
Palatino, Barbosdl, Modern No.20,
Rotuns, Onyx, Interstate, Modern,
Monod, American Typewriter,
Franklin Gothic, Optima, Poster,
Clarendon, Garamond, Rockwell,
Linkin, Century Gothic, Charcoal,
Cooper New, Trade Gothic, OCR A,
Stencil, Univers, News Gothic, Studio
Text, Letter Gothic, Century, ITISA,
Alternative Script, Goudy Old Style,
Comic Sans, Times, Arnhem SDR,
Cheletera, & Barnard Century Modern

W

Typeface: Symbol, WingDoo,
Historia, Helvetica Neue, Cheltan
Grasse Modern ornamental & Barnard
Century Modern

Identity

DESIGN Ryan Crouchman, Toronto **ART DIRECTION** Ryan Crouchman and Lisa Greenberg **CREATIVE DIRECTION** Lisa Greenberg and Judy John **CHIEF CREATIVE OFFICER** Judy John **COPYWRITER** Steve Persico **DIGITAL ART DIRECTION** Ryan Crouchman **STYLIST** Ryan Crouchman and Lisa Greenberg **PHOTOGRAPHY** Rob Fiocca and Arash Moallemi **PRINTING HOUSE** Somerset Graphics and Webnews Printing **URL** leoburnett.ca **TWITTER** @LeoBurnettTor **AGENCY** Leo Burnett Toronto **CLIENT** House-Maison **PRINCIPAL TYPE** Kane and Futwora **DIMENSIONS** 11.5 × 17 in. (9.2 × 43.2 cm)

Packaging

CREATIVE DIRECTION Shaobin Lin, Guangdong, China **DESIGN COMPANY** Lin Shaobin Design **CLIENT** Xinlin Tea House **PRINCIPAL TYPE** Custom **DIMENSIONS** 13.8 × 9.8 × 3.5 in. (35 × 25 × 8.8 cm) 14.2 × 5.9 × 3.2 in. (36 × 15 × 8.2 cm)

茶舍

潮汕 老埠 工夫茶文化 1791

备器｜候汤｜热罐｜醒茶｜泡茶｜温杯｜洒茶｜品韵｜洗茶

古树茶宋种正山小种
龙井绿茶神金俊眉茶
韵品茶洒杯温茶泡茶
安溪铁观音凤凰单丛
云南普洱茶武夷岩茶
单丛茶碧螺春大红袍
一尺发山如舍居屋堂
问八呆海是东施弱西

Exhibition

DESIGN Yoon-Young Chai,
Jesse Kidwell, Jaeyoon Kim,
and Abbott Miller, New York
ART DIRECTION Abbott Miller•
ASSOCIATE Jesse Kidwell **URL**
pentagram.com **TWITTER**
@pentagram **DESIGN FIRM**
Pentagram• **CLIENT** The
Jewish Museum **PRINCIPAL**
TYPE Schmalfette Grotesk
DIMENSIONS Various

Posters

DESIGN Anna Bühler, Ole
Jenssen, Nina Odzinieks,
and Pit Stenkhoff, Berlin **URL**
neuegestaltung.de **DESIGN**
FIRM Neue Gestaltung
GmbH **CLIENT** Staatstheater
Mainz GmbH **PRINCIPAL**
TYPE Suisse Works, Suisse
Int'l, and handwritten fonts
DIMENSIONS 33.1 × 46.8 in.
(84.1 × 118.9 cm)

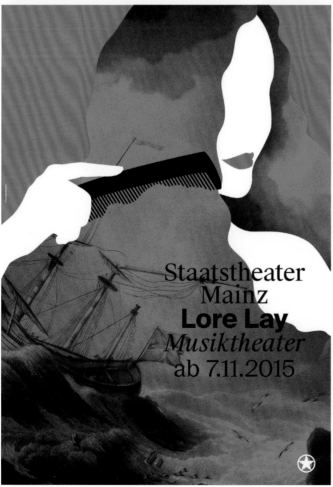

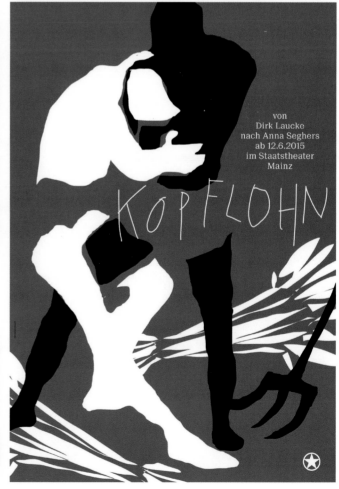

Exhibition

DESIGN Courtney Gooch,
Sarah McKeen, and Paula
Scher,● New York **ART**
DIRECTION Paula Scher
ASSOCIATE Courtney Gooch
URL pentagram.com **TWITTER**
@pentagram **DESIGN FIRM**
Pentagram **CLIENT** Temple
Contemporary at the Tyler
School of Art **PRINCIPAL TYPE**
Handlettering **DIMENSIONS**
Various

Poster

DESIGN Konstantin Eremenko,
Basel **URL** eremenko-vis.com
CLIENT Rappaz Museum Basel
PRINCIPAL TYPE Haas Unica
Pro Heavy **DIMENSIONS**
35.2 × 50.4 in. (89.5 × 128 cm)

Typographie ka__

Design: Konstantin Eremenko. Print: Lézard Graphique

Prints
and Drinks

u–ter
Umstä–de–
lesbar 03
sei–

_

Rappaz Museum,
Dienstag 22.9.2015,
18:30 Uhr

Klingental 11,
4058 Basel

n

Self-Promotion

DESIGN AND CREATIVE DIRECTION Sara Gulzari and Jeff Hester,● Oakland, California **URL** cultpartners. com **DESIGN FIRM** Cult Partners **PRINCIPAL TYPE** Handlettering **DIMENSIONS** 10.25 × 5.2 in. (26 × 13. cm)

Poster

DESIGN AND ART DIRECTION Giorgio Pesce,● Lausanne, Switzerland **URL** atelierpoisson.ch **DESIGN AGENCY** Atelier Poisson **CLIENT** Musée de la Main **PRINCIPAL TYPE** B-Dot, LL Circular, and Trade Gothic **DIMENSIONS** 35.2 × 50.4 in. (89.5 × 128 cm)

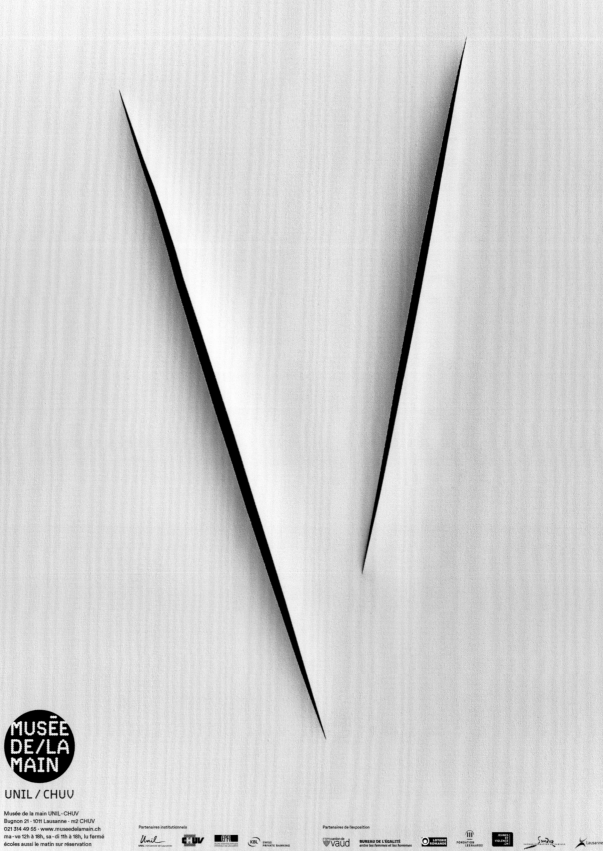

VIOLENCES
1er JUILLET 2015 – 19 JUIN 2016

MUSÉE DE/LA MAIN

UNIL / CHUV

Musée de la main UNIL-CHUV
Bugnon 21 · 1011 Lausanne · m2 CHUV
021 314 49 55 · www.museedelamain.ch
ma - ve 12h à 18h, sa - di 11h à 18h, lu fermé
écoles aussi le matin sur réservation

Partenaires institutionnels

Partenaires de l'exposition

Brochure

DESIGN Rory King, Brooklyn, New York **CREATIVE DIRECTION** Mats Håkansson **ASSOCIATE CREATIVE DIRECTOR** Kara Schlindwein **ASSOCIATE DIRECTOR OF CONTENT DEVELOPMENT** Marion Hammon **SENIOR EDITORIAL MANAGER** Brandhi Williamson **EXECUTIVE DIRECTOR OF COMMUNICATIONS AND MARKETING** Mara McGinnis **URL** pratt.edu **TWITTER** @PrattInstitute **SCHOOL** Pratt Institute **PRINCIPAL TYPE** Aperçu **DIMENSIONS** 9 × 12 in. (22.9 × 30.5 cm)

Book Jacket

DESIGN Spencer Kimble, New York **ART DIRECTION** Jason Booher **PHOTOGRAPHY** Emilio Brizzi **URL** spencerkimble.com **PUBLISHER** Blue Rider Press, Penguin Random House **PRINCIPAL TYPE** Handlettering **DIMENSIONS** 6.1 × 9.25 in. (15.2 × 22.89 cm)

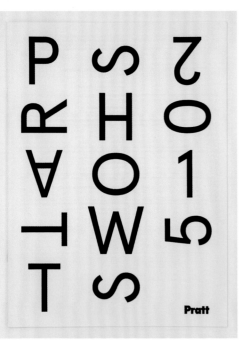

The Life
and Death
of
Sophie Stark

A Novel

Anna North

Annual Report

DESIGN Annabel Huml, Tobias Nusser, and Stephanie Zehender, Stuttgart **ART DIRECTION AND URL** Tobias Nusser **DIRECTOR** Beate Flamm **PRODUCTION** Peter Hoppe and Andreas Rimmelspacher **PRINT** Eberl Print GmbH **URL** strichpunkt-design.de/en **TWITTER** @STRICHPUNKT **DESIGN AGENCY** Strichpunkt **CLIENT** adidas AG **PRINCIPAL TYPE** AdiHaus and Ostrich Sans **DIMENSIONS** 11.1 × 8.7 in. (28.5 × 22 cm)

Annual Report

DESIGN Sven Lindhorst-Emme,• Raúl Kokott, and Josh Schaub, Berlin **ART DIRECTION** Björn Wolf and Fons Hickmann• **CREATIVE DIRECTION** Professor Fons Hickmann and Professor Gabriele Kiefer **URL** m23.de **TWITTER** @FonsHickmannM23 **STUDIO** Fons Hickmann m23 **CLIENT** TU Braunschweig, Architecture Department **PRINCIPAL TYPE** Suisse **DIMENSIONS** 6.7 × 9.4 in. (17 × 24 cm)

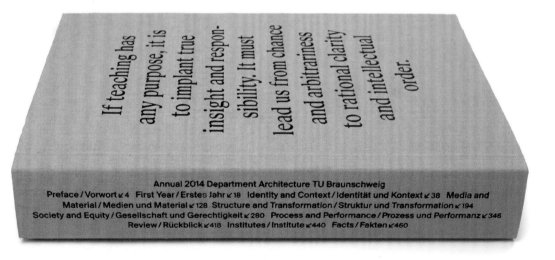

Posters

DESIGN Rob Alexander and Nate Luetkehans, San Francisco **CREATIVE DIRECTION** Rob Alexander and Jill Robertson **PRODUCTION ARTIST** Dominique Mao **WRITERS** Ben McNutt and Jill Robertson **URL** visitoffice.com **STUDIO** Office **CLIENT** Wee Society **PRINCIPAL TYPE** Futura (modified) and handlettering **DIMENSIONS** 16 × 21 in. (40.6 × 53.3 cm)

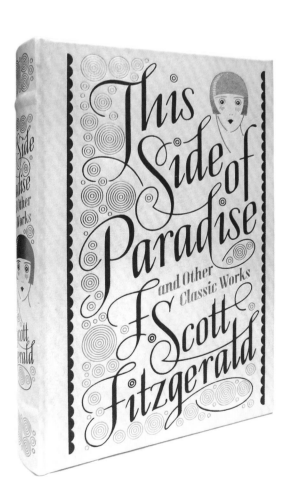

Book jacket

DESIGN Roberto de Vicq de Cumptich,• New York **ART DIRECTION** Patrice Kaplan **CREATIVE DIRECTION** Jo Obarowski **URL** devicq.com/this_side.html **DESIGN FIRM** de Vicq design **CLIENT** Sterling Publishing **PRINCIPAL TYPE** Jeeves and Sperling FY **DIMENSIONS** 6.25 × 9.25 in. (15.9 × 23.5 cm)

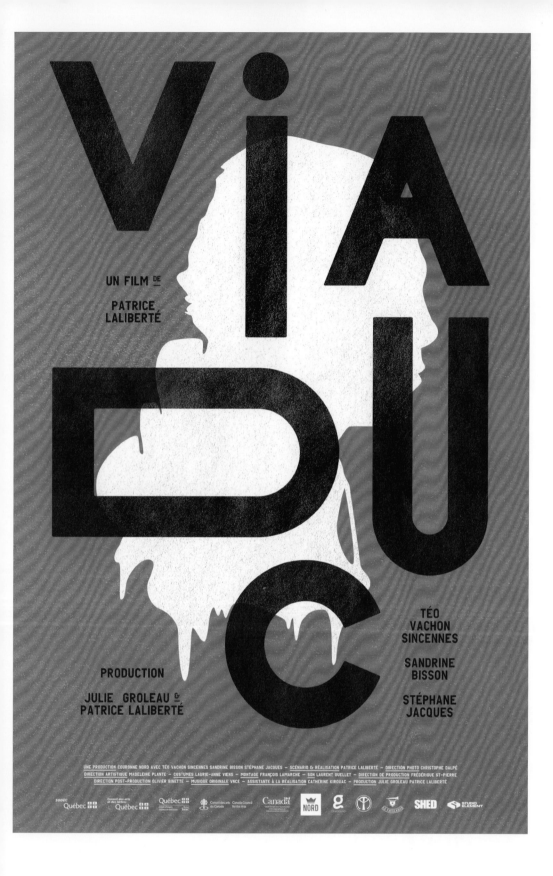

Poster

CREATIVE DIRECTION
Justin Lortie, Montréal
PHOTOGRAPHY Danny Taillon
SILKSCREEN PRINTING Atelier
BangBang **URL** wedge.work
DESIGN FIRM Wedge **CLIENT**
Couronne Nord **PRINCIPAL**
TYPE Plaque Découpée
Universelle and custom

Posters

GRAPHIC DESIGN Boris
Brumnjak and Rikke Landler,
Berlin **ART DIRECTION** Boris
Brumnjak **URL** brumnjak.com
DESIGN FIRM BRUMNJAK
– Studio für Design **CLIENT**
Gallery Print **PRINCIPAL TYPE**
Helvetica **DIMENSIONS**
23.4 × 33.1 in. (59.4 × 84.1 cm)

Gallery Print

Gallery Print

Book

DESIGN Matthew Boyd,
Toronto **CREATIVE DIRECTION**
Diti Katona **URL** concrete.ca
DESIGN FIRM Concrete **CLIENT**
Wayward Arts **PRINCIPAL**
TYPE Cactus, Druk, Jean-Luc,
Plak, Plakat, and Swiss 721
DIMENSIONS Various

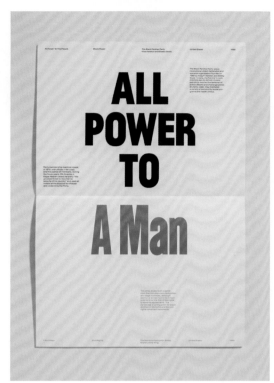

Logotype

DESIGN DIRECTOR Ralph
Kenke, Sydney **URL**
2-design.net **CLIENT** SONA
Architecture **PRINCIPAL**
TYPE Akzidenz-Grotesk BQ
and Alte Haas Grotesk

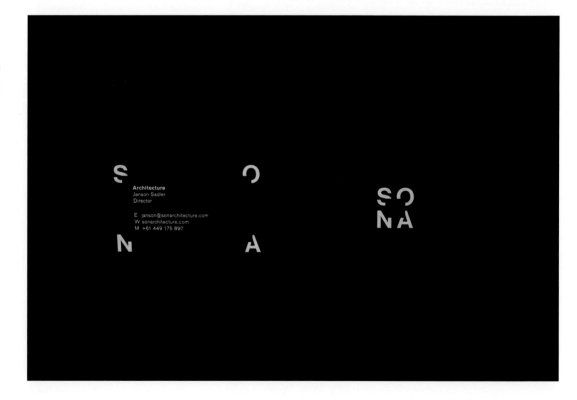

Experimental

DESIGN Satoru Yamamoto,
Tokyo **PRINTER** Toppan
Printing **PRINCIPAL TYPE**
Helvetica Neue Bold
DIMENSIONS 28.6 × 40.5 in.
(72.6 × 103 cm)

TOKYO DRIFT Inspired by Shinya Fujiwara

Book Jacket

DESIGN AND ART DIRECTION
Ariane Spanier, Berlin **URL**
arianespanier.com **DESIGN**
FIRM Ariane Spanier Design
CLIENT Fukt Magazine for
Contemporary Drawing
PRINCIPAL TYPE Curla and
Gira Sans **DIMENSIONS** 6.5 ×
9.1 in. (16.5 × 23 cm)

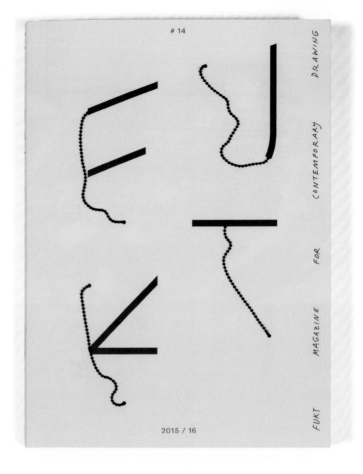

Book

DESIGN Kim Walker and
Abbott Miller,• New York
ART DIRECTION Abbott Miller
ASSOCIATE Kim Walker **URL**
pentagram.com **TWITTER**
@pentagram **DESIGN FIRM**
Pentagram• **CLIENT** The
Barnes Foundation **PRINCIPAL**
TYPE Leitura and Vanitas
DIMENSIONS 13.1 × 15.9 in.
(33.3 × 40.4 cm)

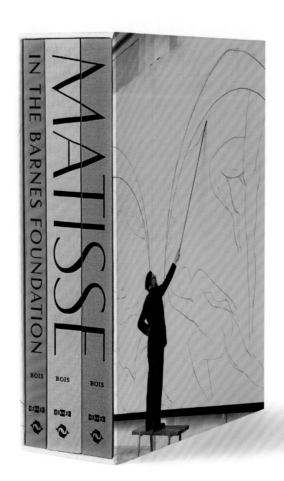

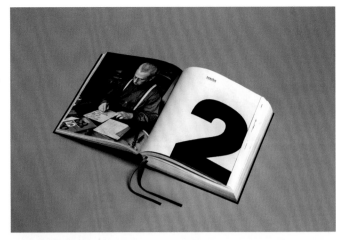

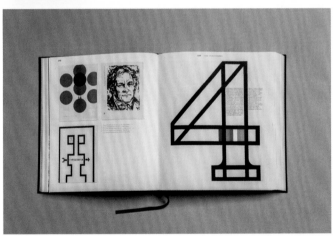

Book

DESIGN AND EDITOR Barbora Toman Tylová, Prague **STUDIES** Iva Knobloch, Jan Rous, and Barbora Toman Tylová **PHOTOGRAPHS** (in the book) Filip ŠSach **PHOTOGRAPHER** (of the book) Filip Györe **RETOUCHING AND** **POSTPRODUCTION** Jiří Toman **URL** oldrichhlavsa.cz and toman-design.com **STUDIO** Toman Design **PUBLISHER** UMPRUM, Akropolis **PRINCIPAL TYPE** Corridor **DIMENSIONS** 9.3 × 11 in. (23.5 × 27cm)

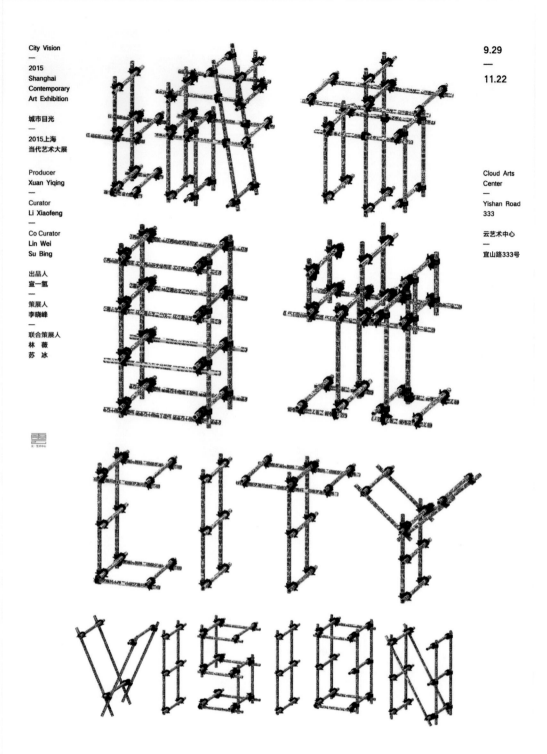

City Vision
—
2015
Shanghai
Contemporary
Art Exhibition

城市目光
—
2015上海
当代艺术大展

Producer
Xuan Yiqing
—
Curator
Li Xiaofeng
—
Co Curator
Lin Wei
Su Bing

出品人
宣一氢
—
策展人
李晓峰
—
联合策展人
林 薇
苏 冰

9.29
—
11.22

Cloud Arts
Center
—
Yishan Road
333

云艺术中心
—
宜山路333号

Poster

DESIGN Zheng Bang-qian,
Shanghai **DESIGN FIRM** dx
studio

Posters

DESIGN AND ART DIRECTION
Kevin Cantrell,• Salt Lake City
LETTERING Kevin Cantrell
TYPOGRAPHY CONSULTING
Arlo Vance **URL** kevincantrell.
com **TWITTER** @kevinrcantrell
DESIGN FIRM Kevin Cantrell
Studio **CLIENT** Legion Paper

PRINCIPAL TYPE Cottonhouse
Slab and custom **DIMENSIONS**
18 × 24 in. (45.7 × 61 cm)

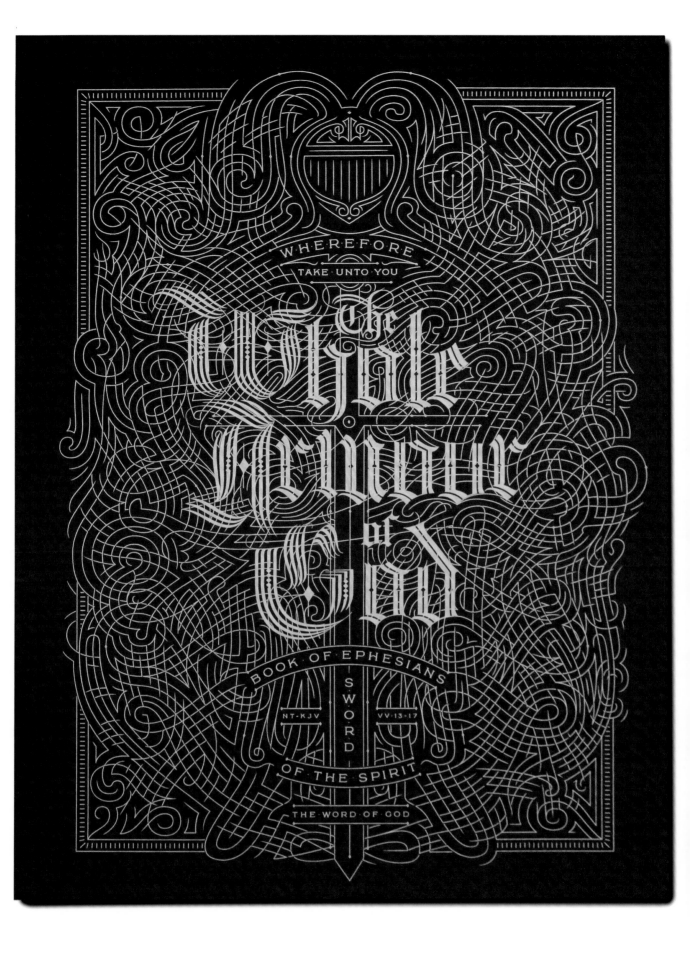

WHEREFORE
TAKE·UNTO·YOU
The Whole Armour of God
BOOK·OF·EPHESIANS
S·W·O·R·D
NT·KJV   VV·13-17
OF·THE·SPIRIT
THE·WORD·OF·GOD

Magazine

DESIGN Nuria Cabrera, Giovanni Cavalleri, Pablo Martín, Rafa Roses, and Astrid Stavro Palma de Mallorca, Balearic Islands, Spain **ART DIRECTION** Pablo Martín and Astrid Stavro **EDITOR IN CHIEF** Marc Valli **URL** designbyatlas. com **TWITTER** @designbyatlas **DESIGN FIRM** Atlas **CLIENT** Frame Publishers **PRINCIPAL TYPE** Bella, Founders Grotesk, and Plantin Pro **DIMENSIONS** 8.7 × 11 in. (22 × 28 cm)

Posters

DESIGN AND ART DIRECTION Yukichi Takada,● Osaka **URL** cid-lab.info **DESIGN FIRM** CID Lab **CLIENT** Hirakawacho Music Executive Committee **PRINCIPAL TYPE** Helvetica and custom **DIMENSIONS** 23.4 × 33.1 in. (59.4 × 84.1 cm)

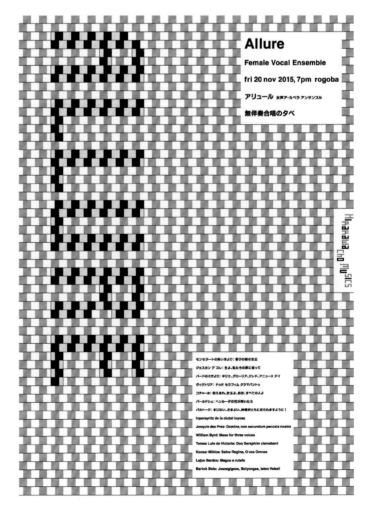

Book Jacket

DESIGN Aurial Lee, Liquan Liew, Vanessa Lim, and Yah-Leng Yu, Singapore **ART DIRECTION** Liquan Liew, Vanessa Lim, and Yah-Leng Yu **CREATIVE DIRECTION** Yah-Leng Yu **ILLUSTRATION** Aurial Lee and Estella Ng **WRITERS** Marcus Leong, Stephanie Peh, Caroline Elisabeth Wong, and Yvonne Xu **PHOTOGRAPHY** Jovian Lim and Rebecca Toh **DESIGN FIRM** Foreign Policy Design Group **URL** foreignpolicydesign.com **TWITTER** @foreignpolicydg **INSTAGRAM** @foreignpolicydg **CLIENT** Foreign Policy Design Group **PRINCIPAL TYPE** Futura Bold, Hoefler Text, and Simple **DIMENSIONS** 7.1 × 9.4 in. (18 × 24 cm)

Book

DESIGN Liquan Liew, Vanessa Lim, Aurial Lee, and Yah-Leng Yu, Singapore **ART DIRECTION** Liquan Liew, Vanessa Lim, and Yah-Leng Yu **CREATIVE DIRECTION** Yah-Leng Yu **ILLUSTRATION** Aurial Lee and Estella Ng **PHOTOGRAPHY** Jovian Lim and Rebecca Toh **WRITERS** Marcus Leong, Stephanie Peh, Caroline Elisabeth Wong, and Yvonne Xu **URL** foreignpolicydesign.com **TWITTER** @foreignpolicydg **INSTAGRAM** @foreignpolicydg **DESIGN FIRM** Foreign Policy Design Group **PRINCIPAL TYPE** Futura Bold, Hoefler Text, and Simple **DIMENSIONS** 7.1 × 9.4 in. (18 × 24 cm)

CREATIVE DIRECTION
Paul Garbett, Sydney
URL garbett.com.au **TWITTER**
@garbettdesign **DESIGN**
FIRM Garbett **CLIENT** Sydney
Opera House **PRINCIPAL**
TYPE LL Brown and custom
DIMENSIONS 33.1 × 46.8 in.
(84.1 × 118.9 cm)

ART DIRECTION Lukas Betzler,
Simon Bork, and Armin Roth,
Stuttgart **URL** studiopanorama.
de **CLIENT** Theater Rampe
PRINCIPAL TYPE AT Schneidler
DIMENSIONS 23.4 × 33.1 in.
(59.4 × 84.1 cm)

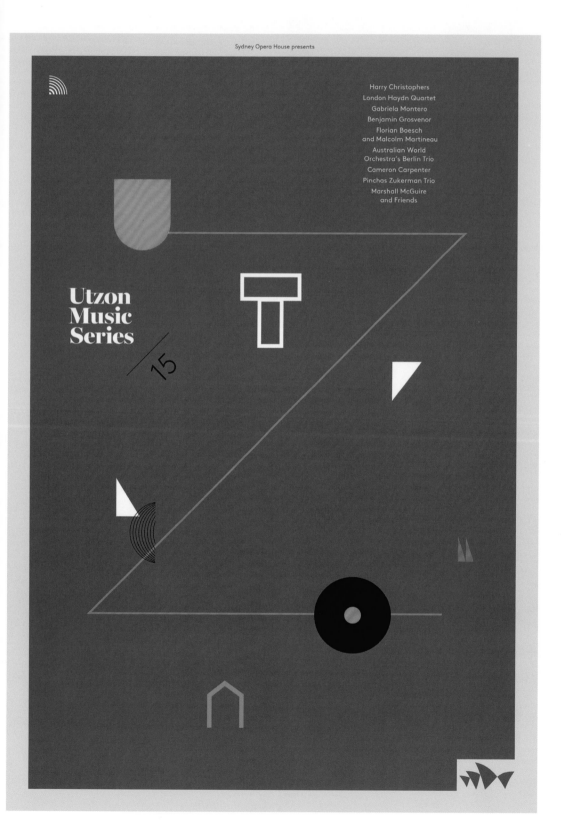

WHY MAKE SENSE

Student Work

DESIGN AND EDITORIAL Sarah
Fricke, Lisa Petersen, and Lea
Sievertsen, Halle, Germany
EDITORS Anna Berkenbusch,•
Sarah Fricke, Lisa Petersen,
and Lea Sievertsen
PUBLISHER Hochschulverlag
Burg Giebichenstein
Kunsthochschule Halle
PROFESSORS Anna
Berkenbusch and Ferdinand
Ulrich **SCHOOL** Burg
Giebichenstein University of
Art and Design **PRINCIPAL
TYPE** Larish Neue and Suisse
Int'l **DIMENSIONS** 6.3 × 9.4 in.
(16 × 24 cm)

Magazine

DESIGN Colin Doerffler and
Martin Major, Bielefeld,
Germany **PROFESSORS** Kai
Duenhoelter and Dirk Fütterer•
URL gestaltung-bielefeld.de
SCHOOL Fachhochschule
Bielefeld, Fachbereich
Gestaltung **PRINCIPAL
TYPE** Favorit and Speed
DIMENSIONS 7.9 × 10.6 in.
(20 × 27 cm)

Magazine

DESIGN AND ART DIRECTION
Luke Tonge, London **CREATIVE
DIRECTION** James Fooks-Bale
URL monotype.com **TWITTER**
@monotype **FOUNDRY**
Monotype **PRINCIPAL TYPE**
Various **DIMENSIONS**
8.8 × 11 in. (22.4 × 27.9 cm)

Identity

DESIGN Marcelo Hong and Peter Lee, Toronto **ART DIRECTION** Marcelo Hong, Peter Lee, and Laure Stromboni **CREATIVE DIRECTION** Lisa Greenberg **CHIEF CREATIVE OFFICER** Judy John **GROUP CREATIVE**

DIRECTOR Ryan Crouchman **COPYWRITER** Jessica Mori **AGENCY PRODUCER** Laurie Filgiano **PRINT PRODUCER** Gord Cathmoir and Anne Peck **GROUP ACCOUNT DIRECTOR** Allison Litzinger **ACCOUNT EXECUTIVE** Maura

Kelly **PLANNER** Tahir Ahmad **PHOTOGRAPHY** Saty + Pratha **URL** leoburnett.ca **TWITTER** @LeoBurnettTor **AGENCY** Leo Burnett Toronto **PRINCIPAL TYPE** Walsheim **DIMENSIONS** 12 × 9 in. (30.5 × 22.9 cm)

Magazine

DESIGN AND ART DIRECTION
Mariela Hsu, Washington, D.C.
CREATIVE DIRECTION Jake
Lefebure and Pum Lefebure●
URL designarmy.com **TWITTER**
@designarmy **AGENCY** Design
Army **CLIENT** The One Club
PRINCIPAL TYPE AvenyT,
Chronicle Display, and LL
Circular **DIMENSIONS** 11 × 16
in. (28 × 40.5 cm)

Identity

DESIGN Luisa Milani and Walter Molteni, Milan **URL** latigre.net **TWITTER** twitter.com/latigremilano **DESIGN STUDIO** La Tigre **CLIENT** Revolution Department **PRINCIPAL TYPE** Aperçu and Austin **DIMENSIONS** Various

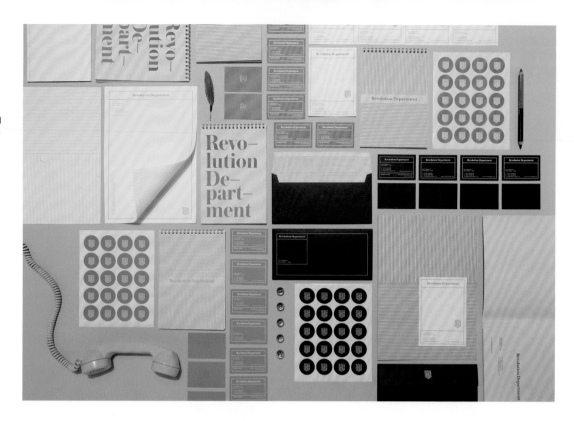

Book

DESIGN Lisa Drechsel, Sascha Lobe,• and Sven Thiery, Stuttgart **URL** L2M3.com **STUDIO** L2M3 Kommunikationsdesign GmbH **CLIENT** Daimler AG, Mercedes-Benz Classic **PRINCIPAL TYPE** Corporate S **DIMENSIONS** 10.9 × 14.4 in. (27.8 × 36.5 cm)

Student Work

DESIGN Erkin Karamemet,
Bielefeld, Germany **URL**
karamemet.com **PROFESSOR**
Dirk Fütterer● **INSTRUCTOR**
Johannes Breyer **SCHOOL**
FH Bielefeld University of
Applied Sciences **PRINCIPAL**
TYPE EK Buhara and EK Max
DIMENSIONS 7.9 × 10.8 in.
(20 × 27.5 cm)

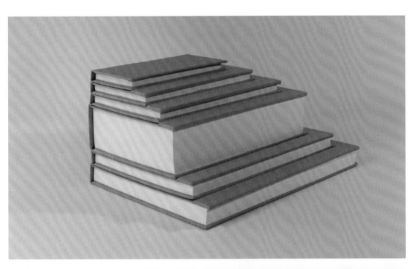

Student Work

DESIGN Kawisara
Vacharaprucks, Bangkok **URL**
kawisara.com **TWITTER**
@kawisaravach **PROFESSOR**
Paul McNeil **SCHOOL** London
College of Communication,
University of the Arts London
PRINCIPAL TYPE Walbaum
DIMENSIONS Various

Student Work

DESIGN Tatjana Burka, Philipp Elsner, and Emily Henderson, Munich **PROFESSOR** Sybille Schmitz **SCHOOL** MD.H Media Design Hochschule **PRINCIPAL TYPE** Kabel, DSKlingspor Regular and Titel; DSKoch-Fraktur, and Titel, and Marathon LT Book **DIMENSIONS** Various

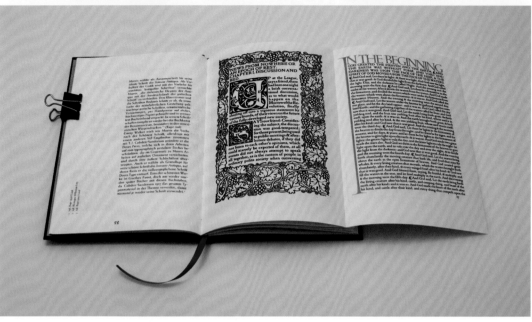

Student Work

DESIGN Matthias Christ and Philipp Schmidt, Stuttgart **URL** matthiaschrist.net and pehjott.net **EDITORS** Felix Ensslin and Charlotte Klink **PROFESSOR** Uli Cluss **SCHOOL** Stuttgart State Academy of Art and Design **PUBLISHER** Sternberg Press **PRINCIPAL TYPE** FF Super Grotesk **DIMENSIONS** 5.8 × 8.3 in. (14.8 × 21 cm)

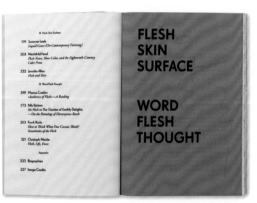

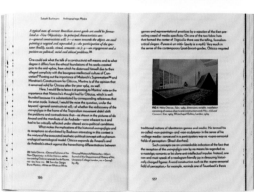

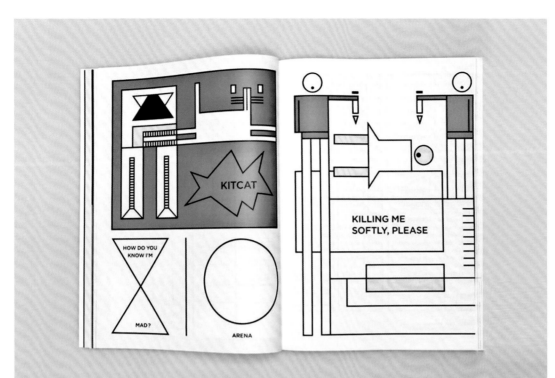

Student Work

DESIGN Franziska Loos,
Berlin **URL** franziskaloos.com
PROFESSOR Fons Hickmann•
SCHOOL Berlin University
of the Arts **PRINCIPAL TYPE**
Gotham **DIMENSIONS**
11.4 × 15 in. (29 × 38.1 cm)

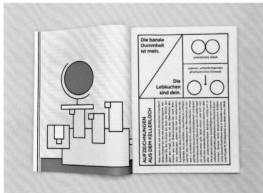

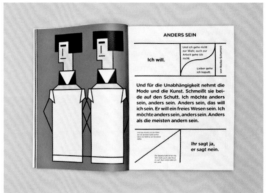

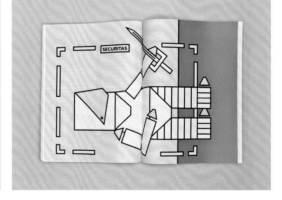

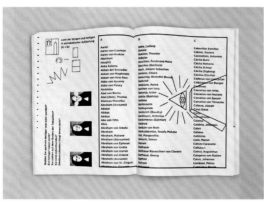

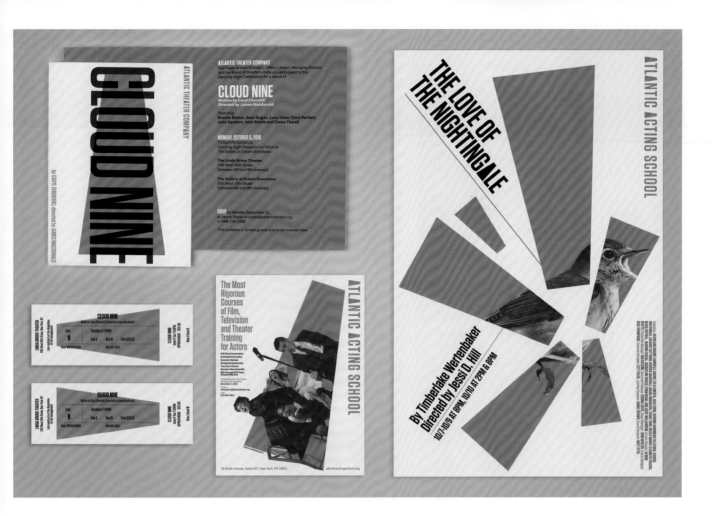

Identity

DESIGN Paula Scher● and
Rory Simms,● New York **ART
DIRECTION** Paula Scher **URL**
pentagram.com **TWITTER**
@pentagram **DESIGN FIRM**
Pentagram● **CLIENT** Atlantic
Theater Company **PRINCIPAL
TYPE** Tungsten **DIMENSIONS**
Various

Identity

DESIGN Mats Kubiak and Andreas Steinbrecher, Düsseldorf **ILLUSTRATION** Andreas Steinbrecher **URL** matskubiak.com and andreassteinbrecher.de **PROFESSOR** Andreas Uebele● **SCHOOL** Peter Behrens School of Arts, Düsseldorf **CLIENT** Aquazoo Löbbecke Museum **PRINCIPAL TYPE** Aquatype and Georgia **DIMENSIONS** Various

Poster

DESIGN AND ART DIRECTION
Stephan Bundi, Bern **URL**
atelierbundi.ch **DESIGN FIRM**
Atelier Bundi AG **CLIENTS**
Architekturforum Bern and
Bernisches Historisches
Museum **PRINCIPAL TYPE**
Neue Helvetica **DIMENSIONS**
37.2 × 50.4 in. (94.5 × 128 cm)

Posters

DESIGN David Arzt, Ina Bauer,
Sascha Lobe,• and Mark
Schulze, Stuttgart **STUDIO**
L2M3 Kommunikationsdesign
GmbH **URL** L2M3.com **CLIENT**
Schmuckmuseum Pforzheim
PRINCIPAL TYPE Simple
DIMENSIONS 33.1 × 46.8 in.
(84.1 × 118.9 cm)

anziehend
von der
fibel
zur
brosche
20.11.15
bis
21.02.16

schmuckmuseum
pforzheim

jahnstraße 42 d-75173 pforzheim öffnungszeiten: di-so und feiertags 10.00-17.00 uhr pforzheim www.schmuckmuseum.de außer heiligabend und silvester im reuchlinhaus tel.+49(0)7231|39 21 26

---

zwischen
natur und
künstlichkeit
**schmuck von
daniel kruger**
27.03.
bis
14.06.15

schmuckmuseum
pforzheim

jahnstraße 42 d-75173 pforzheim öffnungszeiten: di-so und feiertags 10.00-17.00 uhr pforzheim www.schmuckmuseum.de außer heiligabend und silvester im reuchlinhaus tel.+49(0)7231|39 21 26

**erhobenen
hauptes**
kopf-
schmuck
aus aller
welt
30.11.14
bis
22.02.15

schmuckmuseum
pforzheim

jahnstraße 42 d-75173 pforzheim öffnungszeiten: di-so und feiertags 10.00-17.00 uhr pforzheim www.schmuckmuseum.de außer heiligabend und silvester im reuchlinhaus tel.+49(0)7231|39 21 26

**erhobenen
hauptes**
kopf-
schmuck
aus aller
welt
30.11.14
bis
22.02.15

schmuckmuseum
pforzheim

jahnstraße 42 d-75173 pforzheim öffnungszeiten: di-so und feiertags 10.00-17.00 uhr pforzheim www.schmuckmuseum.de außer heiligabend und silvester im reuchlinhaus tel.+49(0)7231|39 21 26

Book Jacket

DESIGN Katharina Godbersen, Hamburg **URL** tomleiferdesign. de **DESIGN FIRM** Tom Leifer Design GmbH **CLIENT** Awards Unlimited **PRINCIPAL TYPE** Drescher Grotesk and Poynter Oldstyle Text **DIMENSIONS** 8.1 × 10.4 in. (20.5 × 26.5 cm)

Book

DESIGN Pierre Pané-Farré, Leipzig, Germany **TWITTER** @panefarre **STUDIO** Pierre Pané-Farré – Studio for Graphic and Typedesign **CLIENT** Institut für Buchkunst Leipzig **PRINCIPAL TYPE** Edel Grotesk and Grotesque Condensed **DIMENSIONS** 8.7 × 12.2 in. (22 × 31 cm)

Book Jacket

DESIGN AND URL Richard Ljoenes,● New York **URL** reganarts.com **DESIGN FIRM** Regan Arts **PRINCIPAL TYPE** Replica **DIMENSIONS** 5.6 × 8.5 in. (14.2 × 21.6 cm)

Journal

DESIGN Brendan Campbell and Derek Schusterbauer, Providence, Rhode Island **ART DIRECTION** Derek Schusterbauer **PHOTOGRAPHY** Erik Gould **EDITORS IN CHIEF** Sarah Ganz Blythe and S. Hollis Mickey **EDITOR** Amy Pickworth **PRINTER** Meridian Printing **URL** risdmuseum. org/portfolio **STUDIO** RISD Museum Graphic Design **PUBLISHER** RISD Museum **PRINCIPAL TYPE** Arnhem and Calibre **DIMENSIONS** 7.25 × 9.5 in. (18.4 × 24.1 cm)

Poster

CHIEF CREATIVE OFFICER
Stewart Devlin,• New York
**ASSOCIATE CREATIVE
DIRECTOR** Rafael Medina
SENIOR DESIGNER Lingxiao
Tan **GROUP ACCOUNT
DIRECTOR** Jillian Booty
PRODUCTION DIRECTOR Steve

Lipman **DESIGN FIRM** Red
Peak **PRINCIPAL TYPE** Gotham
Book and Gotham Bold
DIMENSIONS 24 × 26 in.
(61 × 91.5 cm)

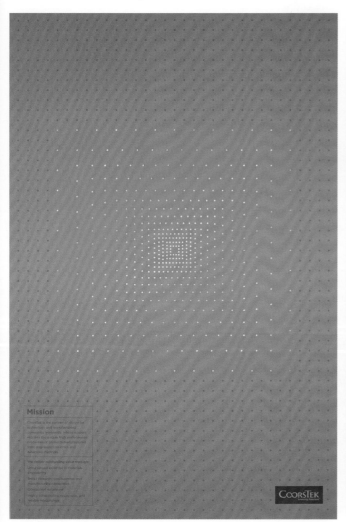

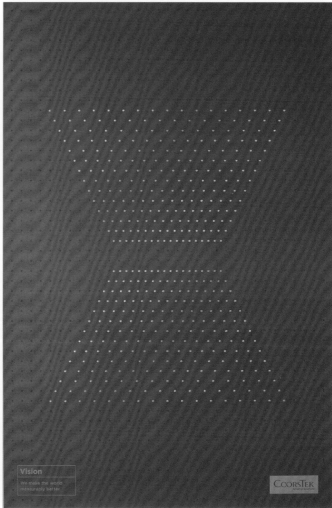

196

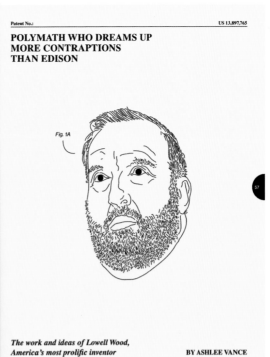

Patent No.: US 13,897,765

POLYMATH WHO DREAMS UP MORE CONTRAPTIONS THAN EDISON

Fig. 1A

The work and ideas of Lowell Wood, America's most prolific inventor

BY ASHLEE VANCE

Magazine Spread

DESIGN Alexander Shoukas, New York **CREATIVE DIRECTION** Robert Vargas● **DEPUTY CREATIVE DIRECTOR** Tracy Ma **DIRECTOR OF PHOTOGRAPHY** Clinton Cargill **PUBLICATION** *Bloomberg Businessweek* **PRINCIPAL TYPE** BW Haas Agate **DIMENSIONS** 15.75 × 10.5 in. (40 × 26.7 cm)

Magazine Spread

DESIGN Robert Vargas,● New York **DEPUTY CREATIVE DIRECTOR** Tracy Ma **DIRECTOR OF PHOTOGRAPHY** Clinton Cargill **PUBLICATION** *Bloomberg Businessweek* **PRINCIPAL TYPE** BW Druk, BW Druk XX Condensed, BW Druk XXX Condensed, and BW Druk XXXX Condensed **DIMENSIONS** 15.75 × 10.5 in. (40 × 26.7 cm)

Magazine Cover

ART DIRECTION Kristin Lipman,
Honolulu **CONCEPT AND
LETTERER** Matthew Tapia•
PHOTOGRAPHY Aaron Yoshino
URL matthewtapia.com
TWITTER @masaotapia
INSTAGRAM @matthewtapia
STUDIO Matthew Tapia
Graphics & Lettering **CLIENT**
Honolulu Magazine **PRINCIPAL
TYPE** Custom **DIMENSIONS**
8.1 × 10.9 in. (20.6 × 27.7 cm)

Page Opener

DESIGN DIRECTOR Chris
Dixon, New York **DEPUTY ART
DIRECTOR** Tonya Douraghy
TYPOGRAPHER Anton
Ioukhnovets **URL** vanityfair.
com **TWITTER** @VanityFair
PUBLICATION *Vanity Fair*
PRINCIPAL TYPE VF Didot
and New Grotesk Square
DIMENSIONS 7.75 × 10.9 in.
(19.7 × 27.7 cm)

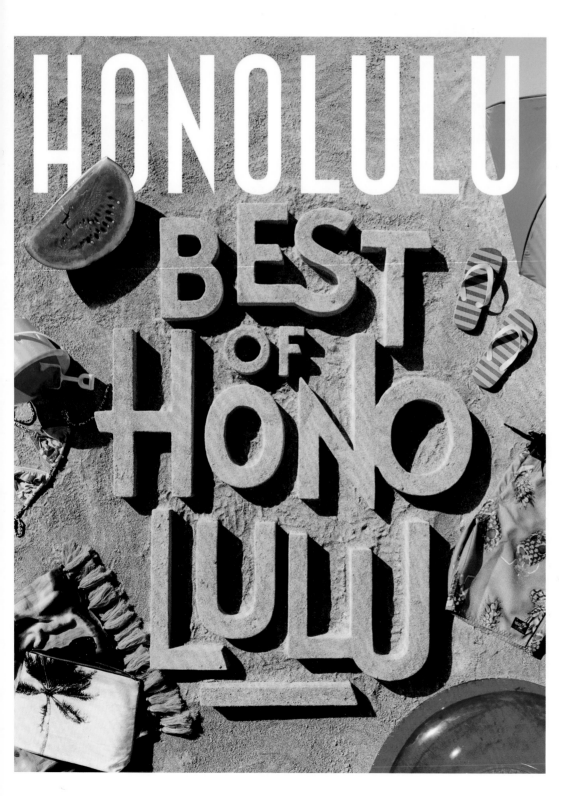

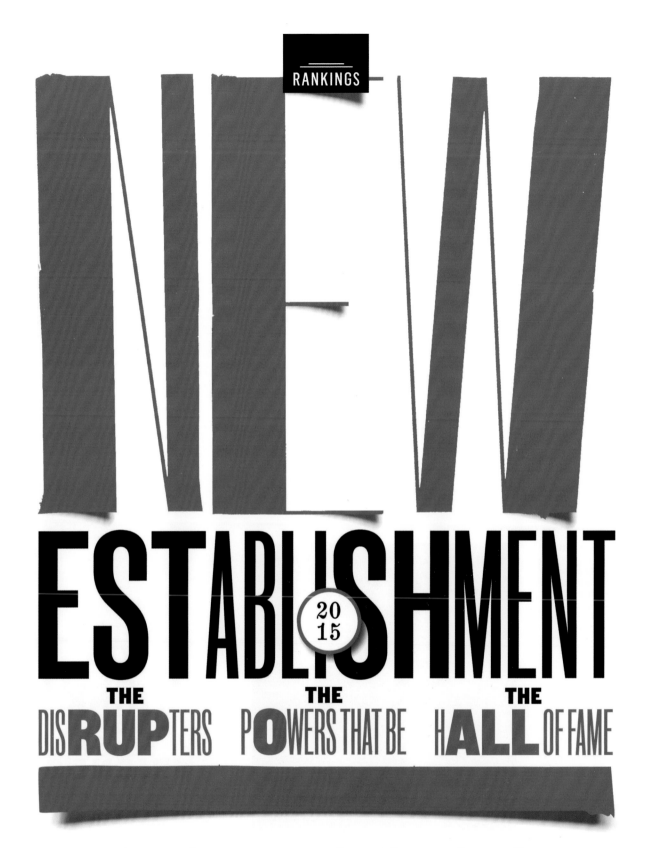

NEW

ESTABLISHMENT

20 15

THE
DIS**RUP**TERS

THE
P**O**WERS THAT BE

THE
H**ALL** OF FAME

A posse of top reporters run the numbers—and unearth
some surprising facts—for the most important visionaries, investors,
and cultural leaders in "the Year of the Unicorn"

TYPOGRAPHY BY ANTON IOUKHNOVETS

Magazine Spread

DESIGN Jamie Prokell, New York **CREATIVE DIRECTION** Debra Bishop● **DIRECTOR OF PHOTOGRAPHY** Natasha Lunn **PHOTOGRAPHY** Peter Hapak **PHOTO EDITOR** Gabrielle Sirkin **PUBLICATION** *More* **PRINCIPAL TYPE** Graphik **DIMENSIONS** 18 × 10.9 in. (45.7 × 27.6 cm)

IF YOU REVEAL GOVERNMENT SECRETS IN AN ATTEMPT TO EXPOSE GOVERNMENT WRONGDOING, DOES THAT MAKE YOU A HERO OR A TRAITOR? ATTORNEY JESSELYN RADACK STANDS UP FOR SOME OF THE WORLD'S MOST REVILED WHISTLE-BLOWERS— THINK EDWARD SNOWDEN, JULIAN ASSANGE—BECAUSE FOR HER, IT'S PERSONAL

COURTING CONTROVERSY

BY SUZANNA ANDREWS
PHOTOGRAPHED BY PETER HAPAK

98
MORE APRIL 2015

Magazine Spread

DESIGN AND ART DIRECTION Jamie Prokell, New York **CREATIVE DIRECTION** Debra Bishop● **ILLUSTRATION** Kelly Blair **PUBLICATION** *More* **PRINCIPAL TYPE** Graphik **DIMENSIONS** 18 × 10.9 in. (45.7 × 27.6 cm)

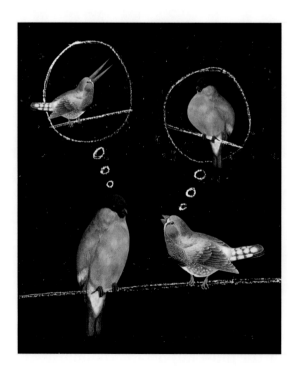

BEST BUD · OFFICE PAL
FRENEMY · SOUL MATE
SIDEKICK · BFF

WHAT YOU (REALLY) THINK ABOUT YOUR FRIENDS

WE ASKED. MORE THAN 1,000 OF YOU ANSWERED.
HERE'S WHAT YOU SAID ABOUT HOW YOU GET, KEEP, TREASURE, RECONNECT
WITH—AND SOMETIMES DROP—FRIENDS

ILLUSTRATED BY KELLY BLAIR

107
MORE APRIL 2015

BY
GENEVIEVE MONSMA

PHOTOGRAPHED BY
HANNAH KHYMYCH

BE
AU
TY

WHEN LESS IS MORE

GET READY TO PARE DOWN YOUR ROUTINE—AND LOOK PRETTIER. AN EASIER, MORE
NATURAL AESTHETIC, PROMINENT ON FALL FASHION RUNWAYS, IS A TREND WE'RE ALL RALLYING BEHIND.
BUT ONE CAVEAT: "LOW MAINTENANCE" DOES NOT MEAN "GIVE UP." SO WHAT'S
THE LEAST YOU CAN GET AWAY WITH WHILE STILL SPORTING GORGEOUS HAIR, MAKEUP AND NAILS?
HERE, YOUR MINIMALIST MANIFESTO

95
MORE SEPTEMBER 2015

DESIGN Jamie Prokell, New York **CREATIVE DIRECTION** Debra Bishop● **DIRECTOR OF PHOTOGRAPHY** Natasha Lunn **PHOTOGRAPHY** Peter Hapak **PHOTO EDITOR** Gabrielle Sirkin **PUBLICATION** *More* **PRINCIPAL TYPE** Graphik **DIMENSIONS** 18 × 10.9 in. (45.7 × 27.6 cm)

THE BIAS HUNTER
THE BIAS HUNTER
THE BIAS HUNTER
THE BIAS HUNTER
THE BIAS HUNTER
THE BIAS HUNTER
THE BIAS HUNTER
THE BIAS HUNTER
THE **BIAS** HUNTER
THE BIAS HUNTER
THE BIAS H**U**N**TE**R
THE BIAS **HUN**TER
THE BIAS HUN**TE**R
THE BIAS HUN**T**ER
THE BIAS HUNTER
THE BIAS HUNTER

MOST OF US WOULD LIKE TO BELIEVE we can see past **RACE, GENDER,
SEXUAL ORIENTATION,** etc. But new American Bar Association president **PAULETTE BROWN,**
who has spent her life fighting for diversity and fairness, wants all of us—
including herself—to look deep inside for the subtler stereotypes that could color our thinking.
WOULD YOU PASS THE TEST? BY LISA MILLER

PHOTOGRAPHED
BY
PETER HAPAK

101
MORE SEPTEMBER 2015

DESIGN Jamie Prokell, New York **CREATIVE DIRECTION** Debra Bishop● **DIRECTOR OF PHOTOGRAPHY** Natasha Lunn **PHOTOGRAPHY** Hannah Khymych **PHOTO EDITOR** Stephanie Swanicke Slater **PUBLICATION** *More* **PRINCIPAL TYPE** Graphik **DIMENSIONS** 18 × 10.9 in. (45.7 × 27.6 cm)

Magazine Spread

DESIGN AND CREATIVE DIRECTION Debra Bishop,• New York **DIRECTOR OF PHOTOGRAPHY** Natasha Lunn **PHOTOGRAPHY** Jan Welters **PHOTO EDITOR** Stephanie Swanicke Slater **PUBLICATION** *More* **PRINCIPAL TYPE** Domaine Text, Domaine Display, and Graphik **DIMENSIONS** 18 × 10.9 in. (45.7 × 27.6 cm)

Magazine Spread

DESIGN Jamie Prokell, New York **CREATIVE DIRECTION** Debra Bishop• **DIRECTOR OF PHOTOGRAPHY** Natasha Lunn **PHOTOGRAPHY** Dan Winters **PHOTO EDITOR** Stephanie Swanicke Slater **PUBLICATION** *More* **PRINCIPAL TYPE** Graphik **DIMENSIONS** 18 × 10.9 in. (45.7 × 27.6 cm)

PHOTOGRAPHED BY ANDREW B. MYERS / ILLUSTRATED BY LA TIGRE

REAL-LIFE REINVENTION SECRETS

SOME REINVENTED BY CHOICE, OTHERS BY NECESSITY. BUT THESE SMART, GUTSY WOMEN, INCLUDING HUNDREDS OF READERS SURVEYED ON MORE.COM, ALL MADE CHANGES THAT ULTIMATELY LED THEM TO GREATER SUCCESS AND HAPPINESS. LET THEIR LIVES BE YOUR GUIDE

CAREER RECALIBRATIONS

IN OUR SURVEY,

92%

of you said you changed your life sometime in the past five years.

84%

tweaked your job or career. Most popular moves: creating (or buying) a business, going back to school.

HOW YOU DID IT

PUSHING PAST FEAR

I left a promising corporate career in June and moved from New York City to Silicon Valley to work for a health and beauty start-up as its director of brand marketing—employee number nine. Unlike corporate America, start-up life is undefined. There are many sacrifices and trade-offs. But I didn't want to allow the fear of uncertainty—personal, financial, professional—to prevent me from realizing something amazing. I'd prefer to be a complete failure than live in complete fear. I'm a 34-year-old, MBA-educated, strong-minded black female, definitely not the norm for Silicon Valley. But no matter what happens here, I will never look back and wonder, What if. —*Raquel Lachman*

EXCITEMENT FROM THE LAUNCHPAD

1

"BECAME AN Internet social entrepreneur. Early days. The jury is still out."

2

"QUIT MY corporate job and bought my own business—purchased just a week ago!"

3

"I OPENED a store. Women's fitness clothes. It's been in business only three weeks, but I'm loving it."

4

"I REGISTERED a new company name today with the state of New York."

105
MORE FEBRUARY 2015

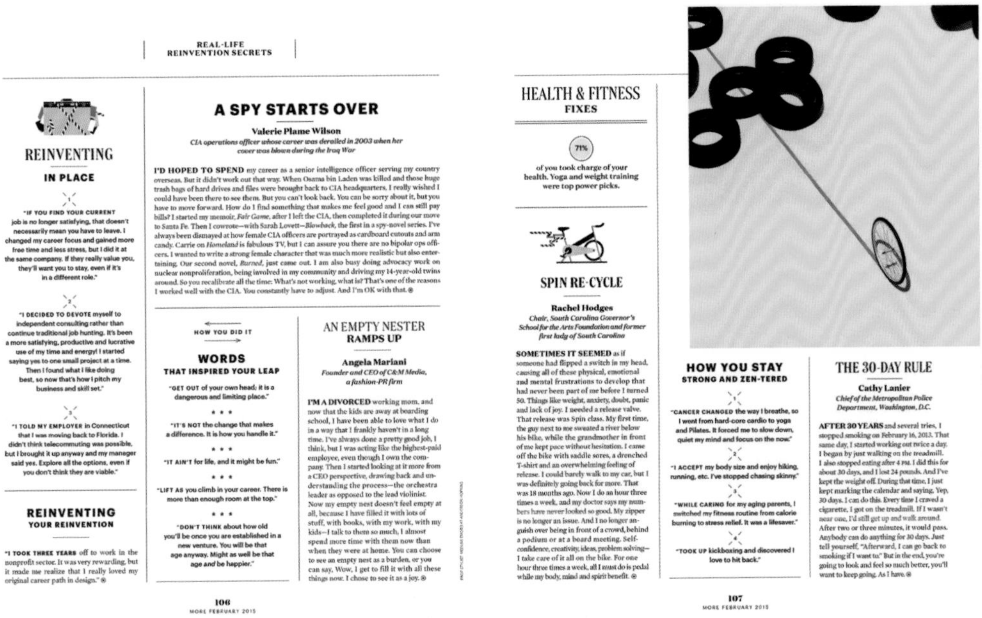

REAL-LIFE REINVENTION SECRETS

REINVENTING IN PLACE

1

"IF YOU FIND YOUR CURRENT job is no longer satisfying, that doesn't necessarily mean you have to leave. I changed my career focus and gained more free time and less stress, but I did it at the same company. If they really value you, they'll want you to stay, even if it's in a different role."

2

"I DECIDED TO DEVOTE myself to independent consulting rather than continue traditional job hunting. It's been a more satisfying, productive and lucrative use of my time and energy! I started saying yes to one small project at a time. Then I found what I like doing best, so now that's how I pitch my business and skill set."

3

"I TOLD MY EMPLOYER in Connecticut that I was moving back to Florida. I didn't think telecommuting was possible, but I brought it up anyway and my manager said yes. Explore all the options, even if you don't think they are viable."

REINVENTING YOUR REINVENTION

"I TOOK THREE YEARS off to work in the nonprofit sector. It was very rewarding, but it made me realize that I really loved my original career path in design."

A SPY STARTS OVER

Valerie Plame Wilson

CIA operations officer whose career was derailed in 2003 when her cover was blown during the Iraq War

I'D HOPED TO SPEND my career as a senior intelligence officer serving my country overseas. But it didn't work out that way. When Osama bin Laden was killed and those huge trash bags of hard drives and files were brought back to CIA headquarters, I really wished I could have been there to see them. But you can't look back. You can be sorry about it, but you have to move forward. How do I find something that makes me feel good and I can still pay bills? I started my memoir, *Fair Game*, after I left the CIA, then completed it during our move to Santa Fe. Then I cowrote—with Sarah Lovett—*Blowback*, the first in a spy-novel series. I've always been dismayed at how female CIA officers are portrayed as cardboard cutouts and arm candy. Carrie on *Homeland* is fabulous TV, but I can assure you there are no bipolar ops officers. I wanted to write a strong female character that was much more realistic but also entertaining. Our second novel, *Burned*, just came out. I am also busy doing advocacy work on nuclear nonproliferation, being involved in my community and driving my 14-year-old twins around. So you recalibrate all the time: What's not working, what is? That's one of the reasons I worked well with the CIA. You constantly have to adjust. And I'm OK with that.

HOW YOU DID IT

WORDS THAT INSPIRED YOUR LEAP

"GET OUT of your own head; it is a dangerous and limiting place."

* * *

"IT'S NOT the change that makes a difference. It is how you handle it."

* * *

"IT AIN'T for life, and it might be fun."

* * *

"LIFT AS you climb in your career. There is more than enough room at the top."

* * *

"DON'T THINK about how old you'll be once you are established in a new venture. You will be that age anyway. Might as well be that age *and* be happier."

AN EMPTY NESTER RAMPS UP

Angela Mariani

Founder and CEO of C&M Media, a fashion-PR firm

I'M A DIVORCED working mom, and now that the kids are away at boarding school, I have been able to love what I do in a way that I frankly haven't in a long time. I've always done a pretty good job, I think, but I was acting like the highest-paid employee, even though I own the company. Then I started looking at it more from a CEO perspective, drawing back and understanding the process—the orchestra leader as opposed to the lead violinist. Now my empty nest doesn't feel empty at all, because I have filled it with lots of stuff, with books, with my work, with my kids—I talk to them so much, I almost spend more time with them now than when they were at home. You can choose to see an empty nest as a burden, or you can say, Wow, I get to fill it with all these things now. I chose to see it as a joy.

106
MORE FEBRUARY 2015

HEALTH & FITNESS FIXES

71%

of you took charge of your health. Yoga and weight training were top power picks.

SPIN RE-CYCLE

Rachel Hodges

Chair, South Carolina Governor's School for the Arts Foundation and former first lady of South Carolina

SOMETIMES IT SEEMED as if someone had flipped a switch in my head, causing all of these physical, emotional and mental frustrations to develop that had never been part of me before I turned 50. Things like weight, anxiety, doubt, panic and lack of joy. I needed a release valve. That release was Spin class. My first time, the guy next to me sweated a river below his bike, while the grandmother in front of me kept pace without hesitation. I came off the bike with saddle sores, a drenched T-shirt and an overwhelming feeling of release. I could barely walk to my car, but I was definitely going back for more. That was 18 months ago. Now I do an hour three times a week, and my doctor says my numbers have never looked so good. My zipper is no longer an issue. And I no longer anguish over being in front of a crowd, behind a podium or at a board meeting. Self-confidence, creativity, ideas, problem solving—I take care of it all on the bike. For one hour three times a week, all I must do is pedal while my body, mind and spirit benefit.

HOW YOU STAY STRONG AND ZEN-TERED

1

"CANCER CHANGED the way I breathe, so I went from hard-core cardio to yoga and Pilates. It forced me to slow down, quiet my mind and focus on the now."

2

"I ACCEPT my body size and enjoy hiking, running, etc. I've stopped chasing skinny."

3

"WHILE CARING for my aging parents, I switched my fitness routine from calorie burning to stress relief. It was a lifesaver."

4

"TOOK UP kickboxing and discovered I love to hit back."

THE 30-DAY RULE

Cathy Lanier

Chief of the Metropolitan Police Department, Washington, D.C.

AFTER 30 YEARS and several tries, I stopped smoking on February 16, 2013. That same day, I started working out twice a day. I began by just walking on the treadmill. I also stopped eating after 4 PM. I did this for about 30 days, and I lost 24 pounds. And I've kept the weight off. During that time, I just kept marking the calendar and saying, Yep, 30 days. I can do this. Every time I craved a cigarette, I got on the treadmill. If I wasn't near one, I'd still get up and walk around. After two or three minutes, it would pass. Anybody can do anything for 30 days. Just tell yourself, "Afterward, I can go back to smoking if I want to." But in the end, you're going to look and feel so much better, you'll want to keep going. As I have.

107
MORE FEBRUARY 2015

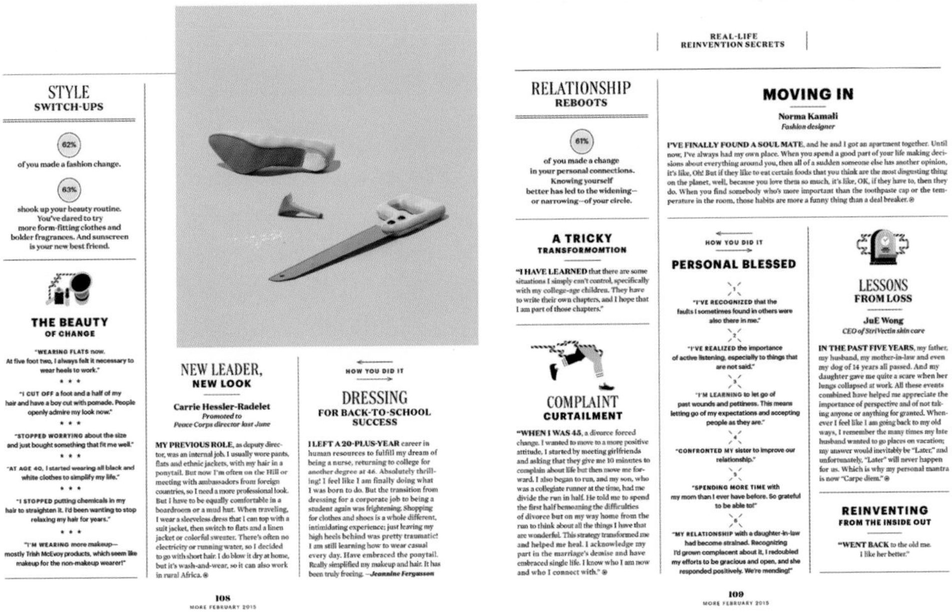

STYLE SWITCH-UPS

62%

of you made a fashion change.

63%

shook up your beauty routine. You've dared to try more form-fitting clothes and bolder fragrances. And sunscreen is your new best friend.

THE BEAUTY OF CHANGE

"WEARING FLATS now. At five foot two, I always felt it necessary to wear heels to work."

* * *

"I CUT OFF a foot and a half of my hair and have a boy cut with pomade. People openly admire my look now."

* * *

"STOPPED WORRYING about the size and just bought something that fit me well."

* * *

"AT AGE 40, I started wearing all black and white clothes to simplify my life."

* * *

"I STOPPED putting chemicals in my hair to straighten it. I'd been wanting to stop relaxing my hair for years."

* * *

"I'M WEARING more makeup—mostly Trish McEvoy products, which seem like makeup for the non-makeup wearer!"

NEW LEADER, NEW LOOK

Carrie Hessler-Radelet

Promoted to Peace Corps director last June

MY PREVIOUS ROLE, as deputy director, was an internal job. I usually wore pants, flats and ethnic jackets, with my hair in a ponytail. But now I'm often on the Hill or meeting with ambassadors from foreign countries, so I need a more professional look. But I have to be equally comfortable in a boardroom or a mud hut. When traveling, I wear a sleeveless dress that I can top with a suit jacket, then switch to flats and a linen jacket or colorful sweater. There's often no electricity or running water, so I decided to go with short hair. I do blow it dry at home, but it's wash-and-wear, so it can also work in rural Africa.

HOW YOU DID IT

DRESSING FOR BACK-TO-SCHOOL SUCCESS

I LEFT A 20-PLUS-YEAR career in human resources to fulfill my dream of being a nurse, returning to college for another degree at 46. Absolutely thrilling! I feel like I am finally doing what I was born to do. But the transition from dressing for a corporate job to being a student again was frightening. Shopping for clothes and shoes is a whole different, intimidating experience; just leaving my high heels behind was pretty traumatic! I am still learning how to wear casual every day. Have embraced the ponytail. Really simplified my makeup and hair. It has been truly freeing. —*Jeannine Fergusson*

108
MORE FEBRUARY 2015

REAL-LIFE REINVENTION SECRETS

RELATIONSHIP REBOOTS

61%

of you made a change in your personal connections. Knowing yourself better has led to the widening—or narrowing—of your circle.

A TRICKY TRANSFORMOMTION

"I HAVE LEARNED that there are some situations I simply can't control, specifically with my college-age children. They have to write their own chapters, and I hope that I am part of those chapters."

COMPLAINT CURTAILMENT

"WHEN I WAS 45, a divorce forced change. I wanted to move to a more positive attitude. I started by meeting girlfriends and asking that they give me 10 minutes to complain about life but then move me forward. I also began to run, and my son, who was a collegiate runner at the time, had me divide the run in half. He told me to spend the first half bemoaning the difficulties of divorce but on my way home from the run to think about all the things I have that are wonderful. This strategy transformed me and helped me heal. I acknowledge my part in the marriage's demise and have embraced single life. I know who I am now and who I connect with."

MOVING IN

Norma Kamali

Fashion designer

I'VE FINALLY FOUND A SOUL MATE, and he and I got an apartment together. Until now, I've always had my own place. When you spend a good part of your life making decisions about everything around you, then all of a sudden someone else has another opinion, it's like, Oh! But if they like to eat certain foods that you think are the most disgusting thing on the planet, well, because you love them so much, it's like, OK, if they have to, then they do. When you find somebody who's more important than the toothpaste cap or the temperature in the room, those habits are more a funny thing than a deal breaker.

HOW YOU DID IT

PERSONAL BLESSED

1

"I'VE RECOGNIZED that the faults I sometimes found in others were also there in me."

2

"I'VE REALIZED the importance of active listening, especially to things that are not said."

3

"I'M LEARNING to let go of past wounds and pettiness. This means letting go of my expectations and accepting people as they are."

4

"CONFRONTED MY sister to improve our relationship."

5

"SPENDING MORE TIME with my mom than I ever have before. So grateful to be able to!"

6

"MY RELATIONSHIP with a daughter-in-law had become strained. Recognizing I'd grown complacent about it, I redoubled my efforts to be gracious and open, and she responded positively. We're mending!"

LESSONS FROM LOSS

JuE Wong

CEO of StriVectin skin care

IN THE PAST FIVE YEARS, my father, my husband, my mother-in-law and even my dog of 14 years all passed. And my daughter gave me quite a scare when her lungs collapsed at work. All these events combined have helped me appreciate the importance of perspective and of not taking anyone or anything for granted. Whenever I feel like I am going back to my old ways, I remember the many times my late husband wanted to go places on vacation; my answer would inevitably be "Later," and unfortunately, "Later" will never happen for us. Which is why my personal mantra is now "Carpe diem."

REINVENTING FROM THE INSIDE OUT

"WENT BACK to the old me. I like her better."

109
MORE FEBRUARY 2015

Magazine Spread

DESIGN AND CREATIVE DIRECTION Debra Bishop,• New York **ILLUSTRATION** La Tigre **DIRECTOR OF PHOTOGRAPHY** Natasha Lunn **PHOTOGRAPHY** Andrew B. Meyers **PHOTO EDITOR** Stephanie Swanicke Slater **PUBLICATION** *More* **PRINCIPAL TYPE** Domaine Text, Domaine Display, and Graphik **DIMENSIONS** 18 × 10.9 in. (45.7 × 27.6 cm)

Exhibition

DESIGN Jewelyn Butron, New York **CREATIVE DIRECTION** Nigel Sielegar● **FABRICATOR** Daniel Gutierrez **URL** corse.nyc **DESIGN FIRM** Corse Design Factory **CLIENT** Typeforce NYC **PRINCIPAL TYPE** Custom, out of newsprint **DIMENSIONS** 10 × 6 ft. (30.5 × 18.3 m)

Architectural and Dimensional Design

DESIGN Pauline Cheng, Daniel Maxfield, and Brad Thomas, San Francisco **FAIA, ARCHITECT** Michael Duncan **LEAD GRAPHIC DESIGNER** Lonny Israel **PROJECT MANAGER** Nicholas Gerstner **URL** som.com **TWITTER** @SOM_Design **DESIGN FIRM** Skidmore, Owings & Merrill **CLIENT** American Conservatory Theater **PRINCIPAL TYPE** Gotham **DIMENSIONS** Various

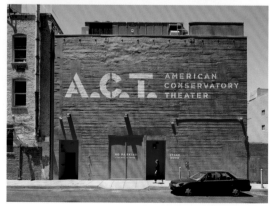

Signage

DESIGN DIRECTION Richard Poulin, New York **PROJECT MANAGER AND SENIOR DESIGNER** Andreina Carrillo **URL** poulinmorris.com **TWITTER** @poulinmorris **DESIGN FIRM** Poulin + Morris **CLIENT** BRIC **PRINCIPAL TYPE** Blender Pro and Freight Sans Pro **DIMENSIONS** Various

Signage

DESIGN Jose Traconis, New York **PRINCIPAL** Graham Hanson● **URL** grahamhanson.com **TWITTER** @ghdnyc **DESIGN FIRM** Graham Hanson Design **CLIENT** Google **PRINCIPAL TYPE** Each letter came from a different New York City neon sign: for Domino Sugar, Colony, Tower Records, Village Vanguard, Apollo Theater, and Katz's Delicatessen **DIMENSIONS** 206 × 57.5 in. (523.2 × 146.1 cm)

Exhibition

DESIGN Damee Yi, Seoul **ART DIRECTION** Jihye Lee **CREATIVE DIRECTION** Hyun Cho **DESIGN FIRM** S/O Project **CLIENT** National Museum of Modern and Contemporary Art

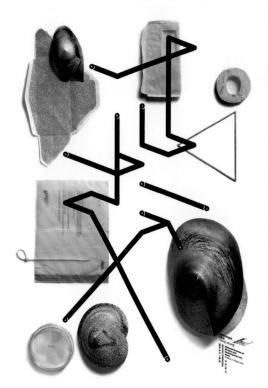

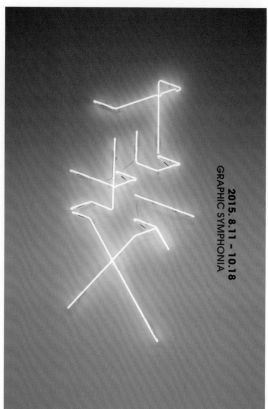

Exhibition

DESIGN, ART DIRECTION, AND CREATIVE PRODUCER Eve Steben, London **PHOTOGRAPHY AND TYPOGRAPHY** Sean Freeman **STAGE DESIGN** Camille Boyer **URL** thereis.co.uk **DESIGN FIRM** THERE IS **CLIENT** SIAM CENTRE **PRINCIPAL TYPE** Wes FY Black **DIMENSIONS** Various

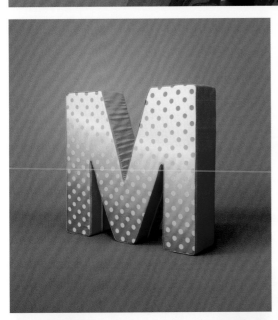

Mural

CREATIVE DIRECTION Douglas Riccardi,• New York **JUNIOR DESIGN** Karan Patel **URL** memo-ny.com **DESIGN FIRM** Memo NY **CLIENT** Schnippers

Signage

DESIGN DIRECTION Adam Tanski, New York **PRINCIPAL** Graham Hanson• **URL** grahamhanson.com **TWITTER** @ghdnyc **DESIGN FIRM** Graham Hanson Design **CLIENT** Capital One **PRINCIPAL TYPE** Custom built out of tools **DIMENSIONS** 192 × 60 in. (487.7 × 152.4 cm)

Exhibition

DESIGN Vanessa Lam, New York **ART DIRECTION** Elle Kim **CREATIVE DIRECTION** Mike Abbink and Hsien-Yin Ingrid Chou **PRODUCTION** Claire Corey **PRODUCTION ARTIST** Paulette Giguere **PHOTOGRAPHY** Martin Seck **URL** momadesignstudio.org **AGENCY** Department of Graphic Design and Advertising, Museum of Modern Art (MoMA) **MUSEUM** Department of Film, Museum of Modern Art (MoMA) **PRINCIPAL TYPE** MoMA Gothic Display and customized MoMA Gothic **DIMENSIONS** Title wall: 71 × 101 in. (180.3 × 256.5 cm)

Exhibition

DESIGN Vanessa Lam, New York **ART DIRECTION AND CREATIVE DIRECTION** Hsien-Yin Ingrid Chou **PRODUCTION** Claire Corey **PRODUCTION ARTIST** Paulette Giguere **SILKSCREEN PRODUCTION** Tom Black **PHOTOGRAPHY** Martin Seck **URL** momadesignstudio.org **AGENCY** Department of Graphic Design and Advertising, Museum of Modern Art (MoMA) **MUSEUM** Department of Photography, Museum of Modern Art (MoMA) **PRINCIPAL TYPE** Plain **DIMENSIONS** 136 × 60 in. (345.4 × 152.4 cm) and 180 × 66 in. (457.2 × 167.6 cm)

Exhibition

DESIGN Eva Bochem-shur and Damien Saatdjian, New York
ART DIRECTION AND CREATIVE DIRECTION Hsien-Yin Ingrid Chou **PRODUCTION ARTIST** Paulette Giguere **PHOTOGRAPHY** Martin Seck **URL** momadesignstudio.org **AGENCY** Department of Graphic Design and Advertising, Museum of Modern Art (MoMA) museum Department of Painting and Sculpture, Museum of Modern Art (MoMA) **PRINCIPAL TYPE** Bureau Grotesque **DIMENSIONS** Title wall: 11.5 × 10.5 ft. (3.5 × 3.2 m) and Time line: 69.2 × 8.7 ft. (21.1 × 2.7 m)

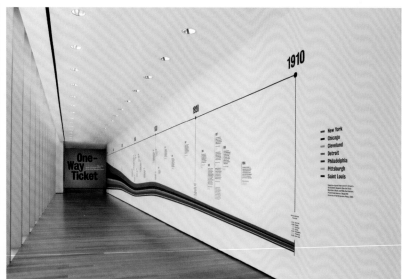

Exhibition

DESIGN Eva Bochem-shur, New York **ART DIRECTION** Tony Lee **CREATIVE DIRECTION** Hsien-Yin Ingrid Chou **PRODUCTION** Claire Corey **PRODUCTION ARTIST** Paulette Giguere **PHOTOGRAPHY** Martin Seck **URL AGENCY** Department of Graphic Design and Advertising, Museum of Modern Art (MoMA) **MUSEUM** Department of Film, Museum of Modern Art (MoMA) **PRINCIPAL TYPE** MoMA Gothic Display and customized MoMA Gothic **DIMENSIONS** 124 × 108 in. (315 × 274.3 cm)

Exhibition

DESIGN In-Hee Bae, New York **ART DIRECTION AND CREATIVE DIRECTION** Hsien-Yin Ingrid Chou **PRODUCTION ARTIST** Paulette Giguere **PHOTOGRAPHY** Martin Seck **URL** momadesignstudio. org **AGENCY** Department of Graphic Design and Advertising, Museum of Modern Art (MoMA) **MUSEUM** Department of Painting and Sculpture, Museum of Modern Art (MoMA) **PRINCIPAL TYPE** Custom **DIMENSIONS** Title wall: 156 × 153 in. (396.2 × 388.6 cm)

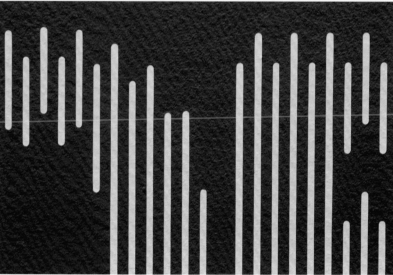

Exhibition

DESIGN Danielle Hall, New York **ART DIRECTION AND CREATIVE DIRECTION** Hsien-Yin Ingrid Chou **PRODUCTION** Claire Corey **PRODUCTION ARTIST** Paulette Giguere **SILKSCREEN PRODUCTION** Tom Black **PHOTOGRAPHY** Martin Seck **URL** momadesignstudio. org **AGENCY** Department of Graphic Design and Advertising, Museum of Modern Art (MoMA) **MUSEUM** Department of Photography, Museum of Modern Art (MoMA) **PRINCIPAL TYPE** MoMA Gothic Display and customized MoMA Gothic **DIMENSIONS** Title wall: 133 × 126 in. (337.8 × 320 cm)

Exhibition

DESIGN AND ANIMATION In-Hee Bae, New York **ART DIRECTION AND CREATIVE DIRECTION** Hsien-Yin Ingrid Chou **PRODUCTION** Althea Penza **PRODUCTION ARTIST** Paulette Giguere **PHOTOGRAPHY** Martin Seck

URL momadesignstudio.org **AGENCY** Department of Graphic Design and Advertising, Museum of Modern Art (MoMA) **MUSEUM** Department of Education, Family Program, Museum of Modern Art

(MoMA) **PRINCIPAL TYPE** MoMA Gothic Display and customized MoMA Gothic **DIMENSIONS** Title wall: 35 × 11.6 ft. (10.7 × 3.5 m)

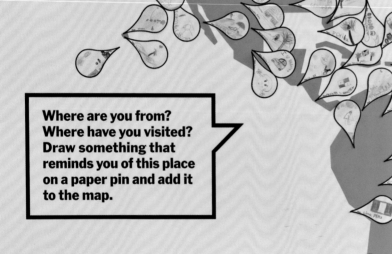

Where are you from? Where have you visited? Draw something that reminds you of this place on a paper pin and add it to the map.

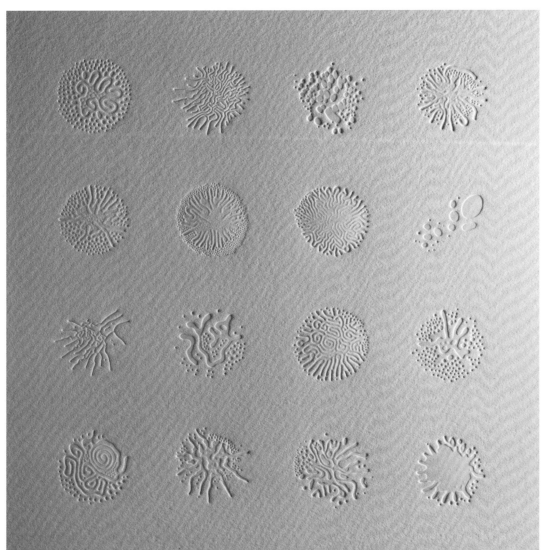

Experimental

CONCEPT, DESIGN, AND ART DIRECTION Craig Ward,• Brooklyn, New York **PHOTOGRAPHY, DEVELOPMENT** Linden Gledhill **PRINTMAKING** Jonathan Selikoff• / Vote For Letterpress **PRINCIPAL TYPE** Custom **DIMENSIONS** Various

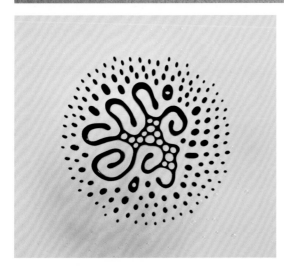

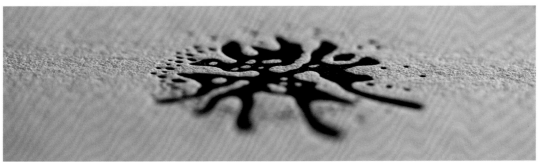

Exhibition

DESIGN Jerome Corgier, Paris, Represented in the United States by the Marlena Agency (marlenaagency.com) **CONCEPTION** Jerome Corgier at Atelier Pariri **PHOTOGRAPHY** Marc Brems Tatti **URL** jeromecorgier.com **TWITTER** @jeromecorgier **TUMBLR** jeromecorgier.tumblr.com

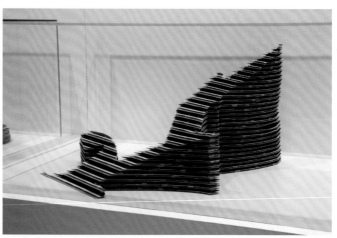

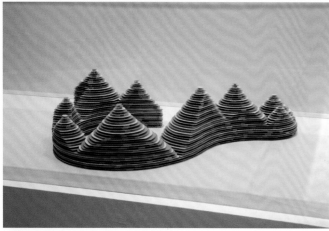

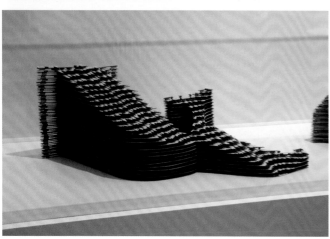

216

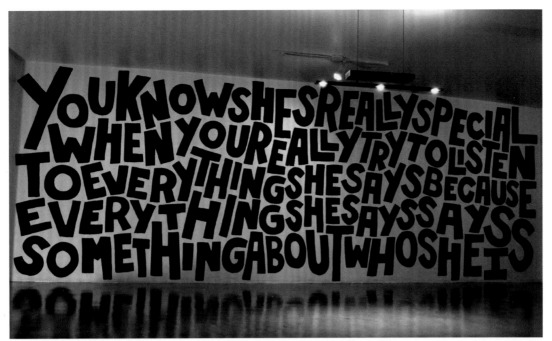

Mural

DESIGNER AND MURALIST Timothy Goodman, New York **ASSISTANT** Julia Parris **PHOTOGRAPHY** Jeremy Preimesbergers **URL** tgoodman.com **TWITTER** @timothyogoodman **CLIENT** CuratorLA **PRINCIPAL TYPE** Handlettering with Matte House Paint **DIMENSIONS** 30 × 10 ft. (9.1 × 2.5 m)

Exhibition

DESIGN Joe Haddad and Lynne Yun, New York **DESIGN DIRECTION** Juan Carlos Pagan● **ART DIRECTION** Erika Kohnen **CREATIVE DIRECTION** Frank Cartagena and Sam Shepherd **CHIEF CREATIVE OFFICER** Kerry Keenan **EXECUTIVE CREATIVE DIRECTOR** Menno Kluin **COPYWRITER** Lauren Cooper **PHOTOGRAPHY** Catalina Kulczar-Marin **URL** deutsch.com **AGENCY** Deutsch **CLIENT** Krylon **PRINCIPAL TYPE** Custom

Exhibition

ASSOCIATE CREATIVE DIRECTOR Ryan O'Keefe **SENIOR ART DIRECTOR** Andre Gidoin **TYPEFACE DESIGNER** Thorbjørn Gudnason **URL** sidlee.com **AGENCY** Sid Lee NY **CLIENT** Absolut Elyx **PRINCIPAL TYPE** Boutique Display and Futura Condensed Light **DIMENSIONS** 6.7 × 11 × 18 ft. (2 × 3.4 × 5.5 m)

Signage

DESIGN David Blumberg, Birmingham, Alabama **CREATIVE DIRECTION** Roy Burns III and Spencer Till **ILLUSTRATION** David Blumberg, Andrew Thomson, and Spencer Till **LETTERER** Spencer Till **URL** lewiscommunications.com **TWITTER** @lewisideas **AGENCY** Lewis Communications **CLIENT** Auto & Truck Services **PRINCIPAL TYPE** Handlettering **DIMENSIONS** Various

Exhibition

FOUNDER AND DESIGNER
Jenna Blazevich, Chicago
URL vichcraft.com **TWITTER**
@Vichcraft **STUDIO** Vichcraft
Design Studio **CLIENT**
Typeforce 6 Chicago
PRINCIPAL TYPE Twenty-seven
thousand .22 caliber bullet
casings **DIMENSIONS** 3 × 6 ft.
(.9 × 1.8 m)

Experimental

**ART DIRECTION AND
LETTERING** Ana Gomez
Bernaus,• Los Angeles **URL**
anenocena.com **TWITTER**
@anenocena **STUDIO**
Anenocena **CLIENT** &Wolf
PRINCIPAL TYPE Handlettering
DIMENSIONS 18 × 24 in.
(45.7 × 61 cm)

Exhibition

DESIGN Clark Bardsley, Jinki Cambronero, Ben Corban, Kelly Dixon, Aaron Edwards, Tessa Harris, George Kahi, Te Rangitākuku Kaihoro, Dean Murray, Tyrone Ohia, Bernie Papa, Dean Poole, Lorna Rikihana, Huhana Turei, and Tanya White, Auckland **CREATIVE DIRECTION** Dean Poole **URL** altgroup.net **DESIGN FIRM** Alt Group **CLIENT** Auckland Council **PRINCIPAL TYPE** Te Oro **DIMENSIONS** 13 × 3.6 ft. (400 × 110 m)

Experimental

DESIGN Tingwei Xing, Nanjing City, China **TWITTER** @Tingwei_X Weibo weibo.com/u/1271573212 **DESIGN STUDIO** XTW Studio **SCHOOL** Nanjing Normal University **DIMENSIONS** 23.4 × 33.1 in. (59.4 × 84.1 cm) and 11.7 × 16.5 in. (29.7 × 42 cm) **PRINCIPAL TYPE** Custom

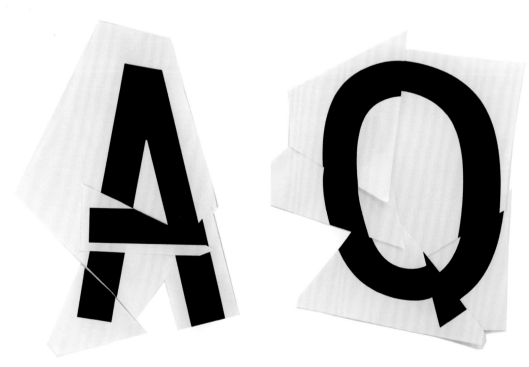

The letter A is composed of four letter pieces

The letter Q is composed of five letter pieces

Signage

DESIGN Nate Coonrod, Brian Metcalf, Serifcan Ozcan, Darren Phillip, and Eden Weingart, New York **CREATIVE** Cory Everett, Erwin Federizo, Eric Helin, Pepe Hernandez, Emily Longfield, Andre Poli, Garrick Sheldon, and Blair Warren **CREATIVE DIRECTION** Mike Giepert, Jimm Lasser, and Gary Van Dzura **EXECUTIVE CREATIVE DIRECTORS** Susan Hoffman, David Kolbusz, and Jaime Robinson **PRODUCERS** Michelle Carman, Pietro Clemente, Orlee Tatarka, Dominic Tunon, Jen Vladimirsky, and Christine Young **HEAD OF ART PRODUCTION** Deb Rosen **SOCIAL STRATEGIST** Jessica Ambercrombie **ACCOUNT TEAM** Jerico Cabaysa, Patty Ehinger, Molly Friedman, and Jacque Sloan **MEDIA TEAM** Karlo Cordova and Justin Lam **PROJECT MANAGEMENT** Sunjoo Ryou **HEAD OF CONTENT PRODUCTION** Nick Setounski **TECH LEAD** Alex Maiorov **DIRECTOR OF TECH** Charles Duncan **QA LEAD** Sean Jones **SENIOR CREATIVE TECHNOLOGIST** Mauricio Ruiz **AGENCY** Wieden+Kennedy New York **CLIENT** Sprite **PRINCIPAL TYPE** Lettering, Sign Painter, and Verlag

Self-Promotion

DESIGN Tina Smith,• New York
URL tinasmithdesign.com
TWITTER @tinasmithdesign
PRINCIPAL TYPE Various
DIMENSIONS 10 × 10 in.
(25.4 × 25.4 cm)

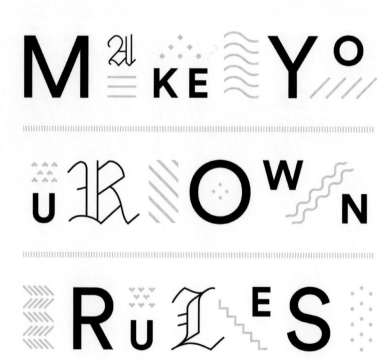

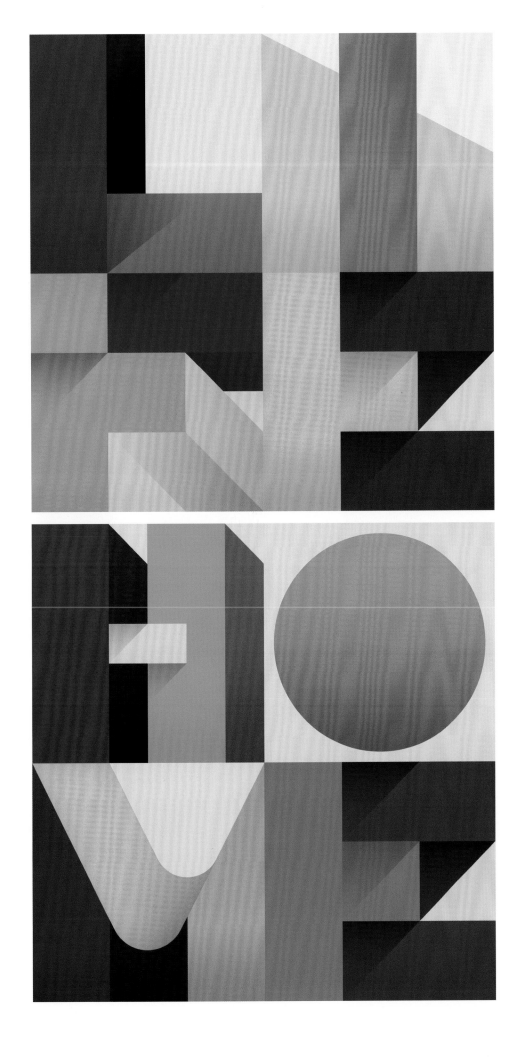

Experimental

TYPE DESIGNER Federico
Landini, Pistoia, Italy
ILLUSTRATOR Ray Oranges,
Florence, Italy **URL**
idependonme.com and
ray-oranges.com **PRINCIPAL
TYPE** Custom **DIMENSIONS**
19.7 × 19.7 in. (50 × 50 cm)

Mural

ARTIST Faust, New York **URL**
faustnewyork.com **INSTAGRAM**
@faustnewyork **CLIENT**
72andSunny **PRINCIPAL TYPE**
Handlettering **DIMENSIONS**
4 × 20 ft. (1.2 × 6.1 m)

Mural

ARTIST Faust, New York **URL**
faustnewyork.com **INSTAGRAM**
@faustnewyork **CLIENT** Spotify
PRINCIPAL TYPE Handlettering
DIMENSIONS 10 × 30 ft.
(3 × 9 m)

Mural

ARTIST Faust, New York
URL faustnewyork.com
INSTAGRAM @faustnewyork
CLIENT NTRPRNRS
PRINCIPAL TYPE Handlettering
DIMENSIONS 25 × 60 ft.
(7.6 × 18.3 m)

Mural

ARTIST Faust, New York
URL faustnewyork.com
INSTAGRAM @faustnewyork
CLIENT Havas Worldwide,
Chicago **PRINCIPAL TYPE**
Handlettering **DIMENSIONS**
8 × 10 ft. (2.4 × 3 m)

Logotype

DESIGN Jon Robbins,●
Brooklyn, New York **ART
DIRECTION** Jon Robbins
COPYWRITER Maddison
Bradley **URL** sidehustle.nyc
DESIGN FIRM Side Hustle
Studios **CLIENT** Paul Bradley
Builders **PRINCIPAL TYPE**
Trade Gothic Extended

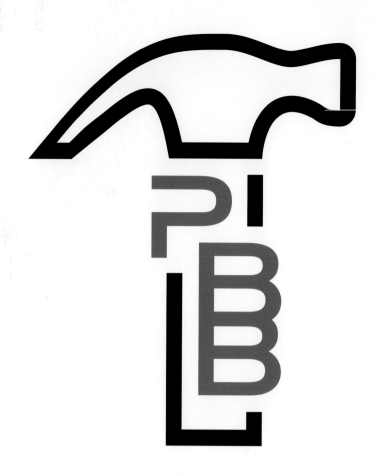

Logotype

**DESIGN AND CREATIVE
DIRECTION** Pharaon Siraj,
Singapore **URL** fifthcolumn.co
DESIGN STUDIO Fifth Column
CLIENT The Rug Maker
PRINCIPAL TYPE
Wordmark and custom

Poster

DESIGN Kirstin Huber, New York **ART DIRECTION** Paula Scher,● Pentagram **URL** kirstinhuber.com **CLIENT** The Public Theater (publictheater. org) **PRINCIPAL TYPE** Knockout **DIMENSIONS** 30.5 × 59 in. (77 × 150 cm)

Logotype

DESIGN AND CONCEPT
Raffinerie AG für Gestaltung,
Zürich **URL** raffinerie.
com **CLIENT** Edition Unik
PRINCIPAL TYPE Warnock Pro

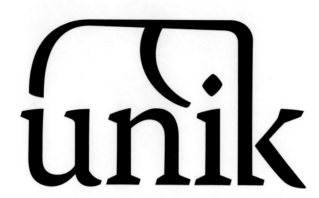

Self-Promotion

DESIGN Thomas G. Uhlein,
Wayne, New Jersey **URL**
uhleindesign.com **TWITTER**
@TGUdesign **DESIGN FIRM**
Uhlein Design

Logotype

CREATIVE DIRECTION Jerald
Saddle and Kate Wang, New
York **CLIENT** Maki Fund

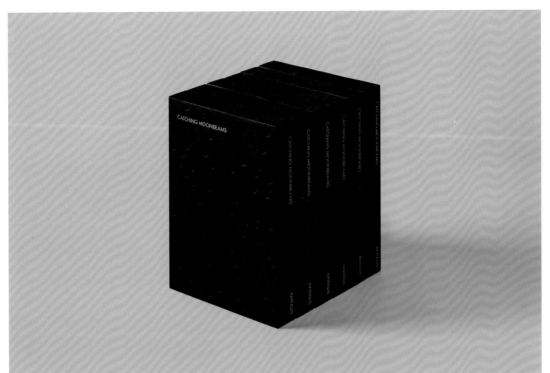

Catalog

DESIGN Fibi Kung and Toby Ng, Hong Kong **CREATIVE DIRECTION** Toby Ng **URL** toby-ng.com **STUDIO** Toby Ng Design **CLIENT** Antalis HK **PRINCIPAL TYPE** Futura Std **DIMENSIONS** 6.6 × 9.1 in. (16.7 × 23 cm)

Packaging

DESIGN AGENCY Saatchi & Saatchi Design Worldwide, Callum Bakker, Michael Bevin, Anushka Bihari, Kane McPherson, and Leah Surynt, Auckland **CREATIVE DIRECTION** Derek Lockwood **CLIENT** Billy Apple **PRINCIPAL TYPE** Futura **DIMENSIONS** Standard can: 355 ml, 4.8 × 2.1 in. (12.2 × 5.3 cm)

Mural

DESIGN Leandro Senna, San Francisco **ADOBE CREATIVE DIRECTOR** Kashka Pregowska-Czerw **URL** leandrosenna. com **TWITTER** @leandrosenna **INSTAGRAM** @senna_leandro **CLIENT** Adobe MAX Conference **PRINCIPAL TYPE** Handlettering **DIMENSIONS** 8 × 14 ft. (2.4 × 4.3 m)

Branding

DESIGN Roberto de Vicq de Cumptich,• New York **CREATIVE DIRECTION** Randi Sirkin **URL** devicq.com/burrito.html **DESIGN FIRM** de Vicq design **CLIENT** Starr Restaurants **PRINCIPAL TYPE** Charcuterie, Eames Century Modern, LiebeDoris, and Sra. Stencil **DIMENSIONS** Various

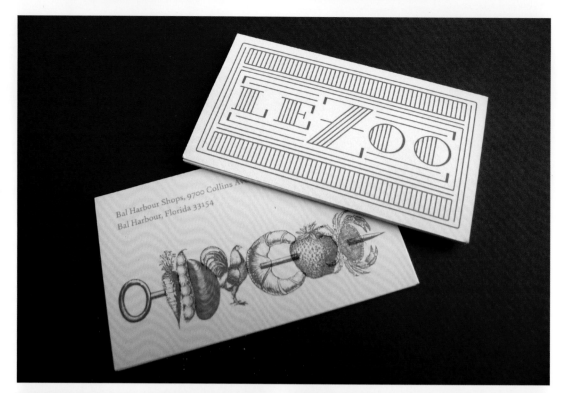

Branding

DESIGN Roberto de Vicq de Cumptich,• New York **CREATIVE DIRECTION** Randi Sirkin **URL** devicq.com/ le_zoo.html **DESIGN FIRM** de Vicq design **CLIENT** Starr Restaurants **PRINCIPAL TYPE** Backhand Script, Burford, Sina, Station, Sweet Sans, and Sweet Sans Titling No. 22 **DIMENSIONS** Various

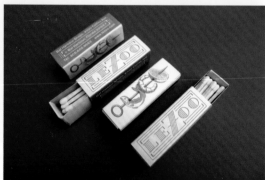

232

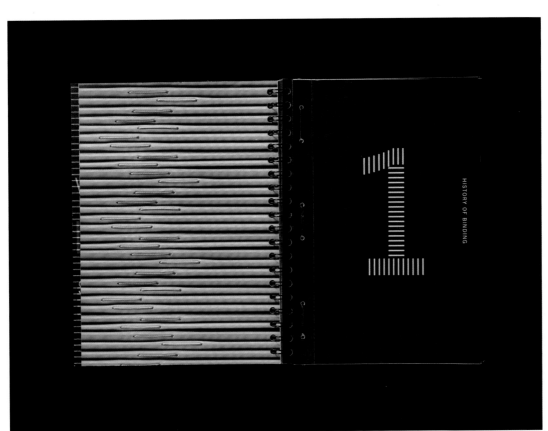

Chapter Dividers

DESIGN Dang Nguyen,
San Francisco **CREATIVE
DIRECTION** Kit Hinrichs•
URL studio-hinrichs.com
STUDIO Studio Hinrichs
CLIENT Sappi **PRINCIPAL
TYPE** News Gothic
DIMENSIONS 15 × 10.25 in.
(38.1 × 26 cm)

Keepsake

DESIGN Taek Hyun Kim,
Baozhen Li, Anna Mort, John
Pobojewski, Bud Rodecker,
Rick Valicenti, and Magdalena
Wistuba, Chicago **DESIGN
DIRECTOR** Rick Valicenti **URL**
3st.com **TWITTER** @3stdesign
STUDIO Thirst **CLIENT**
Classic Color and Smithfield
Properties **PRINCIPAL TYPE**
Custom **DIMENSIONS** 6 × 8 ×
1.25 in. (15.2 × 20.3 × 3.2 cm)

Invitation

ART DIRECTION Daniel
Robitaille, Montréal CREATIVE
DIRECTION Louis Gagnon•
URL paprika.com AGENCY
Paprika CLIENT McCord
Museum PRINCIPAL TYPE
Vittorio DIMENSIONS
5.5 × 8.5 in. (14 × 21.5 cm)

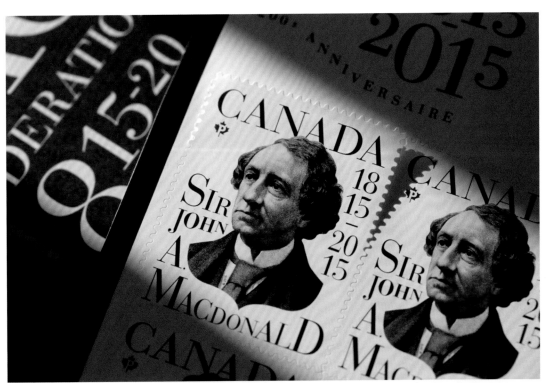

Stamp

ART DIRECTION Daniel Robitaille, Montréal **CREATIVE DIRECTION** Louis Gagnon• **URL** paprika.com **AGENCY** Paprika **CLIENT** Canada Post **PRINCIPAL TYPE** Bodoni **DIMENSIONS** 1.3 × 1.6 in. (3.2 × 4 cm)

Invitation

ART DIRECTION Julien Hebert, Montréal **CREATIVE DIRECTION** Louis Gagnon• **URL** paprika. com **AGENCY** Paprika **CLIENT** Montréal Museum of Fine Arts **PRINCIPAL TYPE** Muller and custom **DIMENSIONS** Various

Identity

DESIGN Katie King Rumford, Brooklyn, New York **CREATIVE DIRECTION** Johnny Selman● **MOTION DESIGN** Calvin Waterman **PRODUCER** Mike Scandiffio **URL** selmandesign.com **TWITTER** @SelmanDesign **STUDIO** Selman Design **CLIENT** Disposable Film

Festival **PRINCIPAL TYPE** DFF Crumple, United Sans Condensed Heavy, and United Sans Regular Medium **DIMENSIONS** Various

Identity

DESIGN Shy Inbar, Pedro Sanches, and Jessica Walsh, New York **ART DIRECTION** Jessica Walsh **CREATIVE DIRECTION** Stefan Sagmeister **PROGRAMMING** Pedro Sanches **DESIGN AGENCY** Sagmeister & Walsh **CLIENT** Fugue **PRINCIPAL TYPE** Maison Neue and GT Sectra **DIMENSIONS** Various

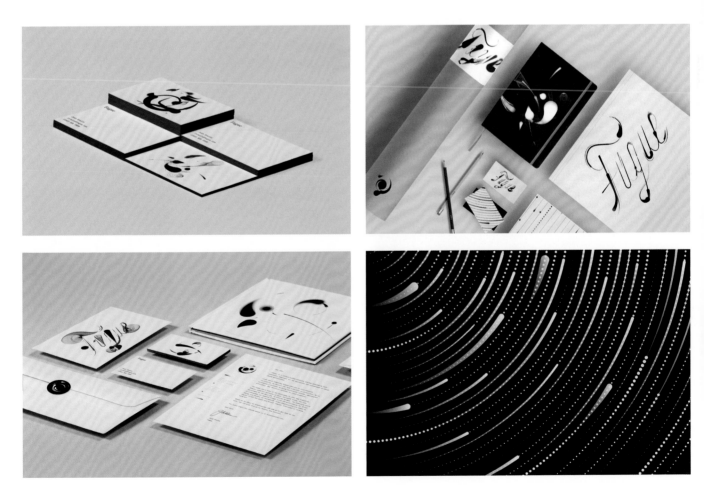

**Exhibition
and Collateral**

**DESIGN AND CREATIVE
DIRECTION** Edward Coffey
and Caroline Kögler
Parramatta, Australia **URL**
raffles.edu.au **SCHOOL**
Raffles College of Design and
Commerce **PRINCIPAL TYPE**
Replica **DIMENSIONS** Various

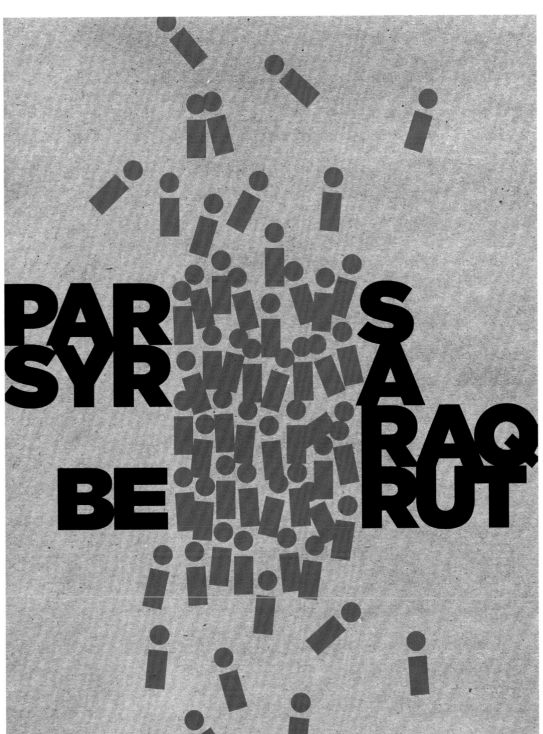

Poster

DESIGN Mohammad Sharaf,•
Brooklyn, New York **URL**
mohammadsharaf.com
TWITTER @MohammadRSharaf
PRINCIPAL TYPE Gotham HTF
DIMENSIONS 19.7 × 27.6 in.
(50 × 70 cm)

Packaging

DESIGN AND CREATIVE DIRECTION Sara Golzari and Jeff Hester,● Oakland, California **URL** cultpartners.com **DESIGN FIRM** Cult Partners **CLIENT** Vintage Wine Estates **PRINCIPAL TYPE** Centaur, Monte Carlo, Numbers Depot, and Tommaso **DIMENSIONS** 3 × 12.75 in. (7.6 × 32.4 cm)

Packaging

DESIGN AND BOOK Ross Clodfelter and Shane Cranford, Winston-Salem, North Carolina **WRITING** Stephanie Campisi and Reid Thorpe **ILLUSTRATION** Dianne Sutherland **PHOTOGRAPHY** Vanessa Rees **URL** wearedevice.com **TWITTER** @WeAreDevice **DESIGN FIRM** Device Creative Collaborative **CLIENT** Piedmont Distillers **PRINCIPAL TYPE** Craw Modern and Gotham Bold **DIMENSIONS** Label: 8.4 × 4.25 in. (21.3 × 10.8 cm) Bottle: 2.75 × 13 in. (7 × 33 cm)

Packaging

CREATIVE DIRECTION Wen Jinheng, Shenzhen, China **URL** red-brand.com **DESIGN FIRM** Shenzhen Lajiao Design **CLIENT** Yunshuchun Tea **PRINCIPAL TYPE** Chinese characters **DIMENSIONS** 5.5 × 5.5 × 5.5 in. (14 × 14 × 14 cm)

Packaging

DESIGN AND CREATIVE DIRECTION Sara Golzari and Jeff Hester,• Oakland, California **URL** cultpartners.com **DESIGN FIRM** Cult Partners **CLIENT** Winery Exchange **PRINCIPAL TYPE** Bank Gothic, Chevalier, Knockout, and Young Gallant **DIMENSIONS** 3.6 × 7.5 in. (9.1 × 9.1 cm)

Packaging

DESIGN DIRECTION Elizabeth Carey Smith,• New York
CLIENT Zady **URL** zady.com
PRINCIPAL TYPE Gotham and Mercury **DIMENSIONS**
12 × 15 in. (30.5 × 38.1 cm) and 17 × 24 in. (43. × 61 cm)

242

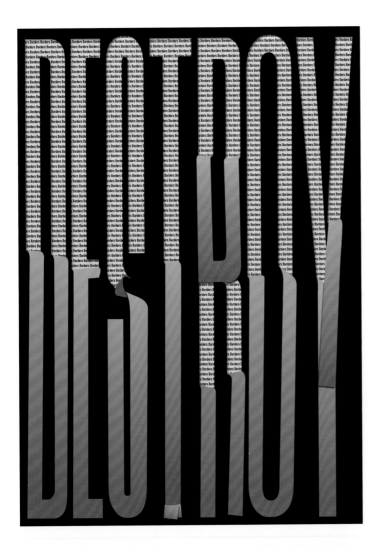

Poster

DESIGN Sven Lindhorst-Emme,• Berlin **URL** lindhorst-emme.de **AGENCY STUDIO** lindhorst-emme **PRINCIPAL TYPE** Custom **DIMENSIONS** 33.1 × 46.8 in. (84.1 × 118.9 cm)

Poster

DESIGN Lea Hinrichs and Sven Lindhorst-Emme,• Berlin **URL** lindhorst-emme.de **AGENCY STUDIO** lindhorst-emme **CLIENTS** Nachteule Productions and Thomas Berghaus **PRINCIPAL TYPE** Akzidenz Grotesk **DIMENSIONS** 33.1 × 46.8 in. (84.1 × 118.9 cm)

Signage

**DESIGN, TYPOGRAPHY, AND
PHOTOGRAPHY** Justin Colt and
Jose Fresneda, New York **ART
DIRECTION** Cade Beaulieu
URL thecollectedworks.xxx
TWITTER @collectedwork
DESIGN STUDIO The
Collected Works **CLIENT**
Nike **DIMENSIONS** 18 × 24 in.
(45.7 × 61 cm)

Packaging

DESIGN AND ART DIRECTION
Justin Colt and Jose
Fresneda, New York **URL**
thecollectedworks.xxx
TWITTER @collectedwork
DESIGN STUDIO The Collected
Works **CLIENT** EMEFE
PRINCIPAL TYPE Platform Bold
DIMENSIONS LP: 12 × 12 in.
(30.5 × 30.5 cm) CD: 5 × 5 in.
(12.7 × 12.7 cm)

Packaging

DESIGN AND ART DIRECTION
Eva Dranaz, Vienna **URL**
3007wien.at **DESIGN STUDIO**
3007 **CLIENT** Heidelinde &
Markus Lang **PRINCIPAL TYPE**
Akzidenz Grotesk Medium
Condensed **DIMENSIONS**
9.4 × 7.9 in. (24 × 20 cm)

Packaging

DESIGN AND ART DIRECTION
Eva Dranaz, Vienna
ILLUSTRATION Jochen Fill **URL**
3007wien.at **DESIGN STUDIO**
3007 **CLIENT** Wiener
Konzerthaus **PRINCIPAL TYPE**
Various **DIMENSIONS**
4.7 × 1.1 in. (12 × 2.8 cm)

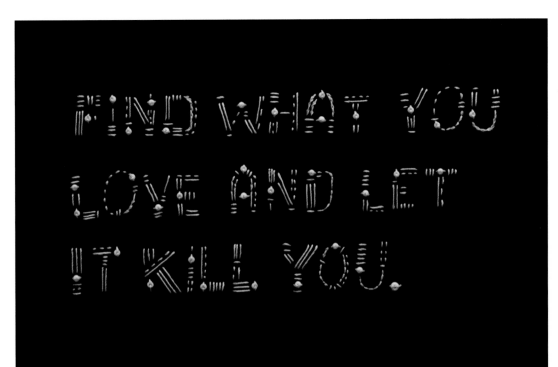

Experimental

DESIGN Nicole Mae Adams,
Brooklyn, New York
INSTAGRAM @_maedin_
STUDIO Maedin **PRINCIPAL
TYPE** Custom **DIMENSIONS**
6 × 3 in. (15.2 × 7.6 cm)

Experimental

ARTIST Faust, New York
URL faustnewyork.com
INSTAGRAM @faustnewyork
PRINCIPAL TYPE Handlettering
DIMENSIONS Various

Packaging

DESIGN Stranger & Stranger,
London, New York, and
San Francisco **STUDIO**
Stranger & Stranger **URL**
strangerandstranger.com/
rio-rum **CLIENT** RIO RUM
PRINCIPAL TYPE
Handlettering **DIMENSIONS**
9.1 × 3.6 in. (23.1 cm × 9.1 cm)

Packaging

DESIGN Stranger &
Stranger, London, New York,
and San Francisco **URL**
strangerandstranger.com/
aultmore **TWITTER**
@strangerstuff **STUDIO**
Stranger & Stranger **CLIENT**
John Dewar & Sons **PRINCIPAL
TYPE** Chronicle Text Grade 1
Semibold and Mrs Eaves
MOD OT Bold **DIMENSIONS**
4.1 × 4.5 in. (10.5 × 11.4 cm)

Packaging

DESIGN Maja Cule, Alison Joseph, and Darren Philip, New York **DESIGN DIRECTION** Serifcan Ozcan **ART DIRECTION** Jeff Dryer and Erwin Federizo **EXECUTIVE CREATIVE DIRECTORS** Susan Hoffman and David Kolbusz **DIRECTOR OF CREATIVE SERVICES** Chris Whalley **HEAD OF CONTENT**

PRODUCTION Nick Setounski **COPYWRITER** Andrew Jasperson **LETTERING** Jeff Bridges and Serifcan Ozcan **PRODUCER** Lisa Delonay and Alison Hill **DIRECTOR OF BRAND STRATEGY** Erik Hanson **BRAND STRATEGIST** Thomas Haslow **ACCOUNT TEAM** Patrick Cahill and Samantha

Wagner **INTERACTIVE STRATEGIST** Tom Gibby **SOCIAL STRATEGIST** Jessica Abercrombie **MEDIA DIRECTOR** David Stopforth **DIRECTOR OF BUSINESS AFFAIRS** Sara Jagielski **PROJECT MANAGERS** Kelly Kraft and Danielle Rounds **TRAFFIC DIRECTOR** Sonia Bisono **PRINT**

PRODUCER Kristen Althoff **CREATIVE TECHNOLOGIST** Craig Blagg **EXECUTIVE INTERACTIVE PRODUCER** Jonathan Percy **INTERACTIVE PRODUCER** Christine Young **UX DESIGNER** Saraswathi Subbaraman **DIRECTOR OF ART PRODUCTION** Deb Rosen **PHOTOGRAPHY** Gary

Land **PRINT PRODUCER** Kristen Althoff **PROJECT MANAGERS** Kelly Kraft and Danielle Rounds **AGENCY** Wieden+Kennedy New York **CLIENT** Squarespace **PRINCIPAL TYPE** Handlettering **DIMENSIONS** 12 × 12 in. (30.5 × 30.5 cm)

A WORLD PREMIERE PRODUCTION BY INVIOLET

WRITTEN BY BIXBY ELLIOT DIRECTED BY STEPHEN BRACKETT

Poster

DESIGN AND PHOTOGRAPHY
Luke Williams,• Brooklyn, New
York **URL** lukelukeluke.com
TWITTER @LLLukeWilliams
CLIENT Bixby Elliot and InViolet
Theater **PRINCIPAL TYPE**
Verlag Bold and custom forms
made from images of human

fingers and bent metal strips
DIMENSIONS
18 × 24 in. (45.7 × 61 cm)

Poster

DESIGN Loana Boppart and
Sven Lindhorst-Emme,• Berlin
CURATION Ana Baumgart
and Forster Herchenbach
TEXT Nikolas Claussen **URL**
lindhorst-emme.de **AGENCY**
studio lindhorst-emme
CLIENT 48h Neukölln Berlin

Art Festival **PRINCIPAL TYPE**
Custom **DIMENSIONS**
33.1 × 46.8 in. (84.1 × 118.9 cm)

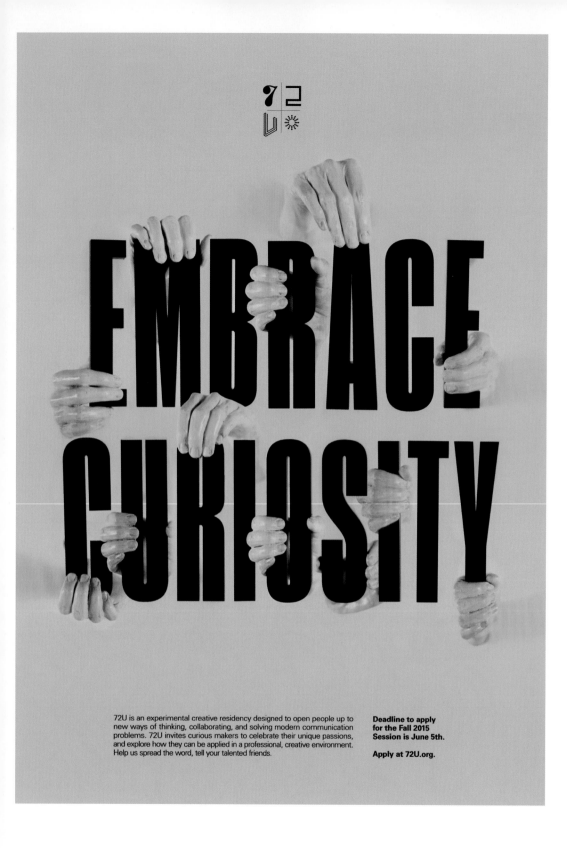

Poster

ART DIRECTION Clare Jensen,
Los Angeles **COPYWRITER**
Natalie Warther
PHOTOGRAPHY Brooke
Frederick **DIRECTOR OF 72U**
Maria Scileppi **2U MANAGER**
Karen Oliveros **URL**
72andsunny.com **AGENCY**
72andSunny **PRINCIPAL TYPE**
Kultur Compressed and
Univers LT Std **DIMENSIONS**
24 × 36 in. (61 × 91.4 cm)

Poster

DESIGN Yuko Ishizaki,●
Toyama, Japan **ART DIRECTION
AND CREATIVE DIRECTION**
Yuko Ishizaki **URL** toy-i.jp
DESIGN FIRM TOY **CLIENT**
Gallery Muryow **PRINCIPAL
TYPE** Tsukushi Gothic
DIMENSIONS 40.6 × 57.3 in.
(103 × 145.6 cm)

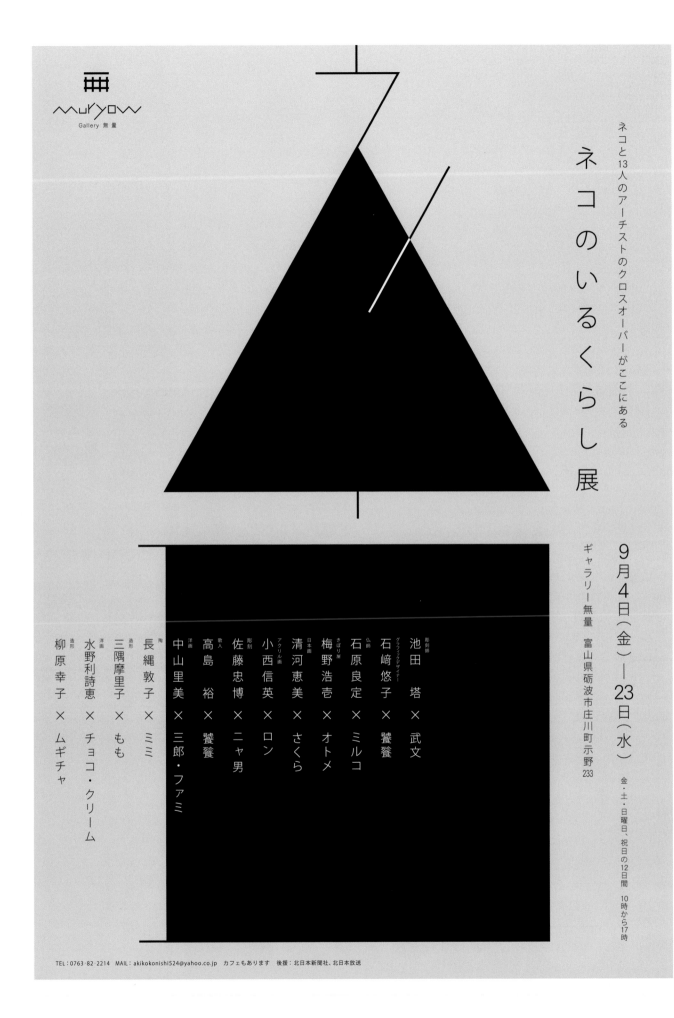

ネコと13人のアーチストのクロスオーバーがここにある

ネコのいるくらし展

ギャラリー無量　富山県砺波市庄川町示野233

9月4日（金）―23日（水）

金・土・日曜日、祝日の12日間　10時から17時

彫刻師
池田　塔　×　武文

グラフィックデザイナー
石﨑悠子　×　饕餮

仏師
石原良定　×　ミルコ

さぼり屋
梅野浩吉　×　オトメ

日本画
清河恵美　×　さくら

アクリル画
小西信英　×　ロン

彫刻
佐藤忠博　×　ニャ男

歌人
高島　裕　×　饕餮

洋画
中山里美　×　三郎・ファミ

陶
長縄敦子　×　ミミ

造形
三隅摩里子　×　もも

洋画
水野利詩恵　×　チョコ・クリーム

造形
柳原幸子　×　ムギチャ

TEL：0763-82-2214　MAIL：akikokonishi524@yahoo.co.jp　カフェもあります　後援：北日本新聞社、北日本放送

Gallery 無量

Posters

DESIGN Felix Kosok, Frankfurt am Main, Germany **URL** felixkosok.de **CLIENT** saint art **PRINCIPAL TYPE** Helvetica Neue **DIMENSIONS** 23.4 × 33.1 in. (59.4 × 84.1 cm)

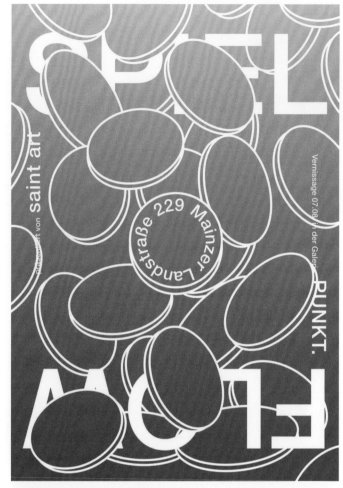

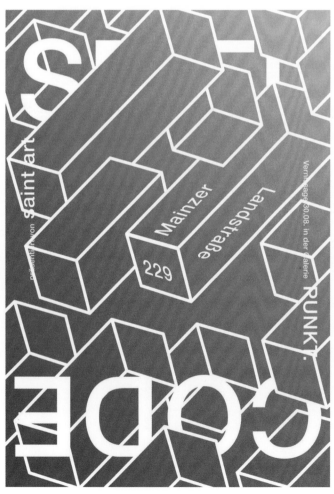

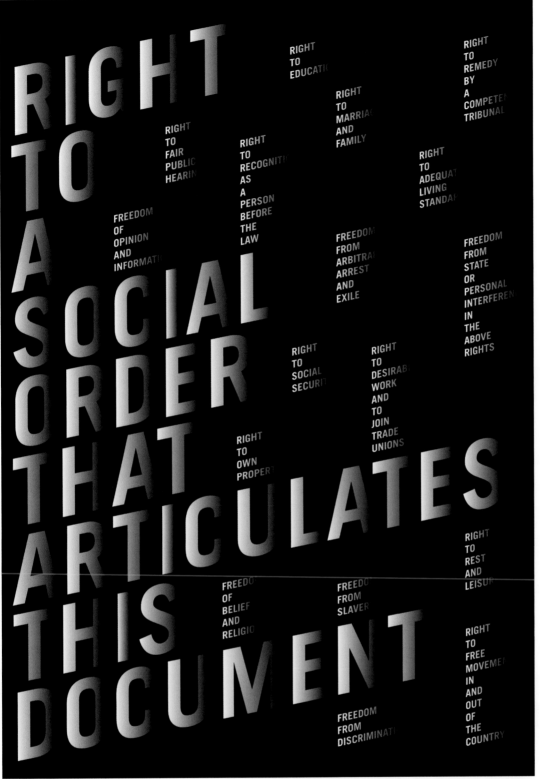

Poster

ART DIRECTION Yu Chen,●
New York and Shanghai **URL**
chenyudesign.org **STUDIO**
ChenyuDesign **CLIENT**
Maryland Institute College
of Art **PRINCIPAL TYPE** Trade
Gothic **DIMENSIONS**
23 × 32.5 in. (58.5 × 83 cm)

Posters

DESIGN Jen Serafini, Chicago **ART DIRECTION** Jen Serafini **SCREEN PRINTING** Mama's Sauce **HANDCRAFTED STICKERS** DieCutStickers. com **PHOTOGRAPHY** Potluck Creative **URL** erafinicreative. com **TWITTER** @jenserafini

INSTAGRAM @serafinicreative **DESIGN FIRM** Serafini Creative **PRINCIPAL TYPE** Ballpoint, Montserrat, and Torque **DIMENSIONS** 18 × 24 in. (45.7 × 61 cm)

Posters

DESIGN, ART DIRECTION, AND CREATIVE DIRECTION Katja Schloz, Stuttgart **URL** katjaschloz.de **STUDIO** Katja Schloz Graphic Design **CLIENT** Karima Klasen **PRINCIPAL TYPE** LL Circular Bold and Oswald Light **DIMENSIONS** 23.4 × 33.1 in. (59.4 × 84.1 cm)

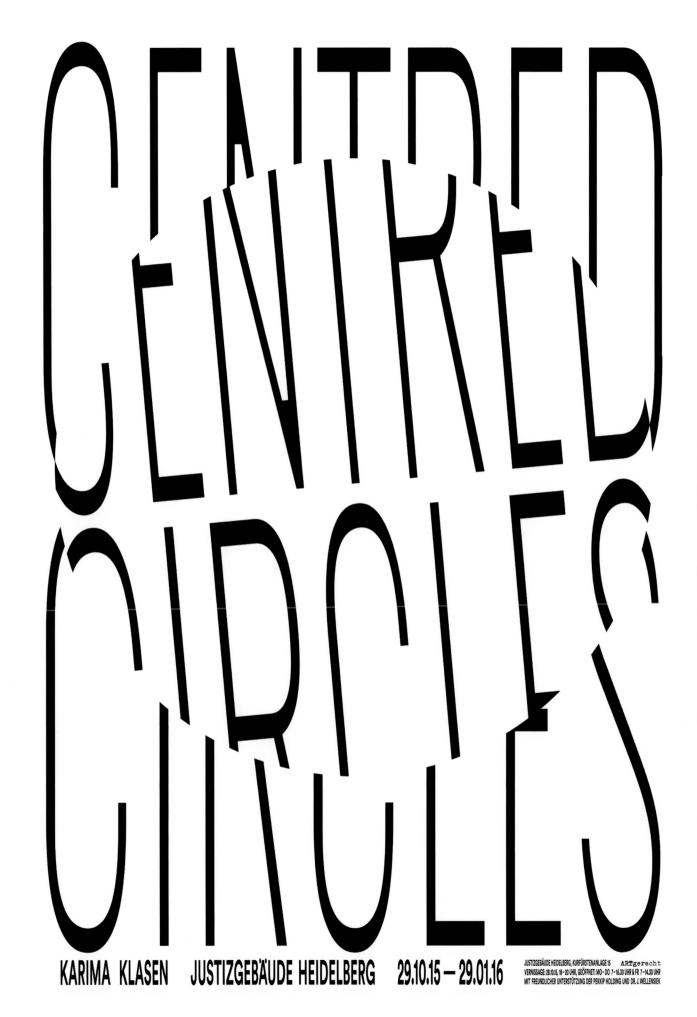

CENTRED CIRCLES

KARIMA KLASEN   JUSTIZGEBÄUDE HEIDELBERG   29.10.15 – 29.01.16

JUSTIZGEBÄUDE HEIDELBERG, KURFÜRSTENANLAGE 15   ARTgerecht
VERNISSAGE: 28.10.15, 18–20 UHR, GEÖFFNET: MO–DO 7–16.30 UHR & FR 7–14.30 UHR
MIT FREUNDLICHER UNTERSTÜTZUNG DER PEKKIP HOLDING UND DR. J. WELLENSIEK

Poster

**DESIGN AND CREATIVE
DIRECTION** Lisa Maione and
Gabriel Melcher, Providence,
Rhode Island **ADVISOR AND
PROFESSOR** Benjamin Shaykin
URL risd.gd **TWITTER** @risdgd
SCHOOL Rhode Island School
of Design **CLIENT** Graphic
Design Department, Rhode
Island School of Design
PRINCIPAL TYPE Atlas Grotesk,
Ivrea, PL Poster, and PL Sans
DIMENSIONS 33 × 22.75 in.
(83.8 × 57.8 cm)

Poster

DESIGN AND PROFESSOR
Chun-liang Leo Lin, Taipei
City **DESIGN FIRM** Leo Lin
Design **CLIENT** College of
Arts, National Taiwan Normal
University **PRINCIPAL TYPE**
Custom **DIMENSIONS**
39.4 × 27.6 in. (100 × 70 cm)

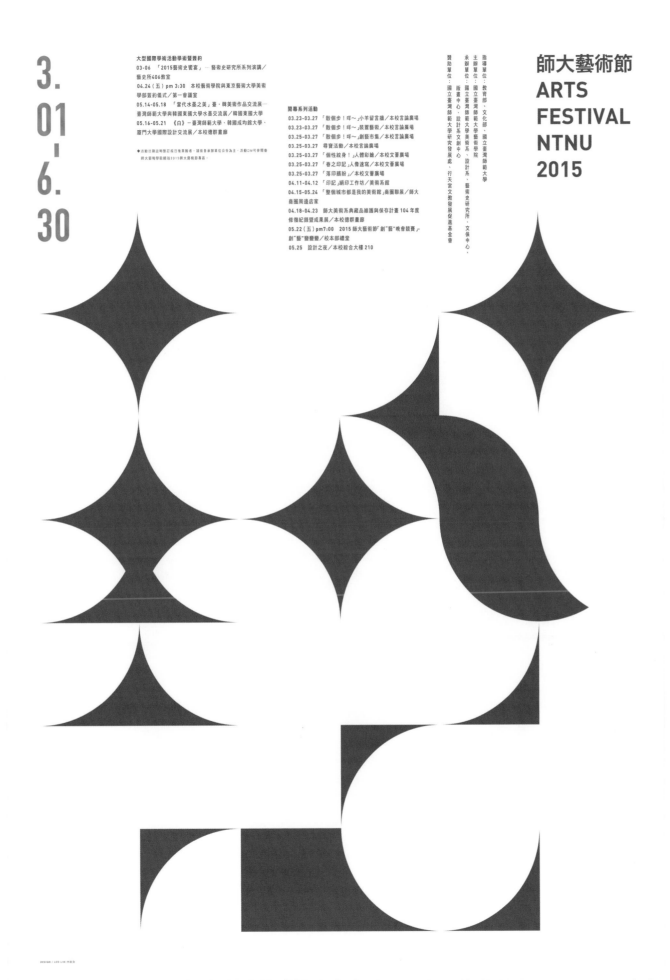

大型國際學術活動學術暨簽約
03-06 「2015藝術史饗宴」─藝術史研究所系列演講／
藝史所406教室
04.24（五）pm 3:30 本校藝術學院與東京藝術大學美術
學部簽約儀式／第一會議室
05.14-05.18 「當代水墨之美」臺‧韓美術作品交流展─
臺灣師範大學與韓國東國大學水墨交流展／韓國東國大學
05.16-05.21 《白》─臺灣師範大學、韓國成均館大學、
廈門大學國際設計交流展／本校德群畫廊

◆ 活動計期日期暨訂或日後實異動者，請依各承辦單位公布為主。活動DM可掃描
師大藝術學院粉絲頁2015師大藝術節專頁。

開幕系列活動
03.23-03.27 「散個步！呼～」小羊留言牆／本校言論廣場
03.23-03.27 「散個步！呼～」裝置藝術／本校言論廣場
03.25-03.27 「散個步！呼～」創藝市集／本校言論廣場
03.25-03.27 尋寶活動／本校言論廣場
03.25-03.27 「個性紋身」人體彩繪／本校文薈廣場
03.25-03.27 「春之印記」人像速寫／本校文薈廣場
03.25-03.27 「落印繽紛」／本校文薈廣場
04.11-04.12 「印記」網印工作坊／美術系館
04.15-05.24 「整個城市都是我的美術館」商圈聯展／師大
商圈周邊店家
04.18-04.23 師大美術系典藏品維護與保存計畫104年度
修復紀錄暨成果展／本校德群畫廊
05.22（五）pm7:00 2015師大藝術節「創"藝"晚會競賽」
創"藝"變變變／校本部禮堂
05.25 設計之夜／本校綜合大樓210

指導單位：教育部、文化部
主辦單位：國立臺灣師範大學
國立臺灣師範大學藝術學院
承辦單位：國立臺灣師範大學美術系、設計系、
藝術史研究所、文保中心、
版畫中心、設計系文創中心
贊助單位：國立臺灣師範大學研究發展處、行天宮文教促進基金會

師大藝術節
ARTS
FESTIVAL
NTNU
2015

DESIGN｜LEO LIHI 林音洪

Poster

**ART DIRECTION AND
LETTERING** David
Clavadetscher, Schwyz,
Switzerland **TYPOGRAPHY**
Michael Kunz **3D RENDERING**
Samuel Trutmann **URL**
clavadetscher.org **TWITTER**
@DClavadetscher **CLIENT**

Jazz Meets Folklore **PRINCIPAL
TYPE** Knockout HTF49-
Liteweight **DIMENSIONS**
35.2 × 50.4 in. (89.5 × 128 cm)

يتحدث باللغة الصينية.

C'est du chinois.

Das ist Chinesisch für mich.

Posters

ART DIRECTION Siyu Mao,
Berlin **URL** siyumao.com
PRINCIPAL TYPE Helvetica
Neue **DIMENSIONS**
23.4 × 33.1 in. (59.4 × 84.1 cm)

DESIGN Joo Hyun Ha,
Gyeonggi-do, South Korea
SCHOOL Hankyong National
University **PRINCIPAL TYPE**
SM KMyungjo **DIMENSIONS**
27.6 × 39.4 in. (70 × 100 cm)

DESIGNER Wael Morcos,[•]
New York **URL** waelmorcos.
com **TWITTER** @waelmorcos
PRINCIPAL TYPE Graphic X
Condensed Bold **DIMENSIONS**
23.4 × 33.1 in. (59.4 × 84.1 cm)

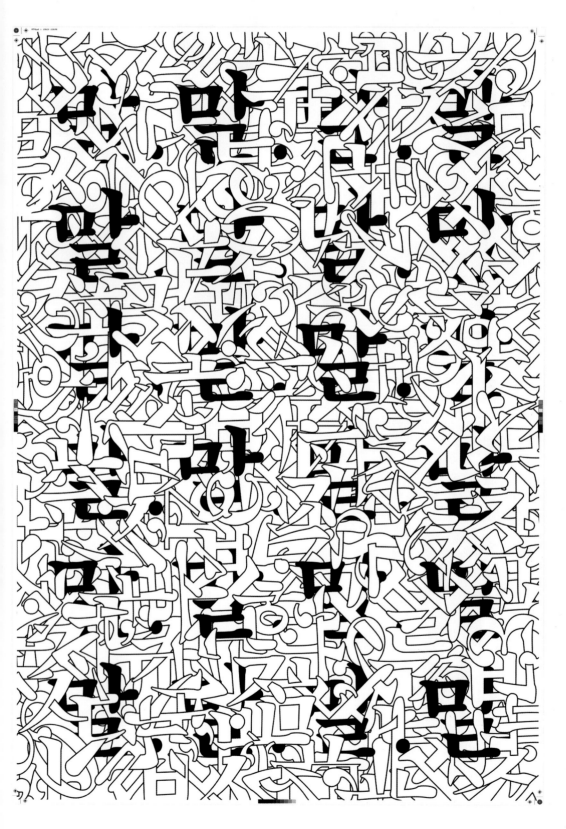

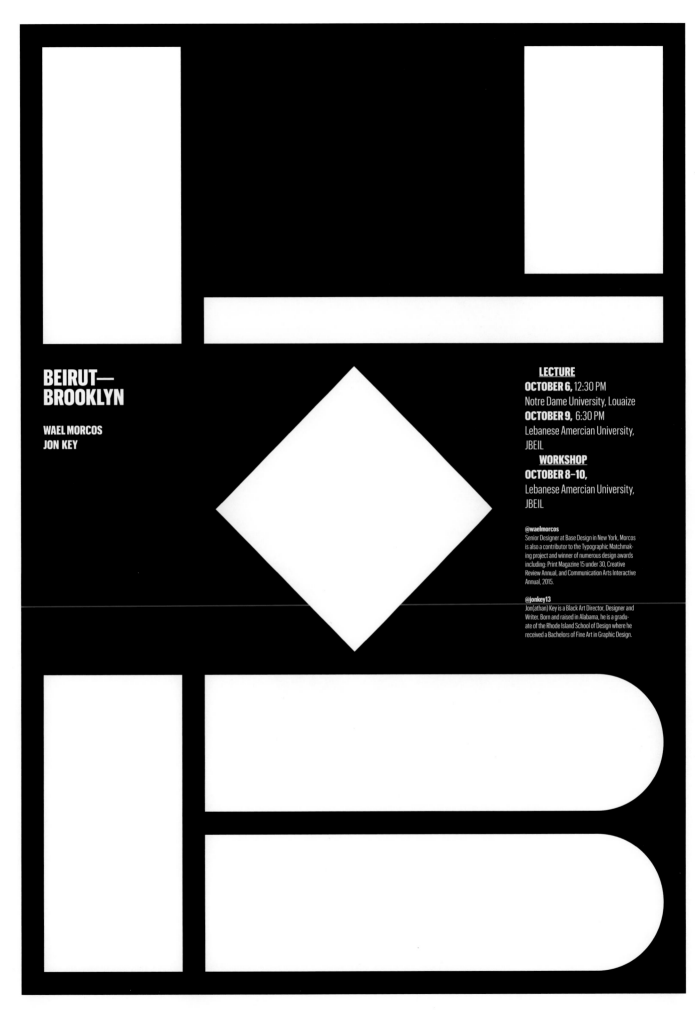

BEIRUT—
BROOKLYN

WAEL MORCOS
JON KEY

LECTURE
LECTURE
OCTOBER 6, 12:30 PM
Notre Dame University, Louaize
OCTOBER 9, 6:30 PM
Lebanese Amercian University,
JBEIL
WORKSHOP
OCTOBER 8–10,
Lebanese Amercian University,
JBEIL

@waelmorcos
Senior Designer at Base Design in New York, Morcos
is also a contributor to the Typographic Matchmak-
ing project and winner of numerous design awards
including: Print Magazine 15 under 30, Creative
Review Annual, and Communication Arts Interactive
Annual, 2015.

@jonkey13
Jon(athan) Key is a Black Art Director, Designer and
Writer. Born and raised in Alabama, he is a gradu-
ate of the Rhode Island School of Design where he
received a Bachelors of Fine Art in Graphic Design.

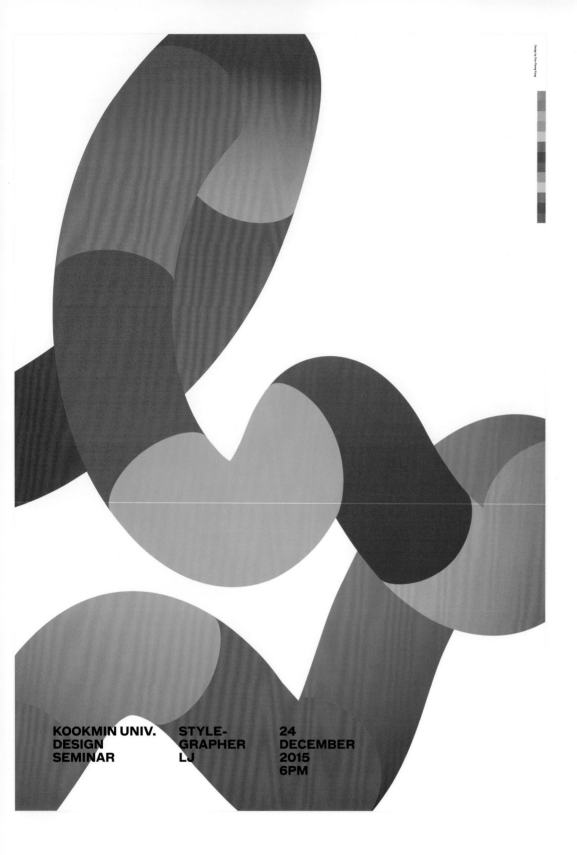

KOOKMIN UNIV. STYLE- 24
DESIGN GRAPHER DECEMBER
SEMINAR LJ 2015
6PM

Design by Goo-Ryong Kang

Poster

DESIGN AND ART DIRECTION
Goo-Ryong Kang, Seoul
TWITTER @griong **DESIGN**
FIRM Chung Choon
CLIENT Kookmin University
PRINCIPAL TYPE FF Bau Bold
DIMENSIONS 27.6 × 39 in.
(70 × 99 cm)

Poster

DESIGN Jim Kühnel, Leipzig
URL jimkuehnel.net **STUDIO**
Jim Kühnel—Studio for
graphic design **CLIENT** Conne
Island and Eine Welt Aus
Hack **PRINCIPAL TYPE** Druk
Condensed **DIMENSIONS**
27.6 × 39.4 in. (70 × 100 cm)

CONNE ISLAND / 5.10.

YOUNG
FATHERS

w/
SUPPORT
BAND
(20 Uhr)

YOUNG-FATHERS.COM
CONNE-ISLAND.DE
EINEWELTAUSHACK.DE

#WMABMT

Posters

DESIGN Zhang Yulian,
Zhongshan City, China
URL blog.sina.com.
cn/u/2722682510 **STUDIO**
Zhang Yulian / Concept Art
and Culture Studio **CLIENT**
Zhongshan Chuangsi Ad
PRINCIPAL TYPE Custom
DIMENSIONS 24.4 × 61 in.
(62 × 155 cm)

Poster

DESIGN AND ART DIRECTION
Goo-Ryong Kang, Seoul
TWITTER @griong **DESIGN
FIRM** Chung Choon **CLIENT**
Yoon Design **PRINCIPAL TYPE**
FF Bau Bold and Yoon Gothic
DIMENSIONS 27.6 × 39 in.
(70 × 99 cm)

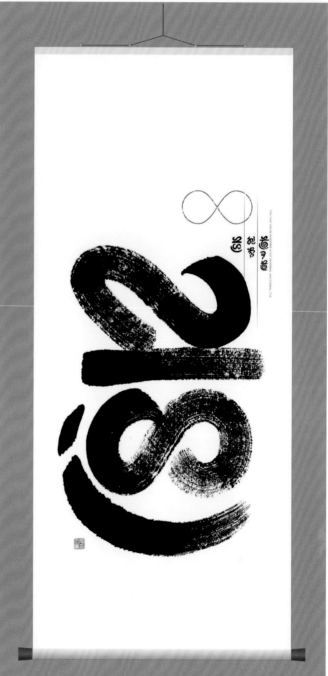

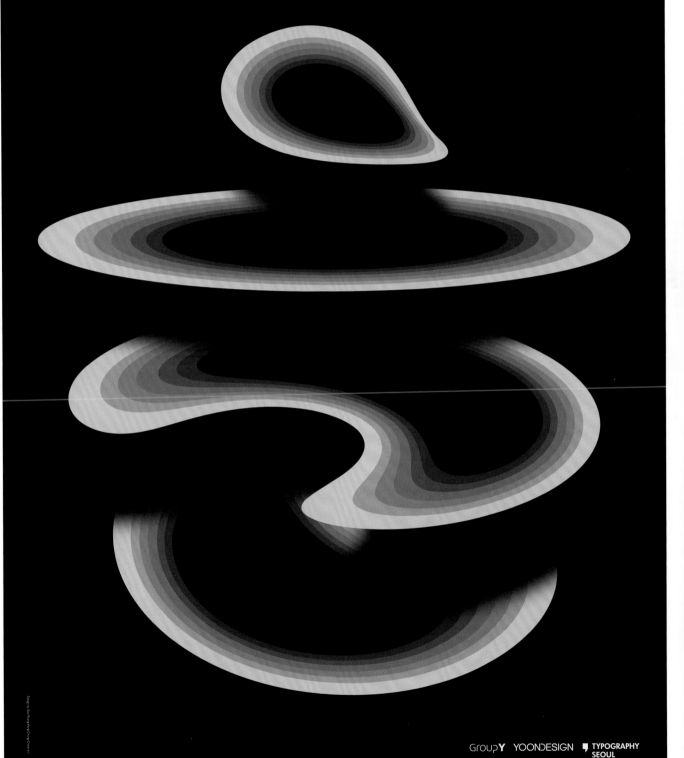

Hangul
Fonts
Original
Form &
Pedigree
1830-
1956

Type
Design
Visiting
Lecture
Hyun Guk
Ryu

일시   2015년 11월 23일 월요일
      저녁 7시 — 9시
장소   (주)그룹와이 (윤디자인연구소)
      빌딩 1층 세미나룸
      서울시 마포구 독막로9길 13

강연자 류현국
       일본츠쿠바기술대학 종합디자인과 교수
입장료 무료
       선착순 30명, 개별 연락 예정
신청   이메일 신청
       director@typographyseoul.com
주최/주관 타이포그래피 서울
후원   (주)그룹와이

GrouⱣY YOONDESIGN ⬤ TYPOGRAPHY
                       SEOUL

267

Posters

DESIGN Ren Wei Huang,
Kaohsiung City, Taiwan
SCHOOL Tung Fang Design
Institute **PRINCIPAL TYPE**
Custom **DIMENSIONS**
24.4 × 33.1 in. (59.4 × 84 cm)

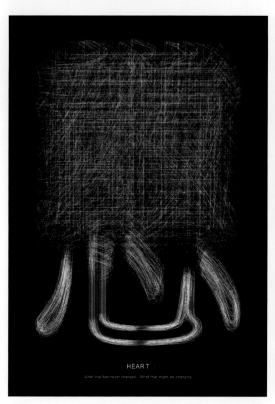

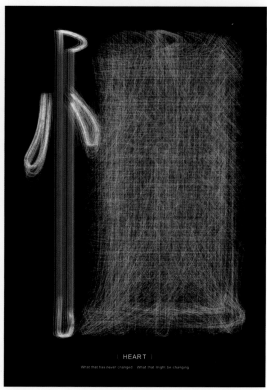

Poster

DESIGN David Minh Nguyen,
San Francisco **URL**
davidminhnguyen.com
FIRM Airbnb **PRINCIPAL TYPE**
Consolas **DIMENSIONS** 18 × 24
in. (45.7 × 61 cm)

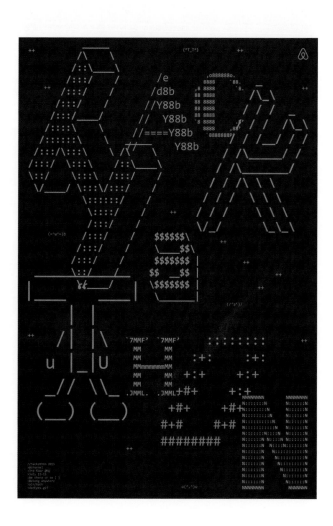

Posters

DESIGN Cyla Costa, Curitiba, Brazil **URL** cylacosta.com and weeklywoody.com **PRINCIPAL TYPE** Custom **DIMENSIONS** 16.5 × 23.5 in. (42 × 60 cm)

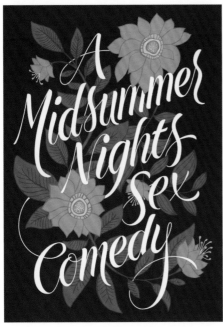

269

Poster

ART DIRECTION Sarah
Déry, Montréal **CREATIVE
DIRECTION** Marie-Élaine
Benoit **TYPEFACE DESIGNER**
Sarah Déry **COPYWRITER**
Caroline Ducharme **ACCOUNT
MANAGER** Flore Valeri **URL**
sidlee.com **AGENCY** Sid
Lee **CLIENT** Maisonneuve-
Rosemont Hospital Foundation
PRINCIPAL TYPE MPV Regular
DIMENSIONS Various

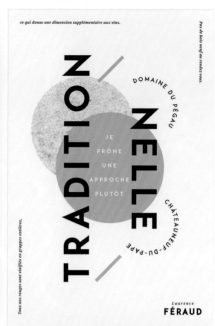

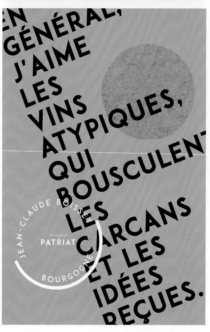

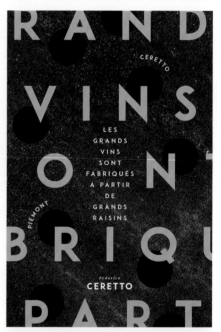

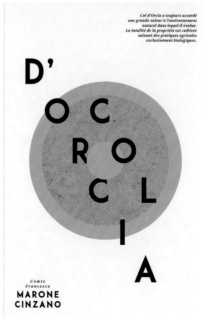

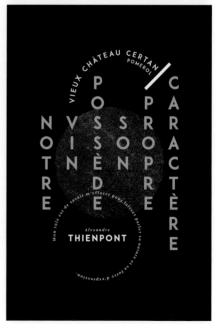

Poster

DESIGN Sam Divers, Ariane Forster, Philipp Lüthi, and Andrea Noti, Bern **URL** heyday.ch **DESIGN STUDIO** Heyday **CLIENT** Lomotion, a film production company **PRINCIPAL TYPE** LL Brown Regular and Euclid Bold **DIMENSIONS** 16.5 × 23.4 in. (42 × 59.4 cm)

Poster

DESIGN Naomi Abel, Lorin Brown, Alison Joseph, and Serifcan Ozcan **CREATIVE DIRECTION** Ian Hart, Jed Heuer, and Serifcan Ozcan **EXECUTIVE CREATIVE DIRECTORS** Susan Hoffman and David Kolbusz **LETTERING** Jeff Bridges and Serifcan Ozcan **COPYWRITER** Garrick Sheldon **MANAGING DIRECTOR** Neal Arthur **ACCOUNT TEAM** Jasmina Almeda and Toby Hussey **PROJECT MANAGER** Erin Bremmer **BUSINESS AFFAIRS** Sara Jagielski **BRAND STRATEGIST** Hayley Parker **CREATIVE SERVICES DIRECTOR** Chris Whalley **PRINT PRODUCER** Nakia Sinclair **STUDIO MANAGER** Jill Kearton **STUDIO PRODUCTION ARTISTS** Russ Brandon, Mike Nesi, and Elfranko Wessels **DIRECTOR OF MEDIA STRATEGY** Christine Mason **MEDIA PLANNER** Gina Chang and Ritesh Gupta **AGENCY** Wieden+Kennedy New York **CLIENT** Cooper Hewitt Smithsonian Design Museum **PRINCIPAL TYPE** Cooper Hewitt and handlettering **DIMENSIONS** 12 × 12 in. (30.5 × 30.5 cm)

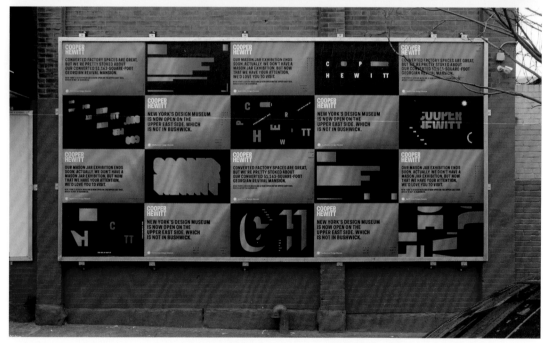

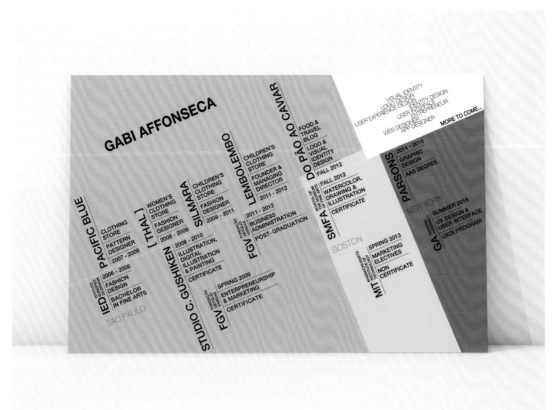

Student Work

DESIGN Gabriela Vianna
Lembo Affonseca, New
York **URL** gabidesign.me
INSTRUCTOR Dmitry Krasny•
SCHOOL Parsons School
of Design **PRINCIPAL TYPE**
Helvetica Neue **DIMENSIONS**
29.8 × 19.3 in. (75.7 × 49 cm)

Self-Promotion

**DESIGN AND CREATIVE
DIRECTION** Nigel Sielegar,•
New York **ILLUSTRATION**
Allie Whitehead **URL** corse.nyc
DESIGN FIRM Corse Design
Factory **PRINCIPAL TYPE**
Custom **DIMENSIONS**
30 × 16 in. (76 × 41 cm)

Self-Promotion

GRAPHIC DESIGNER AND LETTERER Marta Cerdà Alimbau,• Los Angeles **URL** martacerda.com **TWITTER** @MartaCerdaAlimb **CLIENT** 36 Days of Type **PRINCIPAL TYPE** X **DIMENSIONS** 15.7 × 23.6 in. (40 × 60 cm)

Self-Promotion

CREATIVE DIRECTION Joshua Breidenbach and Chi-An De Leo, Ho Chi Minh City **ILLUSTRATION** Huy Le Quoc **URL** rice-creative.com **DESIGN FIRM** Rice Creative **PRINCIPAL TYPE** Univers Bold, Univers Light, and Univers Medium **DIMENSIONS** 10.2 × 2.5 × 2.5 in. (26 × 6.5 × 6.5 cm)

Student Work

DESIGN Hayerin Kim,● New York **URL** irin.kim **INSTRUCTOR** Min Lew **SCHOOL** School of Visual Arts, New York● **PRINCIPAL TYPE** Berthold Akzidenz Grotesk Condensed **DIMENSIONS** Various

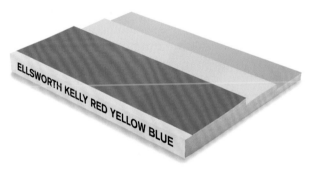

Student Work

DESIGN Hayerin Kim,● New York **URL** irin.kim **INSTRUCTOR** Min Lew **SCHOOL** School of Visual Arts, New York● **PRINCIPAL TYPE** Akzidenz Grotesk

Student Work

DESIGN Katarina Gerritsen, Lauren Moulton, Genevieve Read, and Emily Sneddon, Newcastle, Australia
URL emilysneddon.com
INSTRUCTOR Ralph Kenke
SCHOOL University of Newcastle, Australia
PRINCIPAL TYPE Helvetica Bold and NotCourierSans
DIMENSIONS 8.3 × 11.7 in. (21 × 29.7 cm)

Student Work

DESIGN Francesca Truman,● San Francisco **URL** francescatruman.com
INSTRUCTOR Tom Ingalls
SCHOOL California College of the Arts **PRINCIPAL TYPE** Gotham, Leather, and Neutraface **DIMENSIONS** 3.5 × 14 in. (8.9 × 35.6 cm)

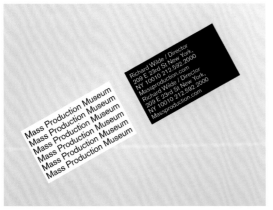

Student Work

DESIGN Hayerin Kim,• New York **URL** irin.kim **INSTRUCTOR** Natasha Jen **SCHOOL** School of Visual Arts, New York• **PRINCIPAL TYPE** Akzidenz Grotesk **DIMENSIONS** Various

Student Work

DESIGN Hayerin Kim,• New York **URL** irin.kim **INSTRUCTOR** Min Lew **SCHOOL** School of Visual Arts, New York• **PRINCIPAL TYPE** Fugue **DIMENSIONS** Various

Student Work

DESIGN Yotam Hadar and
Sasha Portis, New Haven,
Connecticut **CLIENT** Yale
University School of Art
PRINCIPAL TYPE Century Old
Style, Eckmann, and Monotype
Grotesque

2,015 BUT
WHO'S COUNTING:

Yale MFA
Painting/Printmaking
Thesis Exhibition

GROUP TWO
February 13–25

2,015 BUT
WHO'S COUNTING:

Yale MFA
Painting/Printmaking
Thesis Exhibition

Student Work

DESIGN Yotam Hadar,
New Haven, Connecticut
INSTRUCTOR Allen Hori
SCHOOL Yale University School
of Art **PRINCIPAL TYPE** Custom

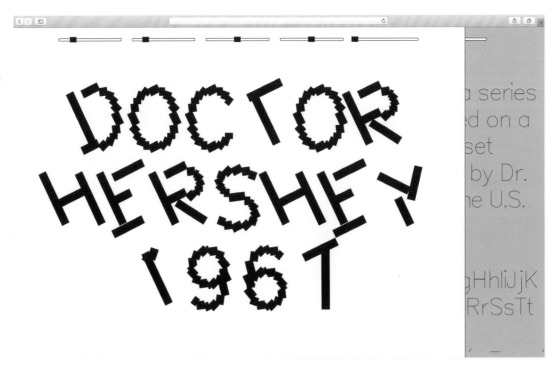

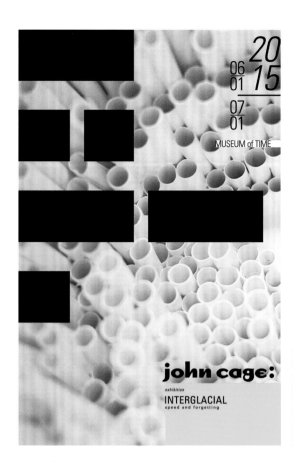

Student Work

DESIGN Minase Yamada, New York **URL** minase.graphics **INSTRUCTOR** Olga Mezhibovskaya● **SCHOOL** School of Visual Arts, New York● **PRINCIPAL TYPE** Dogma Bold and Univers **DIMENSIONS** 24 × 36 in. (61 × 91.4 cm)

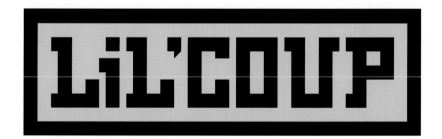

Student Work

DESIGN Mogwon Son, Seoul **INSTRUCTOR** Se Ra Yoon (PSIV) **SCHOOL** Chung-Ang University **DIMENSIONS** Various

Student Work

DESIGN Yong Hyeok Shin,
Seoul **INSTRUCTOR** Se Ra Yoon
URL blog.naver.com/hahooho
SCHOOL Chung-Ang University
PRINCIPAL TYPE DIN Next LT
Pro, Apple SD Neo Gothic, and
SEMA Gothic **DIMENSIONS**
42.2 × 63.5 in. (16.6 × 25 cm)

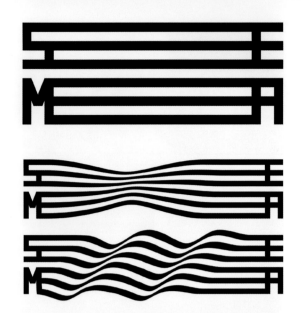

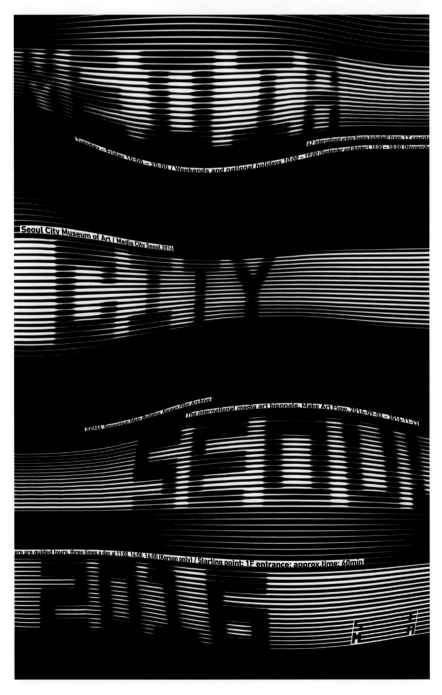

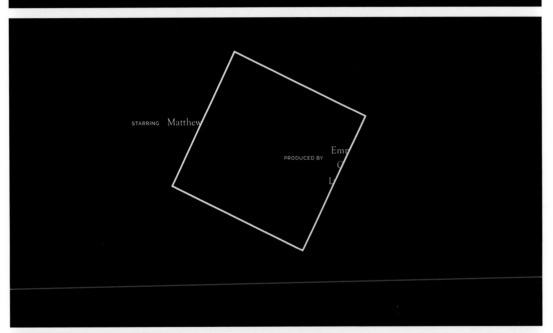

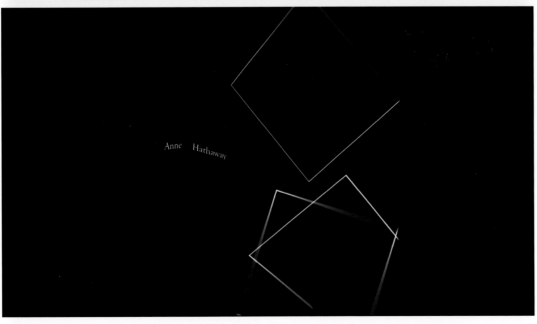

Student Work

DESIGN AND ANIMATION
Rhea Lelina Manglapus **URL**
Rhea-LM.com **INSTRUCTOR**
Ori Kleiner **SCHOOL** School
of Visual Arts, New York•
PRINCIPAL TYPE Goudy Old
Style Regular and Raleway
SemiBold

Student Work

DESIGN Brianna DiFelice,
New York **URL**
www.briannadifelice.com
TWITTER https://twitter.com/
briannadifelice **INSTRUCTOR**
Nic Taylor **SCHOOL** School
of Visual Arts, New York•
PRINCIPAL TYPE Interstate,
Scala Regular, and Scala Sans
Regular **DIMENSIONS** 9 × 12 in.
(22.9 × 30.5cm)

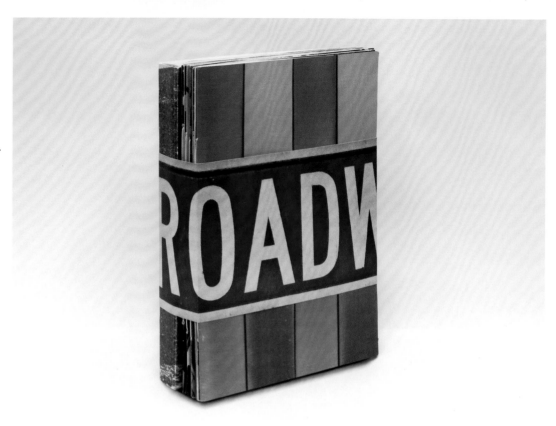

Student Work

**DESIGN, ANIMATION, AND
ILLUSTRATION** Jocelyn Tsaih,
New York **URL** jocelyntsaih.
com **INSTRUCTOR** Natasha
Jen• **SCHOOL** School of Visual
Arts, New York• **PRINCIPAL
TYPE** Handlettering

Student Work

DESIGN Luke Scott, Auckland
EDITORS Megan Au, Elliot
Fergusson, and Alistair
McCready **URL** stemme.co.nz
INSTRUCTOR Jonty Valentine
SCHOOL Auckland University
of Technology **CLIENT** Stemme
PRINCIPAL TYPE Founders
Grotesk and Tiempos
DIMENSIONS 10.4 × 7.5 in.
(26.5 × 19 cm)

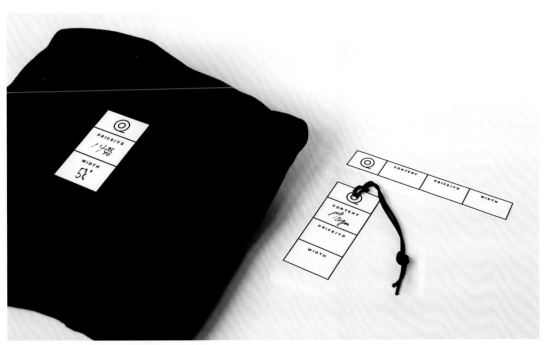

Student Work

DESIGN Jimin Lee, Seoul
INSTRUCTOR Daniel Blackman
SCHOOL School of Visual Arts,
New York● **PRINCIPAL TYPE**
Calibre

Student Work

DESIGN Najeebah Al-Ghadban, New York **ADVISORS** Steven Heller, Warren Lehrer, and Lita Talarico **SCHOOL** School of Visual Arts, MFA Program **PRINCIPAL TYPE** Adobe Garamond

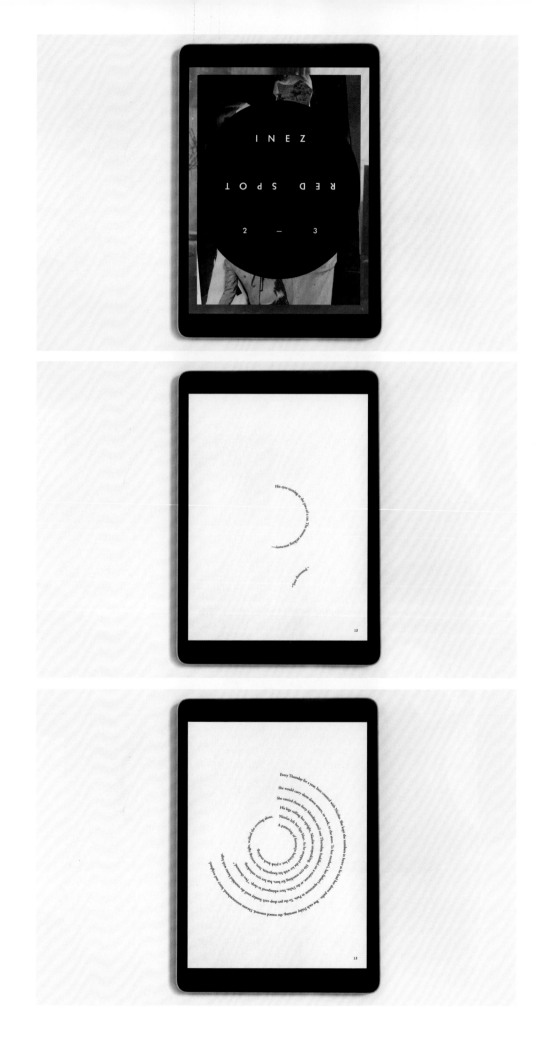

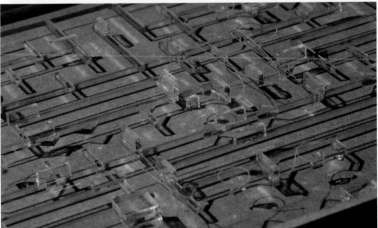

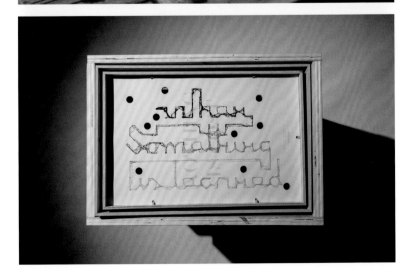

Student Work

DESIGN Anthony Cappetta, New York **URL** gatheredbytheway. com **INSTRUCTOR** Stefan Sagmeister **SCHOOL** School of Visual Arts, New York● **PRINCIPAL TYPE** New Paris Headline Medium **DIMENSIONS** 11 × 17 in. (27.9 × 43.2 cm)

Student Work

DESIGN Qingru Joy Wu,
New York **URL** joy-wu-
2z39.squarespace.com
INSTRUCTOR Carin Goldberg
SCHOOL School of Visual
Arts, New York● **PRINCIPAL
TYPE** My Underwood and
Univers **DIMENSIONS**
16 × 24 in. (40.6 × 61 cm)

WITH A POCKET KNIFE
THEY WILL CUT A RECTANGLE
OUT OF THIN AIR,
RIGHT IN FRONT OF THEM, AND THERE
THE INTERNET WILL BE.
UNFORTUNATELY, MANY PEOPLE WILL
LEAVE PIECES OF SKY

randomfear.com
openthatwindow.com
neogeocity.com
almostcalm.com
papertoilet.com
mechanicalwater.com
slickquick.com

Student Work

DESIGN Danielle Lee, New York **URL** danielle-lee.com **INSTRUCTOR** Min Lew **SCHOOL** School of Visual Arts, New York● **PRINCIPAL TYPE** Challenge Extra Bold

FULFILLED
TO THE
BRIM

ALL
FULFILLED
UP

FIND YOUR HERO BOTTLE.

FULFILL.COM

FIND YOUR HERO BOTTLE.

FULFILL.COM

Student Work

DESIGN Danielle Lee, New York **URL** danielle-lee.com **INSTRUCTOR** Min Lew **SCHOOL** School of Visual Arts, New York● **PRINCIPAL TYPE** LL Brauer Neue

Student Work

DESIGN Brian Lemus,• New
York **URL** brianlemus.com
INSTRUCTOR Skip Sorvino
SCHOOL School of Visual
Arts, New York• **PRINCIPAL
TYPE** Custom **DIMENSIONS**
12 × 20 in. (30.5 × 50.8 cm)

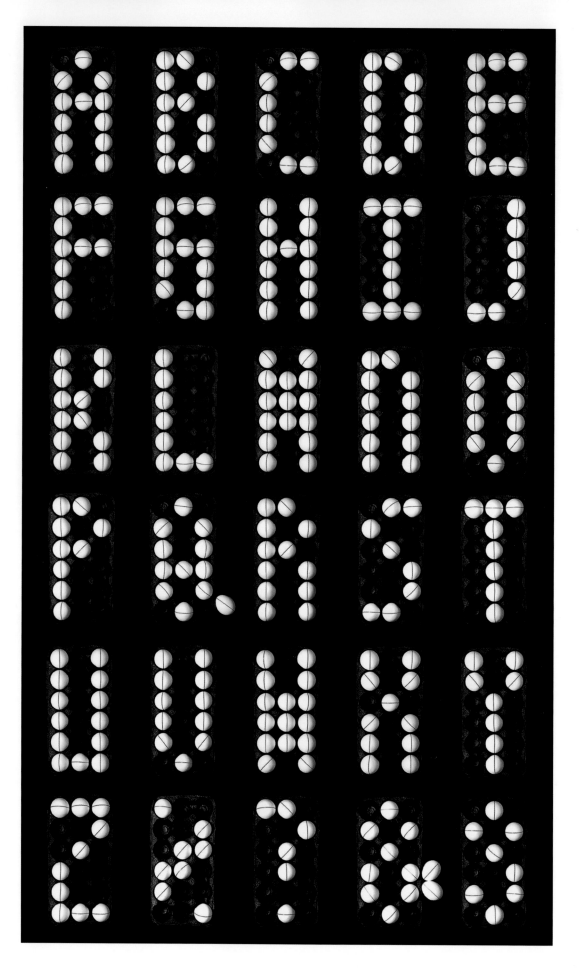

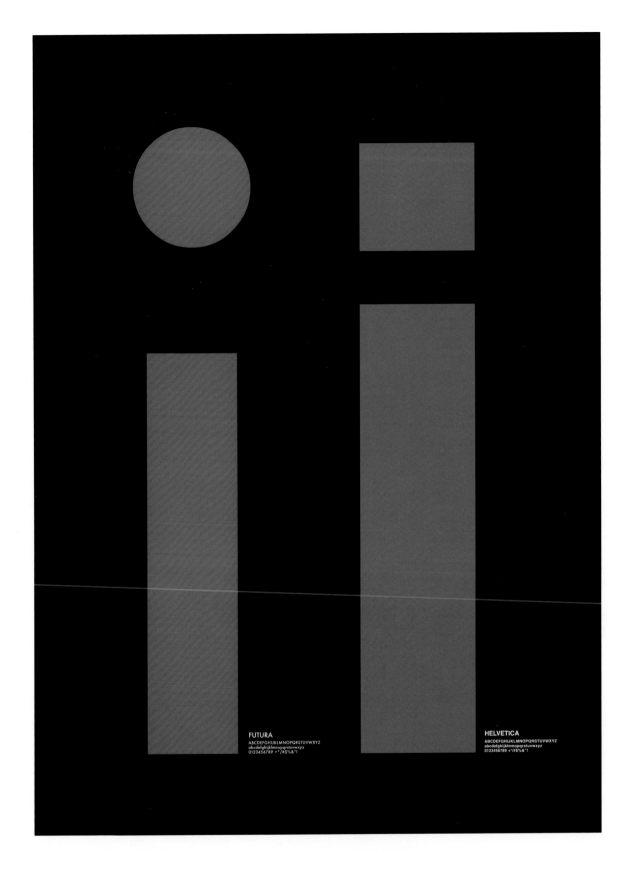

FUTURA
ABCDEFGHIJKLMNOPQRSTUVWXYZ
abcdefghijklmnopqrstuvwxyz
0123456789 +*/#$%&"!

HELVETICA
ABCDEFGHIJKLMNOPQRSTUVWXYZ
abcdefghijklmnopqrstuvwxyz
0123456789 +*/#$%&"!

Student Work

DESIGN Sun Min Chung,
New York **URL** sunminchung.
com/futuraversushelvetica
INSTRUCTOR Natasha Jen●
SCHOOL School of Visual
Arts, New York● **PRINCIPAL
TYPE** Futura and Helvetica
DIMENSIONS 15.75 × 21.5 in.
(40 × 54.6 cm)

Alphabet

DESIGN Dado Queiroz,
Amsterdam **ART DIRECTION**
Fausto Hagen and Fabio
Piucco, Porto Alegre, Brazil
CREATIVE DIRECTION Thiago
Bizarro, Porto Alegre, Brazil
REPRESENTATION AGENCY
Norte (Bárbara Scatolini
and Bruno Narvaez), São
Paulo, Brazil **ADVERTISING
AGENCY** Dez Comunicação,
Porto Alegre, Brazil **URL**
dadoqueiroz.com **DESIGN
FIRM** Dado Queiroz Design
CLIENT AGCO, Massey
Ferguson **PRINCIPAL TYPE**
Helvetica Neue

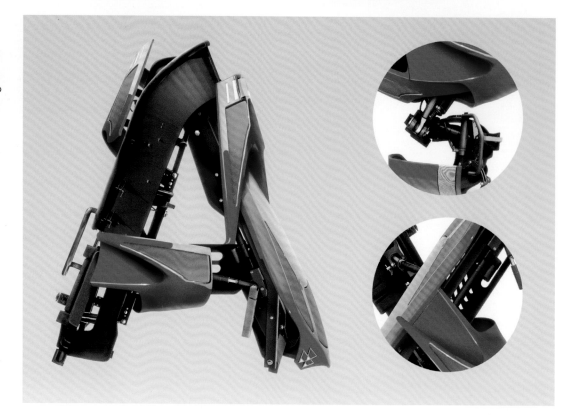

Student Work

DESIGN Jimin Lee,• Seoul
INSTRUCTOR Min Lew **SCHOOL**
School of Visual Arts, New York•
PRINCIPAL TYPE Metric
Bold and Metric Semibold
DIMENSIONS 6.75 × 9.5 in.
(17.1 × 24.1 cm)

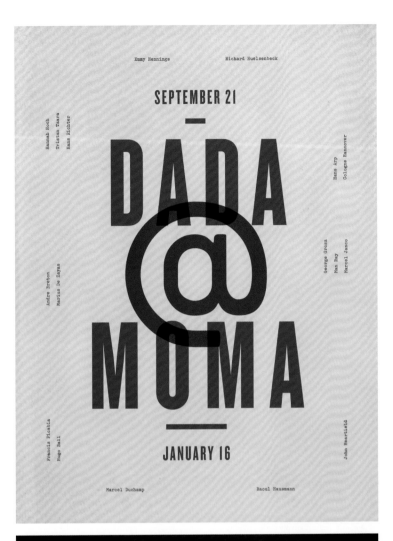

Student Work

DESIGN Jimin Lee,● Seoul
INSTRUCTOR Carin Goldberg
SCHOOL School of Visual Arts,
New York● **PRINCIPAL TYPE**
Garage Gothic and Knockout
(HTF) **DIMENSIONS** 18 × 24 in.
(45.7 × 61 cm)

Student Work

DESIGN Jimin Lee,● Seoul
INSTRUCTOR Carin Goldberg
SCHOOL School of Visual Arts,
New York● **PRINCIPAL TYPE**
Champion Gothic and Ziggurat
DIMENSIONS 18 × 24 in.
(45.7 × 61 cm)

Student Work

MOTION GRAPHIC DESIGN
Ha Lim Kim, New York **URL**
halimkim.com **SCHOOL** School
of Visual Arts, New York●
PRINCIPAL TYPE Learning
Curves and handwriting

Student Work

DESIGN Jimin Lee,● Seoul
INSTRUCTOR Min Lew **SCHOOL**
School of Visual Arts, New York●
PRINCIPAL TYPE LL Brown Std
Bold and Caslon Book BE Bold
DIMENSIONS 18 × 24 in.
(45.7 × 6 cm)

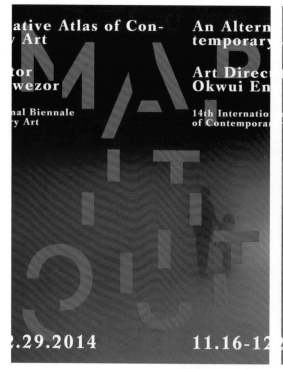

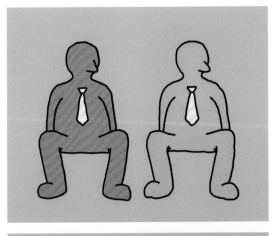
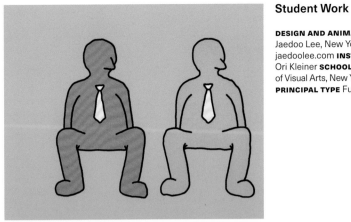
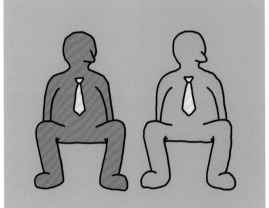

Student Work

DESIGN AND ANIMATION
Jaedoo Lee, New York **URL**
jaedoolee.com **INSTRUCTOR**
Ori Kleiner **SCHOOL** School
of Visual Arts, New York●
PRINCIPAL TYPE Futura

Student Work

DESIGN Sasha Baw Dusky,●
New York **URL** www.behance.
net/sashadusky/ **INSTRUCTOR**
Marianne Klimchuk **SCHOOL**
Fashion Institute of
Technology **PRINCIPAL TYPE**
Custom **DIMENSIONS** 9 × 9 in.
(23 × 23 cm)

Student Work

DESIGN Jaesuk Huh, New York
URL www.jaesukhuh.com
INSTRUCTOR Carin Goldberg
SCHOOL School of Visual Arts,
New York● **PRINCIPAL TYPE**
Custom **DIMENSIONS**
18 × 24 in. (45.7 × 61 cm)

Student Work

DESIGNER Íñigo López
Vázquez, Pueblo, Mexico **URL**
ilvz.net **TWITTER** @inigolv
INSTRUCTOR Paul Soulellis
SCHOOL Rhode Island School
of Design **PRINCIPAL TYPE**
Ivrea **DIMENSIONS** Various

IVREA IS A TYPEFACE,
TYPEWRITER AND TEXT
EDITOR DESIGNED
FOR DRAWING;

A À Á Â Ã Ä Å B Ç D E È É Ê Ë F G H I Ì Í Î Ï J K L M N Ñ O
Ò Ó Ô Õ Ö P Q R S Š T U Ù Ú Û Ü V W X Y Ý Ÿ Z Ž Æ Ð Ø Þ Ł Œ
Δ Ω a à á â ã ä å b c ç d e è é ê ë f g h i ì í î ï j k l m
n ń ñ o ò ó ô õ ö p q r s š t u ù ú û ü v w x y ý ÿ z ž ª º
fi fl ß æ ð ø þ ı ł œ µ π 0 1 2 3 4 5 6 7 8 9 ¹ ² ³ ¼ ½ ¾ ( )
[ ] { } # % ‰ % † ‡ ! ¡ ¿ ? ‹ › « » ∫ @ $ ¢ £ ¤ ¥ € ƒ ⊢ ⊣ ₺
/ \ ⁄ | ¦ & § ¶ · • + − ± ÷ × = < > ≤ ≥ ≈ ≠ ∂ Π Σ
H T T P : / / W W W . I V R E A . X Y Z /

IT IS INSPIRED BY
OLIVETTI TYPEWRITERS
& THE DRAWINGS
CREATED WITH THEM.

295

FRANCIS PICABIA HANNAH HOCH KURT SCHWITTERS
HANNAH HOCH MARCEL DUCHAMPS JEAN ARP
GEORGE GROSZ HANS RICHTER ARTHUR SEGAL ELT MESENS JEAN ARP
KURT SCHWITTERS MARCEL DUCHAMPS ELT MESENS MAN RAY
ARTHUR SEGAL SALVADOR DALI ARTHUR SEGAL
SALVADOR DALI ARTHUR SEGAL SALVADOR DALI
GEORGE GROSZ SALVADOR DALI
ANDREE MASSON GEORGE GROSZ
JOHANNES BAADER
GEORGE GROSZ

DADA
THE MUSEUM
MODERN ART
11 WEST
53 STREET
NEW YORK
NEW YORK

HANS RICHTER GEORGE GROSZ HANS RICHTER
JOHANNES BAADER MARCEL DUCHAMPS ELT MESENS

Student Work

DESIGN Chloé R. Bush, New
York **URL** chloerbush.com
INSTRUCTOR Carin Goldberg
SCHOOL School of Visual
Arts, New York● **PRINCIPAL**
TYPE Impact **DIMENSIONS**
18 × 24 in. (45.7 × 61 cm)

Student Work

DESIGN Chloé R. Bush, New
York **URL** chloerbush.com
INSTRUCTOR Carin Goldberg
SCHOOL School of Visual
Arts, New York● **PRINCIPAL**
TYPE ITC Caslon 224 Book
DIMENSIONS 18 × 24 in.
(45.7 × 61 cm)

296

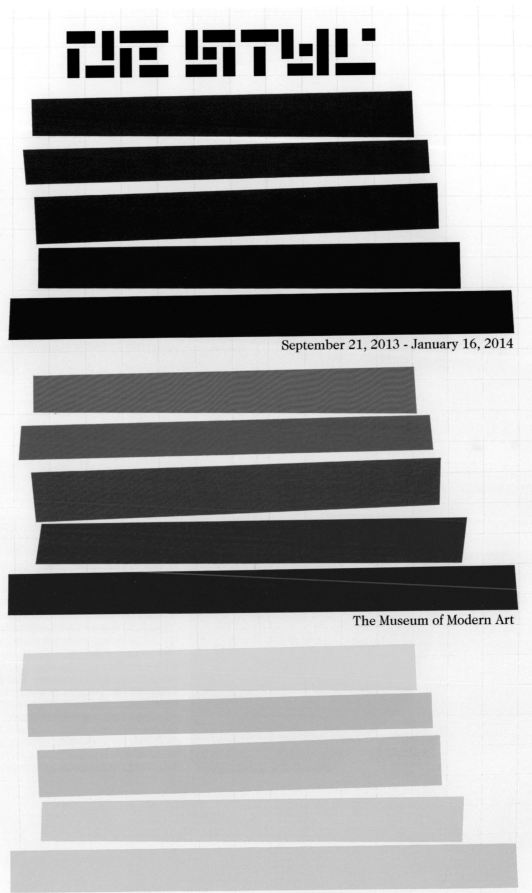

September 21, 2013 - January 16, 2014

The Museum of Modern Art

11 West 53 Street. New York, NY 10019

Student Work

DESIGN AND ILLUSTRATION
Tricha Tan (alias: Tricha
Trains), Brighton **URL** behance.
net/trichatrains **TWITTER**
@TrichaTrains **INSTRUCTOR**
Gavin Ambrose **SCHOOL**
University of Brighton
PRINCIPAL TYPE FF DIN
DIMENSIONS 4.5 × 6.3 in.
(11.5 × 16 cm)

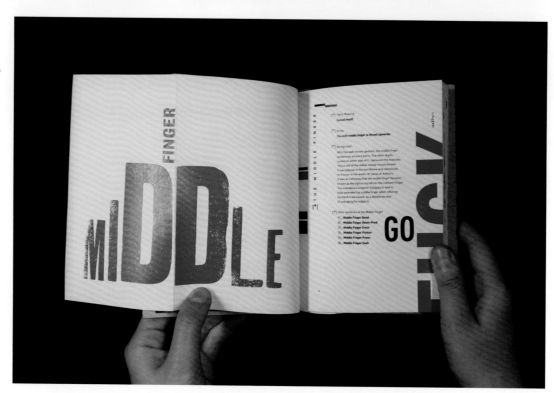

Student Work

DESIGN Ariana Ambrico,
Bridgewater, New Jersey
INSTRUCTOR Olga
Mezhibovskaya● **SCHOOL**
School of Visual Arts, New
York● **PRINCIPAL TYPE**
Cubano **DIMENSIONS** Album
covers 12 × 12 in. (30.5 × 30.5
cm) Logo/Podcast 4 × 4 in.
(10.2 × 10.2 cm)

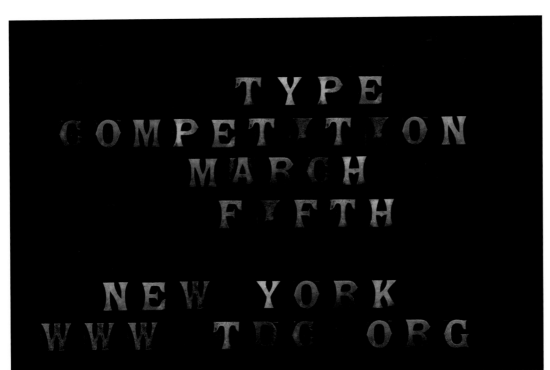

Student Work

DESIGN Hyunsik Kim **URL**
hyunsikkim.com/typography36
SCHOOL School of Visual Arts,
New York● **INSTRUCTOR** Gail
Anderson● **PRINCIPAL TYPE**
Helvetica Neue and wooden
type slugs **DIMENSIONS**
24 × 15.5 in. (60.5 × 38.75 cm)

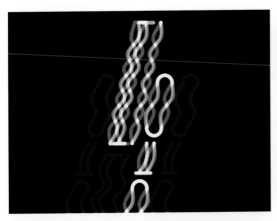

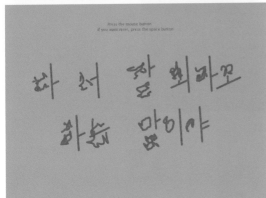

Student Work

DESIGN SunAh Hwang,
Shinjae Jung, Jinyeong Kim,
Wheekyun Kim, Yu Jin Kim,
Minsu Lee, Saebom Lee,
Sungho Lee, Yeonsu Lee,
Cheol Jun Lim, Jiyoung Lim,
YunSeon Lim, Jinsung Moon,
Seung Je Nam, Chaeryun
Park, Gun Hyung Park,
Se Yeon Park, and Hyolim
Sohn, Seoul **DIRECTORS**
Jiwon Lee and Dae In Chung
SCHOOL Kookmin University,
Department of Visual
Communication Design,
Type and Media Group
PRINCIPAL TYPE Custom

Student Work

DESIGN Chin I Lee, San Francisco **URL** chinilee. com **PHOTOGRAPHY RETOUCHER** Hsuan-Jung Hung **INSTRUCTOR** Gina Chang **SCHOOL** Academy of Art University, School of Graphic Design **PRINCIPAL TYPE** Brothers, Fenway Park JF, Sentinel, and Vitesse **DIMENSIONS** 3.4 × 3.4 × 5.2 in. (8.5 × 8.5 × 13 cm)

Student Work

DESIGN Chin I Lee, San Francisco **PHOTOGRAPHY RETOUCHER** Hsuan-Jung Hung **MODEL** Olya Rostov **URL** chinilee.com **INSTRUCTOR** Christopher Morlan **SCHOOL** Academy of Art University, School of Graphic Design **PRINCIPAL TYPE** Gotham, ITC Lubalin Graph, and Mercury Text **DIMENSIONS** 7.9 × 9.9 in. (20 × 25 cm)

Student Work

DESIGN Rik Watkinson, Berlin **PROFESSORS** Steffen Schuhmann and Wim Westerveld **BOOKBINDING** Jan Christodulow **PRINT PRODUCTION** Olaf Kriseleit **PROOFREADING (INTERVIEWS)** Kristina MacVicar **URL** buerowatkinson.de **SCHOOL** Weißensee School of Art, Berlin **PRINCIPAL TYPE** Calibre Light and Gerbera Regular

Student Work

DESIGN Chin I Lee, San Francisco **PHOTOGRAPHY RETOUCHER** Hsuan-Jung Hung **MODEL** Olya Rostov **URL** chinilee.com **INSTRUCTOR** Gina Chang **SCHOOL** Academy of Art University, School of Graphic Design **PRINCIPAL TYPE** Gotham and FF Super Grotesk **DIMENSIONS** 2.5 × 1.75 × 9 in. (6.4 × 4.5 × 22.9 cm)

Student Work

DESIGN Leon Butler, Galway,
Ireland **INSTRUCTOR** Angela
Riechers **SCHOOL** School
of Visual Arts, New York●
PRINCIPAL TYPE Generative
Sans

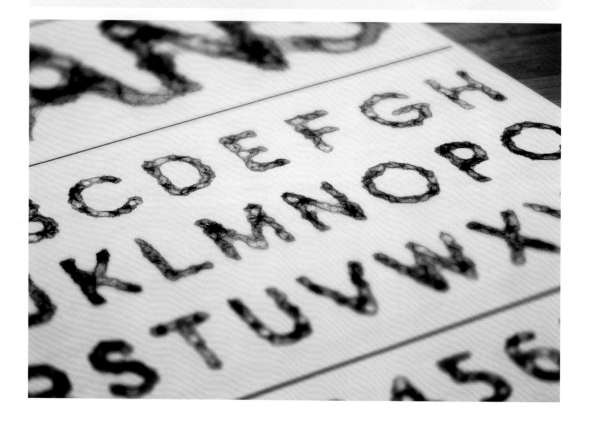

Student Work

DESIGN Zach Harter, New York
URL zachharterdesign.com
INSTRUCTOR Natasha Jen●
SCHOOL School of Visual Arts,
New York● **PRINCIPAL TYPE**
Futura Bold, Futura Book, and
Processed Display

Student Work

DESIGN Alayna Citrin, Baltimore **URL** alaynacitrin.com **TWITTER** @alaynacitrin **INSTRUCTOR** Brockett Horne **SCHOOL** Maryland Institute College of Art **PRINCIPAL TYPE** Job Shop Gothic, Knockout, and hand-carved script blocks from posters created by the Globe Poster Printing Corporation **DIMENSIONS** Various

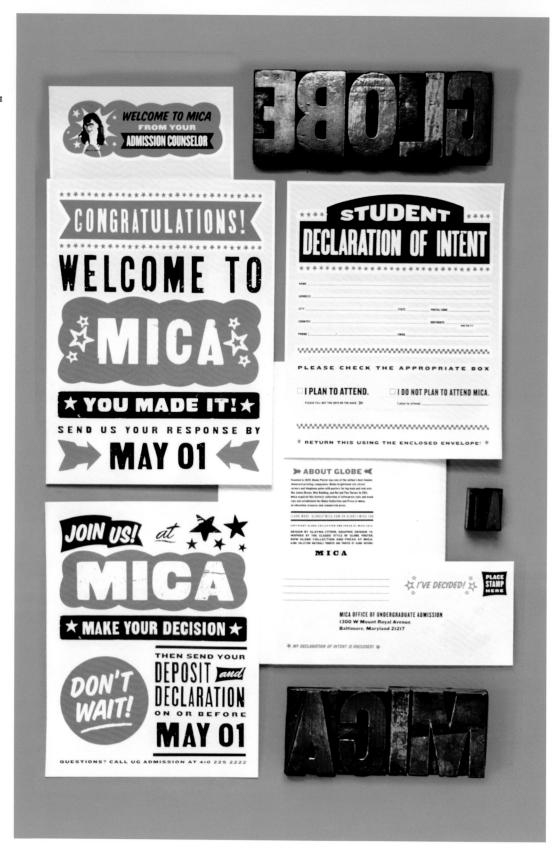

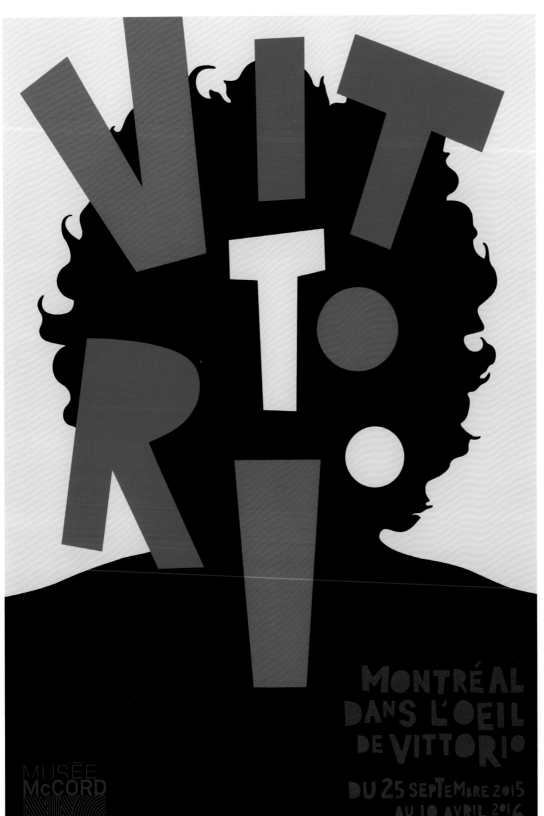

Poster

ART DIRECTION Daniel Robitaille, Montréal **CREATIVE DIRECTION** Louis Gagnon● **URL** paprika.com **DESIGN FIRM** Paprika **CLIENT** McCord Museum **PRINCIPAL TYPE** Vittorio **DIMENSIONS** 24 × 36 in. (61 × 91.5 cm)

Student Work

DESIGN Bianca Ng, Ann Arbor, Michigan, and London
INSTRUCTOR Kira Salter
SCHOOL Central Saint Martin
PRINCIPAL TYPE Handlettering **DIMENSIONS** 32 × 5 ft. (9.8 × 1.5 m)

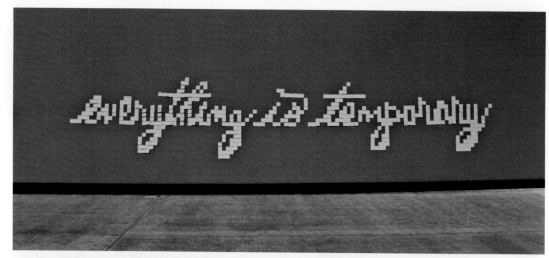

Student Work

DESIGN Scott Biersack, Phoenix **PHOTOGRAPHY** Brian Dunham **URL** scottbiersack. com **TWITTER** @youbringfire **INSTRUCTOR** Jarred Elrod **SCHOOL** Arizona State University **PRINCIPAL TYPE** FM Bolyar Pro and Paradigm **DIMENSIONS** Various

306

T-Shirt

DESIGN Bob Aufuldish,• San Anselmo, California **PRINTER** Katrina Herman, All Gold **URL** aufwar.com **DESIGN FIRM** Aufuldish & Warinner **CLIENT** All Gold **PRINCIPAL TYPE** Helvetica **DIMENSIONS** 32 × 29 in. (82 × 75 cm)

Student Work

DESIGN Ori Elisar, Jerusalem **URL** orielisar.com **TWITTER** twitter.com/orielisar **INSTRUCTORS** Michal Sahar and Eran Yuval **SCHOOL** Bezalel Academy of Art and Design, Jerusalem

Student Work

DESIGN AND ANIMATION
Minhyung Chun, New York
URL minhyungchun.com
INSTRUCTOR Daniel Oeffinger
SCHOOL School of Visual Arts,
New York● **PRINCIPAL TYPE**
Futura Medium Condensed

Student Work

DESIGN Fenghe Luo, New
York **URL** fenghe-luo.com
INSTRUCTORS Gail Anderson●
and Joshua Hester● **SCHOOL**
School of Visual Arts, New
York● **PRINCIPAL TYPE** Fedra
Nine

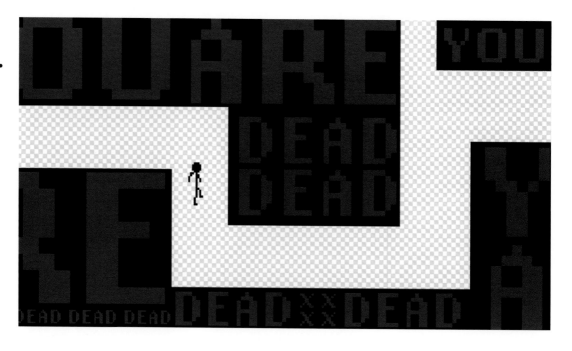

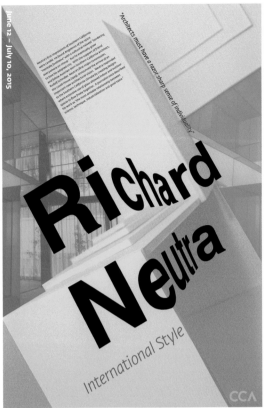

Student Work

DESIGN Hyelin Kim (Erin), Providence, Rhode Island **TEACHING ASSISTANT** Prin Limphongpand **INSTRUCTOR** Ernesto Aparicio **SCHOOL** Rhode Island School of Design **PRINCIPAL TYPE** Fedra Sans and Helvetica Neue **DIMENSIONS** 24 × 36 in. (61 × 91.4 cm)

Student Work

DESIGN Beatrice D'Agostino, Berlin and Milan **URL** beatricedagostino.com **TWITTER** @BeaDagostino **PROFESSORS** Marta Bernstein and Christoph Dunst **SCHOOL** Politecnico di Milano **PRINCIPAL TYPE** Garamond, Ludmilla, and Simoncini **DIMENSIONS** 8.6 × 5.2 in. (21.8 × 13.2 cm)

Television Campaign

DESIGN Courtney Hufhand and Amelia Irwin, New York **ART DIRECTION** Kristen Williams **CREATIVE DIRECTION** Jennifer Cast and Matthew Duntemann **SENIOR VICE PRESIDENT BRAND** Matthew Duntemann **VICE PRESIDENT BRAND DESIGN** Jennifer Cast **SENIOR ANIMATION DIRECTOR** Christopher Papa **SET FABRICATION** Julia Rosner **ANIMATION / 3D MODELING** Scott Kennell and Ross Norton **STUDIO GRAPHICS MANAGER** Alessandra Sutera **COMPANY** Nickelodeon

Apps

DESIGNER AND DEVELOPER Dae In Chung, Seoul **URL** paperdove.com **TWITTER** @cdaein

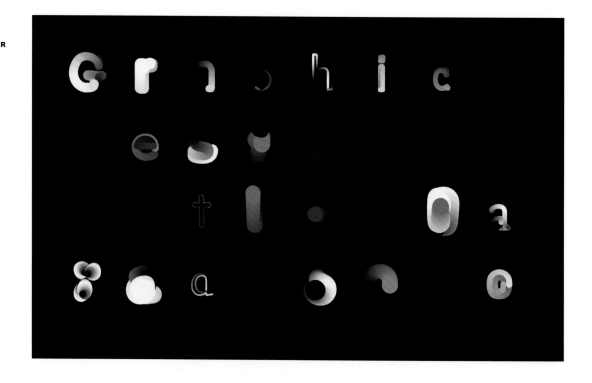

Monotype Fonts Technology **Expertise** Company   Search

Insights and resources from some of the brightest minds in the business

All Case Studies Webinars Articles
Best Practice

Website

DESIGN Jenn Contois,•
Nicola Jones, Colin Kersley,
and Information Architects,
Woburn, Massachusetts;
Cardiff, Wales; and Zürich
BOOK Information Architects
CREATIVE DIRECTION James
Fooks-Bale **DIRECTOR** Mark
Boulton **PROJECT MANAGER**
Emily Fenech **COPYWRITER**
Michael Evamy **ILLUSTRATION**
SEA Design **URL** monotype.
com **TWITTER** @monotype
FOUNDRY Monotype
PRINCIPAL TYPE Kootenay
and Malabar

New from old: the why and how of reviving a typeface

Legibility in quick glance environments

dddddddd
88888888

11:17

MESSAGES

Rich Evans
I'm running late...
be there in 10
minutes.

Website

DESIGN Michael McNeive,
Baltimore **CREATIVE
DIRECTION** Michael McNeive
DEVELOPMENT Daniel Givens
and Dustin Pfeifer **URL** drxlr.
com **TWITTER** @drxlr **DESIGN
FIRM** Drexler **CLIENT** Oliver
Brewing Co **PRINCIPAL TYPE**
Engravers Gothic, GT Pressura,
and GT Pressura Mono

Website

DESIGN Ludovic Balland and
Thomas Petit, Basel **ART
DIRECTION** Ludovic Balland
CODING Gael Hugo **URL**
pprocess.ch/?live **DESIGN
FIRM** Ludovic Balland
Typography Cabinet **CLIENT**
Centre culturel suisse Paris
PRINCIPAL TYPE NEXT Book,
NEXT Poster Regular, Medium,
and Italic

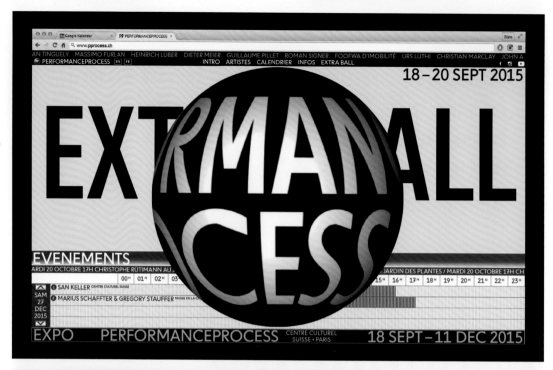

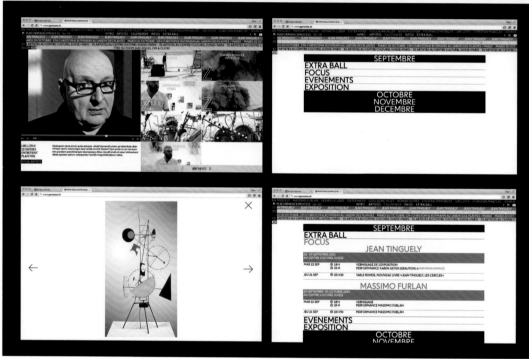

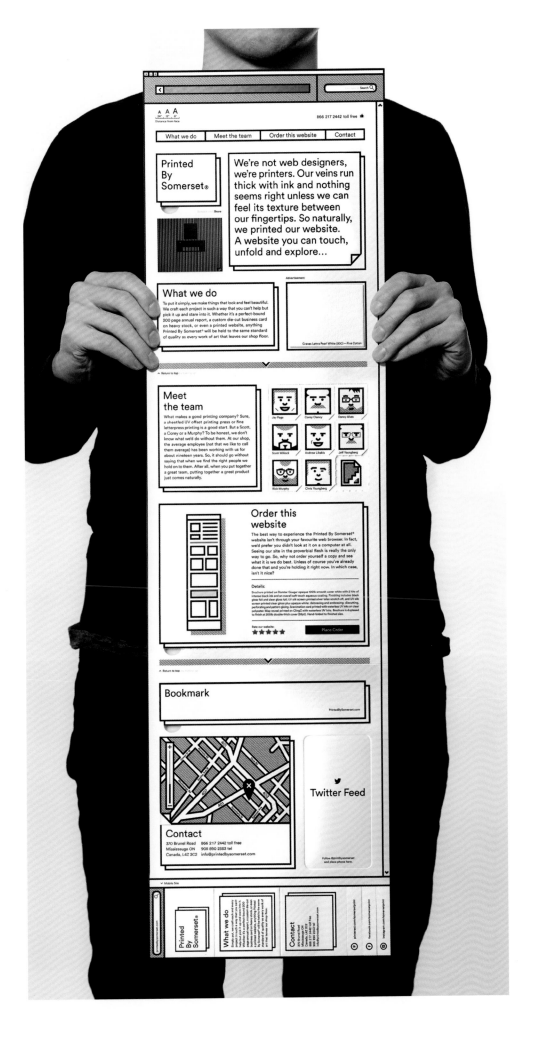

Website

DESIGN Ryan Crouchman, Dejan Djuric, Pedro Izzo, and Jeff Waktins, Toronto **ART DIRECTION** Ryan Crouchman, Dejan Djuric, Chris Duchaine, Pedro Izzo, and Scott Leder **DIGITAL ART DIRECTION** Ryan Crouchman, Dejan Djuric, and Pedro Izzo **CREATIVE DIRECTION** Lisa Greenberg and Judy John **CHIEF CREATIVE OFFICER** Judy John **GROUP CREATIVE DIRECTION** Ryan Crouchman, Lisa Greenberg, and Sean Ohlenkamp **COPYWRITERS** Andrew Caie and Marty Hoefkes **ILLUSTRATION** Dejan Djuric and Kristina Marija Valiunas **DEVELOPERS AND WEB/FLASH DEVELOPERS** Jacqueline Adediji and Dan Purdy **DIRECTOR, CREATIVE TECHNOLOGY** Felix Wardene **AGENCY PRODUCERS** Sabrina DeLuca and Laurie Filgiano **ACCOUNT EXECUTIVE** Kayla Osmond **PLANNER** Joshua Hansen **PROJECT MANAGER** Tracy Wrightman **PHOTOGRAPHY** Luis Albuquerque and Arash Moallemi **URL** leoburnett. ca **TWITTER** @LeoBurnettTor **AGENCY** Leo Burnett Toronto **PRINCIPAL TYPE** LL Circular

Website

DESIGN Soobin Park, New York **DESIGN DIRECTION** Scott Galbraith **ART DIRECTION** Woonji Kim **CREATIVE DIRECTION** Charles Marrelli **GROUP CREATIVE DIRECTOR** Can Misirlioglu **ACD, EXPERIENCE DESIGN** Joseph Mcheffey **SOCIAL STRATEGIST** Katie Campo and Rachel Korenstein **SENIOR DIGITAL PRODUCER** Anna Santiago **SENIOR DIGITAL PRODUCER** Michael Bucchino **EXECUTIVE PRODUCER** Stuart Culpepper **EXECUTIVE PRODUCER** Nick Williams **AUDIO ENGINEER** Brandon Jiaconia **SENIOR WEB DEVELOPER** Dalton Ridenhour **LEAD CREATIVE TECHNOLOGIST** Jad Mintun **CREATIVE TECHNOLOGIST** Jian Xu **WEB DEVELOPER** Angus Lo **QA ENGINEER** Michael Shagalov **URL** http://ny.havasworldwide.com **AGENCY** Havas Worldwide NY **CLIENT** Tom Mullen, Director, Digital Marketing, Legacy Recordings, Sony Music Entertainment **PRINCIPAL TYPE** Univers LT Std

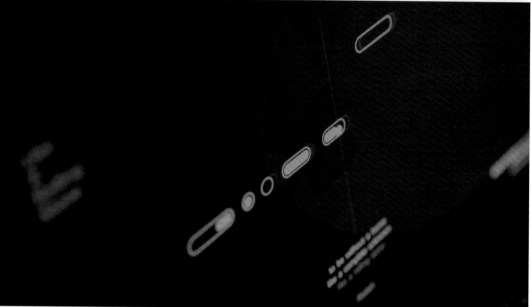

Website

CREATIVE DIRECTION Todd
Albertson, Washington, D.C.,
Port Moody, British Columbia
USER EXPERIENCE DESIGNER
Todd Albertson **URL**
weaponofchoicetype.com
DESIGN FIRM Weapon
of Choice Type Foundry
PRINCIPAL TYPE Various

: **No. 48 Display / No.48 Stencil**

A geometric sans originally made for the Society of Publication Designers 48th design annual.
Two styles for the price of one: roman and stencil.

: Complete character set below : single weight : two styles : otf only

Total Computers
1–3 $50.00 USD
Buy Now

315

DESIGN Kirstin Huber,
New York **ART DIRECTION**
Paula Scher,• Pentagram•
URL kirstinhuber.com
PHOTOGRAPHY Tammy Shell
(tammyshell.com) **PHOTO**
ASSISTANT Kameron Neal
(kameronneal.com) **CLIENT**
The Public Theater
(publictheater.org) **PRINCIPAL**
TYPE Knockout **DIMENSIONS**
30.5 × 59 in. (77 × 150 cm)

Poster

DESIGN Kirstin Huber, New York **ART DIRECTION** Paula Scher,● Pentagram● **URL** (kirstinhuber.com) **CLIENT** The Public Theater (publictheater.org) **PRINCIPAL TYPE** Knockout **DIMENSIONS** 30.5 × 59 in. (77 × 150 cm)

Poster

DESIGN Kirstin Huber, New York **ART DIRECTION** Paula Scher,● Pentagram● **URL** kirstinhuber.com **CLIENT** The Public Theater (publictheater.org) **PRINCIPAL TYPE** Knockout **DIMENSIONS** 30.5 × 59 in. (77 × 150 cm)

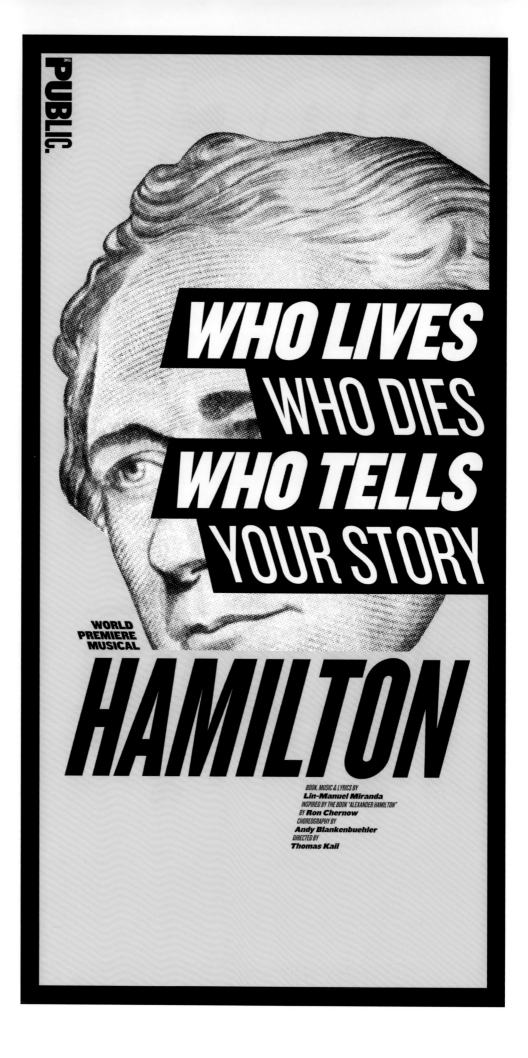

Poster

DESIGN Kirstin Huber,
New York **ART DIRECTION**
Paula Scher,● Pentagram●
PHOTOGRAPHY Tammy
Shell **URL** tammyshell.com
PHOTO ASSISTANT Kameron
Neal kameronneal.com **URL**
kirstinhuber.com **CLIENT**
The Public Theater
publictheater.org **PRINCIPAL**
TYPE Knockout **DIMENSIONS**
30.5 × 59 in. (77 × 150 cm)

Website

DESIGN AND DEVELOPMENT
Nick Sherman,• New York **URL**
nicksherman.com **TWITTER**
@NickSherman **JAVASCRIPT**
DEVELOPMENT Chris Lewis,
Seattle **FONT-LOADING**
OPTIMIZATION Bram Stein,
Copenhagen **TEXT** John D.
Berry,• Seattle **ADDITIONAL**
TEXT Robert Slimbach,
Mountain View, California
EDITING Sally Kerrigan
San Francisco **PROJECT**
COORDINATION Nicole
Miñoza,• Bainbridge Island,
Washington **ADDITIONAL**
PROJECT COORDINATION
Greg Veen, San Francisco
HISTORICAL IMAGES
Letterform Archive, San
Francisco **LETTERPRESS**
SAMPLES Dafi Kühne, Zürich
CLIENT Adobe Systems
PRINCIPAL TYPE Acumin

ACUMIN

Intro   Design   History   Usage   Preview   Get Acumin

DETAILS	**Mind**	Clearly	**PAGE**	Defining
Closed	**Think**	BATHS	**Being**	Broader
Voices	**ROOM**	Palace	**Forms**	FORMS
SHOPS	Inside	Mostly	**MARK**	Naming
Floral	Found	AVOID	Britain	Version
Today	TASKS	**Styles**	Nearly	**STOOD**
MOLD	Range	**Fifties**	HAND	**Revival**
Itself	Others	**JOINS**	Master	**What's**
Such	GOTHIC	**Plays**	Widths	**FORM**

Acumin is a versatile sans-serif typeface family designed by Robert Slimbach, intended for a balanced and rational quality. Solidly neo-grotesque, it performs beautifully at display sizes but also maintains an exceptional degree of sensitivity for text sizes.

Intro   Design   History   Usage   Preview

GET ACUMIN

 Acumin is part of the <u>Adobe Originals</u> series of typefaces, developed with the highest standards for aesthetic value, technical quality, and typographic functionality.

Copyright 2015 Adobe Systems Incorporated.
All rights reserved. Subject to <u>terms of use</u> and <u>privacy policy</u>.

Student Work

DESIGN Enle Li, New York
VOICE-OVER Neil Degrasse
Tyson **INSTRUCTOR** Daniel
Oeffinger **SCHOOL** School
of Visual Arts, New York•
PRINCIPAL TYPE Custom

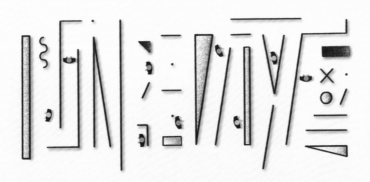

Typeface
Design
TDC MMXVI

Chairman's Statement

Making a typeface is an intricate design project. It's like peeling the onion. It may seem simple at first, but the layers of understanding and the stages of perfecting are quite possibly limitless. Where other design projects are sprints, designing a typeface is a marathon, sometimes a relay race, sometimes an Ironman. Making a single typeface takes time and patience; making a career of designing typefaces takes complete and utter devotion.

I've come to know a lot of typeface designers and their work. I have great admiration for people who do it well. Mastery of letterforms is magical.

It's been an honor to chair the judging of the 2015 TDC competition. This year's judges included Alexander Tochilovsky, curator of the Herb Lubalin Study Center and a typographer by training, typeface designers Veronika Burian of TypeTogether, Petr van Blokland of TypeNetwork, and Stéphane Elbaz, currently a web designer at The Intercept, and also a fine typeface designer in his own right.

We could not have done justice to the submissions of Cyrillic, Greek, Arabic, Hebrew, Chinese, Japanese, or Korean without the help of Maxim Zhukov, who coordinated a team of experts to give counsel and perspective on these designs.

It is amazing to watch a group of such exquisitely observant people look at type. For the winners of this year's competition, I say you are few and you should be very proud. These judges were seriously looking for excellence. Congratulations.

Cara Di Edwardo

Judges

Veronika Burian

Veronika Burian studied Industrial Design in Munich and worked in that capacity in Vienna and Milan over a few years. Discovering her true passion for type, she graduated with distinction from the MA in Typeface Design in Reading, UK, in 2003 and worked as type designer at DaltonMaag in London for a few years. After staying for some time in Boulder, USA, and her hometown Prague she is now living and working in Spain.

Veronika Burian is a type designer and co-founder of the independent type foundry TypeTogether, publishing award-winning typefaces and collaborating on tailored typefaces for a variety of clients. She is also involved with Alphabettes.org, a showcase for work and research on lettering, typography, and type design by women and continues to give lectures and workshops at international conferences and universities.

arrows & borders & ornaments

Gentlemen

detail & flair

Bereits um 565 wurde es erstmals schriftlich erwähnt

15 kilometers

inspired by *Scotch Romans*

Yellowstone park

Im Jahr 1934 ging ein Bild um die Welt

"**Frebbies**"

*Abril Display · Karmina · Karmina Sans · **Ronnia***

Europamüdigkeit

Понедельник, вторник, среда, четверг, пятница

GROTESK

1st lettering **artist!**

Mrs. Poon, 6940 Laurel Valley Drive, in *Boulder Colorado*

Newsreel

ADVENTURE

I have passed through fire and deep water to arrive

99 bottles of beer on the wall

Adelle · Adelle Sans · Bree Serif · Athelas PE · Crete

Stéphane Elbaz

Originally from Paris, France, Stéphane Elbaz is a graphic and type designer currently living and working in New York City. He recently joined First Look Media where he serves as Head of Product Design, Magazines. In the last few years he devoted much of his time to digital publishing platforms. In addition, he continued his type and brand design practice.

For Code and Theory he led visual design on various projects, including *Vanity Fair* and *GQ* for Condé Nast France, the *LA Times*, *Interview*, and *Art in America*. As an independent designer, Stéphane recently created a brand typeface for Sephora and participated in brand projects for companies in sectors ranging from culture and fashion to the energy industry. In 2009 he was awarded the Certificate of Excellence in Type Design from the Type Directors Club of New York for his type family Geneo.

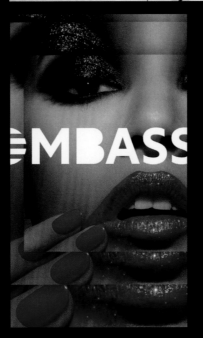

Alexander Tochilovsky

Alexander Tochilovsky is a graphic designer, typographer, curator, and educator, with nearly twenty years of professional design experience, and ten years of experience teaching typography. He graduated with a BFA from The Cooper Union, and holds an MFA from Cranbrook Academy of Art. He is currently the Curator of the Herb Lubalin Study Center of Design and Typography. In 2009 he cocurated the exhibition *Lubalin Now*, and since 2010 he has curated five other exhibitions: Appetite (2010), *Pharma* (2011), *Type@Cooper* (2012), *Image of the Studio* (2013), and *Thirty* (2015). Since 2007 he has taught typography and design at the Cooper Union School of Art, and also teaches the history of typeface design at Type@ Cooper, the postgraduate certificate program he co-founded in 2010.

NEW (...and Then)

CRANBROOK ART MUSEUM
SATURDAY, OCTOBER 15, 2011

Productus

Book *Italic* 01234 ©Typetr & Branding (@¥$€)
Medium *Italic* 01234 ©Typetr & Typography (@¥$€)
Semibold *Italic* 01234 ©Typetr & Coherency (@¥$€)
Bold *Italic* 01234 ©Typetr & Identity (@¥$€)
Black *Italic* 01234 ©Typetr & Diversity (@¥$€)

Proforma

Ultralight *Italic* 012345: ©Typetr & Branding
Light *Italic* 012345: ©Typetr & Typography
Book *Italic* 012345: ©Typetr & Coherency
Medium *Italic* 012345: ©Typetr & Identity
Semibold *Italic* 012345: ©Typetr & Diversity
Bold *Italic* 012345: ©Typetr & Synergy

Petr van Blokland

Petr van Blokland (1956) is the owner, together with Claudia Mens, of Buro Petr van Blokland + Claudia Mens, founded in 1980 and working in cooperation with a network of participating designers and engineers, depending on the type of projects. He studied at the Royal Academy of Arts—cum laude—in The Hague and studied Industrial Design at Delft Technical University. His special interest is in typography, type design, designing the design process, automation of design, developing software tools for designers, and design theory. He developed live design games at various art schools and conferences around the world and published columns in design magazines on various topics.

Van Blokland lectured at the Department of Graphic Design of the Academy of Arts in Arnhem (1984–1989), at the Department of Graphic Design (1988–2011), and Master Type & Media (1998–present) of the Royal Academy of Arts in The Hague, as well as at the Department of Graphic Design of AKV St. Joost in Breda, Bachelor and Master (2010–present).

Van Blokland received the Charles Peignot Award for typography of Atypl, the Association Typographique International, in 1988 and was Board Member from 1996 to 2003. Together with David Berlow he initiated TypeLab in 1993, which ran as a side program to ATypl conferences for several years.

He was co-founder and CTO of The Health Agency, publisher for online health information, from 2001 to 2006.

Besides lecturing, his current focus is on international projects related to typography and type design. He also is co-founder of webtype.com, for which many typedesign tools were developed.

Tremolo

TYPEFACE DESIGN Nikola Djurek, Zabok, Croatia **FOUNDRY** Typonine **URL** typonine.com **MEMBERS OF TYPE FAMILY** Text, Text Italic, Stencil Text, Stencil Text Italic, Display, Stencil Display **CONCEPT** Tremolo is austere and friendly, loose and tightly wound, brisk and supple—different tones and different voices packed into a single design.

VERONIKA BURIAN In general I am not a big fan of gradients, but this type family struck me as different. By way of interlocking jags they elegantly give depth to the letters and emphasize their playfulness. The design also displays a joy to experiment, strong quality of drawing skills, and a deep understanding of shapes.

Nikola Djurek manages to surprise us by giving to an otherwise stiff blackletter style this somewhat cheeky and frivolous tone, which works surprisingly well even in smaller text sizes.

If I may criticize one thing though, it is the decision to use upright caps in the italic. Surely it is the designer's prerogative to do so, but I feel that the obvious imbalance of weight and spacing is not fully justified here.

The Tremolo type family has eleven individual fonts, but actually only two different weights, and those sit at two extreme ends. Obviously the designer's intention when assembling the family was another than the classic Light to Heavy. I appreciate this approach to question the usual family tree and concentrate on the usage instead.

Tremolo certainly is an interesting addition to the current trend of polychrome typefaces.

different tones and different voices packed into a single desig n

TYPONINE

BC Mikser

DESIGN Filip Kraus, Prague **FOUNDRY** Briefcase Type Foundry (CZ) **URL** briefcasetype.com http://briefcasetype.com/bc-mikser/specimen **TWITTER** @BriefcaseType **CONCEPT**
We rank both contemporary and historic typefaces according to established definitions and categories. If we attempt to describe Mikser in this way, we can say that it is a monolinear, dynamic, sans serif typeface with a uniform character width (in other words, it's monospaced), combining a vertical axis with distinctive modeling of the drawing. We thus acquire a tortuous mix, or rather "miks," which demands the creation of its own typeface category.

STÉPHANE ELBAZ From a practical standpoint, one could find any "mono" totally useless; it is, after all, a design that displays functionalism solely for aesthetic reasons. These constraints are based on functional limitations that no longer exist, and aside from the inherent alignment maniacs that are computer engineers or the tacky interfaces in sci-fi movies, only designers keep their crushes on these peculiar shapes.

This style is historical and persistent. The most respected to the trendiest type foundries propose new mono typefaces every year to meet visual designers' perpetual demands. Going back to the early twentieth century, one finds a variety of "typewriter" typefaces in printers' specimens.

Remember that Gutenberg invented typography as a technology and not as some new "art" of the text. As its design evolved into an art form, it never lost its intimate connection with technology; "Monos" might be the clearest incarnation of this relationship. Whereas in the past, mono design related to mechanization, today it relates to computerization.

The world needed to see the mono version of the Helvetica—isn't this the founding moment of modern type history?—but Mikser is not just a mono and it's definitely not a mono version of something else. This alphabet embraces the mono aesthetic while pushing it further. Without trading the craft and the readability, it manages to integrate something that relates to pop culture. Expressive shapes encapsulated in very limiting containers side by side and displaying an ironic smirk as a whole.

337

Mornic

DESIGNER Nur Muhammad Hasif, Singapore **TWITTER** @nrmdhsif **CONCEPT** Mornic, a single-family display typeface, embodies the spirit of curiosity and is inspired by the designs of Zaha Hadid. The word *Mornic* comes from the term *Modern Organic*. Mornic's bold and dynamic, yet powerful, curving forms stimulate a distinctive fluid motion. The typeface is ambiguous, evoking a sense of curiosity when viewed.

ALEXANDER TOCHILOVSKY
My first impression of this typeface was, "Wow, this is different." I think the other judges felt the same. The texture and the rhythm of the face is so distinct, especially when you see blocks of large text set in it. It feels like it is channeling a little bit of Roger Excoffon's "Choc" and "Calypso," and a little bit of Frutiger's "Stones," with a dash of the Fuse fonts in it. It's no wonder I liked it from the beginning. It reminded me of a lot of what I like about type. When I was just learning that type was designed by someone, and that it can have an idea behind it, these were the faces and ideas I identified with. This typeface brought this all back in a playful and exciting way. It is very present, very graphic, confident, but not rigid.

For such a mannered design, the all-caps settings usually are a terrible idea—think all-caps blackletter tattoos—but in this case it works really well. The letters move in a fluid way, the angles shift and undulate, creating a really lovely rhythm. The variety of angles helps keep the face interesting, and the roundness of the shapes makes it all flow together. I really enjoy the way the cap *E*, cap and lowercase *F*s, and the cap *G* are resolved. The lowercase *t* is an interesting solution. The ampersand is great too. This is a face that I definitely could see having a few contextual alternates, in order to break up the forms whenever letters repeat in a word. It has a very non-Latin feel to it, which lends it a good air of novelty. The eye is surprised but is able to recognize the letters relatively quickly. This is a nice reminder that typefaces are ultimately graphic forms, and that you can still find novel ways of shaping them.

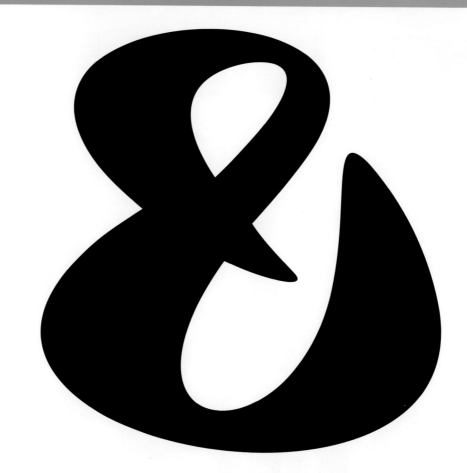

Korova Milkbar

The Miracle of the Snowflake

Yarbles is what I say to him, and I'd chain his glazzies out soon as look

A CLOCKWORK ORANGE

Devotchkas

I Embrace Ye O Ye Millions

Dignified Labourers

He looked a malenky bit poogly when he viddied the four of us like that

And so farewell from your little droog

Bressay

DESIGN Tom Foley, Sebastian Losch, and Spike Spondike, London **DESIGN LEAD AND ENGINEERING** Stuart Brown **HINTING** Michael Cunliffe and Mark Ward **URL** Ron Carpenter and Fabio Haag **FOUNDRY** Dalton Maag **URL** daltonmaag.com **TWITTER** @DaltonMaag **CONCEPT** Bressay is a Scotch Roman design that captures the elegance and sobriety of a style that was popular in the nineteenth century, while meeting the demands of modern print and digital technologies. Scotch Romans are characterized by their vertical stress, high contrast, ball terminals, and bracketed serifs. Bressay takes these features and adds a contemporary twist. The family consists of text and display styles, all optimized for print and screen use, making Bressay ideal for a broad range of applications—from newspaper and editorial typesetting to luxury and fashion branding.

PETR VAN BLOKLAND Where family designs often lack the completeness of different designs for small and large sizes, Bressay does offer this choice, which makes it a complete alternative for other existing "expansion" typefaces. Expansion is Gerrit Noordzij's model name for contrast types that follow writing with the pointed flexible pen: pressure on the pen makes the width of the downstrokes, where the strokes in all other directions are thin.

By changing the width of the thick downstrokes, the different weights are made. By changing the width of all thin strokes, drawings for different sizes are made. Small type needs thicker thin strokes, both for optical reasons and to make sure that the thin lines don't disappear in pixels.

These are classical parameters that also can be found in other expansion type designs. What makes the Bressey special is that it carefully maintains the contrast principle, while in the meantime adding new subtle flavors in line angles, curves, and details such as an alternative characteristic shape for the otherwise circular ball terminals.

The extended glyph set and the weight and size axes make the typeface an interesting candidate to use in a wide range of applications and media, where a subtle but convincing difference with existing expansion typefaces is required.

Bixa

DESIGNER Mark van Wageningen, Amsterdam **FOUNDRY** Novo Typo **URL** novotypo.nl **TWITTER** @NovoTypo **CONCEPT** Novo Typo's Bixa, a digital multicolored font designed for the web, leaves the computer and transforms into an analog wooden typeface. Every letter exists in four colors and thus four printings. The Typewood project shows the entire process: from type design, to the production of the wooden type with a hypermodern CNC milling technique, to the testing and printing of the type specimen on an antique letterpress. This project defines modern techniques and reinvents old techniques.

MATTEO BOLOGNA Bixa is a crazy chromatic font inspired from the wood type era and pushes through our world of pixels at the speed of light.

It's twelve layers of fun that lets the designer to tell her/his story through infinite possibility of color combinations.

It's a font that pushes the envelope not only visually but also technically, being engineered to work as a multicolor font designed for web. I can't wait to use it and to see other designers use it!

TYPEWOOD

WOODTYPE

TYPEWOOD

WOODTYPE

TYPEWOOD

WOODTYPE

TYPEWOOD

WOODTYPE

Typeface Design
Winners

Acanto Regia

TYPEFACE Acanto Regia
DESIGNER Jonathan Cuervo•
Cisneros, Mexico City
FOUNDRY Atypic Co. **URL**
jocuervo.com **CONCEPT**
Acanto is the outcome of a
personal journey through the
blackletter. It arose from a self-
developed blackletter style,
and the calligraphic model
evolved to become a text font
and then a display face. It was
a "taming" process, in which
that wild set of letters turned
into a well-behaved typeface.
Inspired by the Arts and Crafts
Movement, Acanto has a kind
of art nouveau feel. To learn
more about the process and
the other styles that complete
the family, check my website.

Ex Machina

Ars Longa · Vita Brevis

Divine Comedy

-Evangelium des Johannes-

Scripture Quotes

«You can't have Gold without spitting Blood»

Merlot & Syrah 1982

Als der fischäugige Konsul sein Refugium verließ
blikte das hysterische Luxus-Geschöpf zum Matrosen und
verschlang hastig und flink einen Bißen Hochzeitstorte!

abcdéfghijklmñöþqrstŭvwxŷż

ABCDEFGHIJKLMNOPQ

RSTUVWXYZ & 0123456789

¶ § † ‡ * # { @ ß $ £ € ¢ } % ¡ ? © ® ™ a o

romain **Bristly in display sizes, supple for text.**

italic *Faithful partner for the roman, yet independent.*

bold **Oversized to overshadow its neighbors.**

DESIGNER Sandrine Nugue, Paris **DISTRIBUTOR** Centre national des arts plastiques **URL** sandrinenugue.com **TWITTER** @sndrnng **CONCEPT** Infini was commissioned by Centre national des arts plastiques to be downloaded freely by the public. It is more than a typeface; it is a pedagogical project that tells the story of the Latin writing system from its beginnings to the present. This is why Infini finds its foundation in a Greek model popular between the third and first centuries BC. The distinct chiseled marks of stone carving are prevalent in display sizes while being legible and having a dark color in text. The family is composed of a roman with ligatures, an italic, and a bold with twenty-six pictograms.

Froben Antiqua

DESIGNER Ueli Kaufmann, Zürich **URL** uelikaufmann.ch
CONCEPT Froben Antiqua is a serif typeface family intended for character-heavy communication, editorial, and book design. Details and proportions, which bring character to both small and large sizes, are inspired by the works of famous Basel Renaissance printers Johann and Hieronymus Froben. Clear differentiation of round and straight forms and variations in letter width make for distinctive patterns in all styles. There is a strong emphasis on the relationship between text and display and their respective italics, and also the pan-European extensions Cyrillic and Greek. (Froben Antiqua was developed during my MA in Typeface Design program, in 2014–2015, at the University of Reading.)

DISPLAY ITALIC | 384 PT

DISPLAY | 192 PT

R

Que

DISPLAY ITALIC | 96 PT

DISPLAY | 48 PT

Them

Makro

DISPLAY ITALIC | 24 PT

Hans Froben

REGULAR | 384 PT

ITALIC | 192 PT

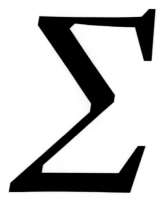

kind

REGULAR | 96 PT

ITALIC | 48 PT

Rudi

Mikro

REGULAR | 24 PT

Desiderius

GREEK ITALIC | 384 PT

GREEK | 192 PT

Σ

αερο

GREEK ITALIC | 96 PT

GREEK | 48 PT

αφίσα

Μικρό

GREEK ITALIC | 24 PT

Έρασμους

Being from different planets, they have to learn each others

897

BLACK

A involontairement donné une très légère inclinaison aux verticales. Imprévue, cette donnée à *PEINE* perceptible sera finalement *c*onservée, dotant l'alphabet d'une très légère dynamique. Après plusieurs années de recherche, la première version disponible du

34

Argentina
Brasil
Colombia
Uruguay
Venezuela
Costa Rica

↓ For the very first time the World-Cup went in **Asia**. And for the very first time it was split between two nations, Japan and *South-Korea*. *A*gentina was the big favourite, followed by the title holders **France**, and as always Brazil. But this turned up to be the World-Cup were the favourites failed. Both *France* and *Argentina* failed to qualify through the first rounds. And an incredible comeback of Ronaldo helped **Brazil** to the final. In the final Brazil faced *Germany* and won 2–0 after two goals by Ronaldo.

WORLD CUP HISTORY IN A NUTSHELL:

&

The **2010** edition promises to be one of the most competetive ever, with both ASIAN and **african** football getting ever more

Zinedine Zidane became the fourth player in World Cup history to score in two different finals, along with Pelé, Paul Breitner and Vavá

SF
GIANTS
San Francisco

SOX ON
EST. 1901
Red Sox
BOSTON

Heading to Miami in search of better help, he got the Heat to the Finals when it wasn't ready to win and then back

Cutch gives up gloves for $3.560

DESIGNER Marko Hrastovec, The Hague FOUNDRY Typotheque URL typotheque.com TWITTER @typotheque CONCEPT I created Zico as part of a graduation project at the Royal Academy of Art, Type and Media program, The Hague.

Bustani

DESIGNER Patrick Giasson
LINGUISTIC TYPOGRAPHER
Kamal Mansour **FOUNDRY**
Monotype Woburn,
Massachusetts (monotype.
com) **TWITTER** @monotype
CONCEPT The Bustani
typeface emulates calligraphic
Naskh style. Words are set on
a slight incline in a manner
similar to a calligrapher's hand.
In addition, the internal
intelligence of Bustani
automatically selects the
appropriate letterforms in their
context according to Naskh
calligraphic rules. Users can
also select alternative forms
from a rich set of letter shapes.
Bustani also handles the
precise placement of vowel
marks and other small
annotations in even the most
fully vocalized text, making the
typeface suitable for all
compositions—from everyday
text to complex scholarly
manuscripts—and in every
language written in the Arabic
script.

Greta Arabic

DESIGNERS Peter Bilak and Kristyan Sarkis, The Hague
MANUFACTURER TPTQ Arabic **URL** TPTQ-Arabic.com
TWITTER @TPTQArabic
CONCEPT Greta Arabic is an unprecedented Arabic super type family in forty styles.

الخيال أكثر أهمية من المعرفة الخيال أكثر أهمية من المعرفة الخيال أكثر أهمية من المعرفة بلا

عندما تصبح المكتبة ضرورة عندما تصبح المكتبة ضرورة عندما تصبح المكتبة ضرورة كالد

يغمسون اقلامهم في قلوب يغمسون اقلامهم في قلوب يغمسون اقلامهم في قلوبنا مر

نصف ما أقوله لك لا مع نصف ما أقوله لك لا معن نصف ما أقوله لك لا معنى له

عندما تصبح المكتبة ض عندما تصبح المكتبة ض عندما تصبح المكتبة ضرورة د

مثل المطر عندما يهطل مثل المطر عندما يهطل مثل المطر عندما يهطل بغزار

إظهر كما أنت وكن ٢ إظهر كما أنت وكن كما أظهر كما أنت وكن كما تظه

يغمسون اقلامهم في يغمسون اقلامهم في يغمسون اقلامهم في قلوبنا

كانَ التَهَكُّمُ في صَو كانَ التَهَكُّمُ في صَوْتِه كانَ التَهَكُّمُ في صَوْتِه واضِح

يين حروفها سم ثعر يين حروفها سم ثعبان أس

DESIGNER Zhang WeiMin,
Shenzhen, China **CLIENT**
NAME WESUN Brand
Consultant **URL** blog.sina.
com.cn/well197338
CONCEPT This font is based
on the Jiao Slavery poem.
The use of cursive with the
Chinese calligraphy pen up
and down is the law. The font
rendering contrasts rough
and fine, smooth lines, and up
and down strokes. Artistically,
the font strokes were
magnificent and sometimes
delicate. The font design
expresses the spirit and
meaning of the poetry.

Greta Sans Hebrew

TYPE DESIGNERS Daniel
Berkovitz and Peter Bilak, The
Hague **FOUNDRY** Typotheque
URL typotheque.com **TWITTER**
@typotheque **CONCEPT**
Greta Sans Hebrew is a super
family of forty styles in five
writing scripts.

הולוגרמה

אהוב נחוץ יכול

בדרום אמריקה

מתוך "סוד תורת הגעגועים" / **אבות ישורון**

ניתן להשיב מכמה וכמה כיוונים, אך לא כאשר לפנינו שיר בודד
שבו האלחיה לספר קהלת כה ברורה. הרי זו שורת הפתיחה של
הספר כולו: "כל הנחלים הולכים אל הים, והים אינו מלא". אם כך
מה עושה המילה נהרות. למה נחלים מפעילים את דמיון המשורר
למעבר מים רחב יותר. מה יש בשיר שיכול לנמק את קריאתו
של אבות ישורון בקהלת כקריאה חדשה ומוצדקת לעצמה? אם
זוכרים שהעברית משקריה או פוגשת את המילה נהרה כמביעה
אור על פני אנשים, אור שהוא גם תנועה או נמצא בתנועה אל
הפנים, אך גם מן הפנים אל העולם, מתאפשרת בשיר הזה קריאה
מושכלת בדרך שבה רואה ישורון את ניסיון חייו. ואין זה ניסיון
שחושף את הכלליות ואת החזרתיות של תופעות במרחב מֶטָה־
היסטורי או על־היסטורי. במידה רבה ישורון מפרק את קהלת

מבפנים, או לוקח אותו כצדה אתו, צדה בשיר, אולי משום שניסיון
חכמתו של הדובר בספר הוא אישר ("וראיתי אני..." אומר קהלת
התנכ"י). כלומר מדבר אחד שראה את העולם מניסיונו שלו,
והביע מחשבה. אך מן הקריאה של השיר של אבות ניתנת לקורא
אפשרות לפרשנות אחרת. אפשר לומר כי את "מוסיף דעת מוסיף
מכאוב" המיר ישורון ב"גאות ושפל", ויתר על כן, במילה געגועים.
כלומר חייו של ישורון חוצים הן את הראייה והן את המחשבה
הכוללנית בגעגועים אל נֲהֲרות הפָּנים, הֶהֲרות של פני המשפחה
שאבדה לו, ולא רק בגעגועים אל אותה סביבה גאוגרפית של
קרסניסטאו, אשר בפולין. אבות סירב לחזור ולבקר באותו מחח
גאוגרפי ל"ביקור שורשים", כלומר סירב לנהור אליו ככל שאר
מחפשי השורשים היוצאים לפולין.

אל תחפש רחוק

במחזה קרוב

על שטיח מעופף

כן ככה זה לאהוב את עצמך

Appendix

Board of Directors 2015–2016

OFFICERS

PRESIDENT
Matteo Bologna
Mucca Design

VICE PRESIDENT
Roberto de Vicq de Cumptich
de Vicq design

SECRETARY/TREASURER
Sean King
Sean King Design

DIRECTORS-AT-LARGE

Gail Anderson
Anderson Newton Design

Paul Carlos
Pure+Applied

Doug Clouse
The Graphics Office

Cara diEdwardo
The Cooper Union

Abby Goldstein
Fordham University

Karl Heine
creativeplacement

Bobby C. Martin Jr.
OCD | The Original Champions
of Design

Bertram Schmidt-Friderichs
Verlag H. Schmidt GmbH Mainz

Nick Sherman
Fonts in Use

Angela Voulangas
The Graphics Office

Craig Ward
Words are Pictures

CHAIRMAN OF THE BOARD
Graham Clifford
Graham Clifford Design

EXECUTIVE DIRECTOR
Carol Wahler

Board of Directors 2016–2017

OFFICERS

PRESIDENT
Doug Clouse
The Graphics Office

VICE PRESIDENT
Paul Carlos
Pure+Applied

SECRETARY/TREASURER
Bobby C. Martin Jr.
OCD | The Original Champions
of Design

DIRECTORS-AT-LARGE

Cara DiEdwardo
The Cooper Union

Abby Goldstein
Fordham University

Karl Heine
creativeplacement

Debbie Millman
Sterling Brands

Joe Newton
Anderson Newton Design

Dan Rhatigan
Type Designer

Douglas Riccardi
Memo NY

Bertram Schmidt-Friderichs
Verlag H. Schmidt GmbH Mainz

Christopher Sergio
Penguin Random House

Elizabeth Carey Smith
Zady

Angela Voulangas
The Graphics Office

CHAIRMAN OF THE BOARD
Matteo Bologna
Mucca Design

EXECUTIVE DIRECTOR
Carol Wahler

Committee for TDC62

CO-CHAIRS
Abby Goldstein and Karl Heine

CALL POSTER DESIGN
Bobby C. Martin Jr.
OCD | The Original Champions
of Design

COORDINATOR
Carol Wahler

ASSISTANTS TO JUDGES
Matteo Bologna, Graham
Clifford, Doug Clouse, Jack
Curry, Roberto de Vicq de
Cumptich, Deborah Gonet,
Cristhan Sabagol, Diego
Vainesman, Allan R. Wahler,
and George Zafiriadis

Committee for TDC 2016

CHAIRMAN
Cara DiEdwardo

ASSISTANTS TO THE JUDGES
Chris Andreola and Maxim
Zhukov

Non-Latin Advisory Board (Nlab)

NLAB is an informal group of
experts that provides guidance
and advice to the judges
of the TDC Type Design
competitions in assessing
typeface designs developed
for non-Latin scripts (Arabic,
Cyrillic, Greek, Indic, and
others).

TDC NON-LATIN ADVISORY BOARD
TDC Non-Latin Advisory Board
included: Huda Smitshuijzen
AbiFarès, Gayaneh
Bagdasaryan, Misha Beletsky,
Charles Bigelow, Patrick
Glasson, Martin Heijra, John
Hudson, Jana Igunma, Dmitriy
Kirsanov, Zoran Kostić, Gerry
Leonidas, Ken Lunde, Klimis
Mastoridis, Ermin Međedović,
Prof. i.R. Dr. Dr. h.c. Heinz
Miklas, Titus Nemeth, Ryoko
Nishizuka, Patrick Norrish,
John Okell, Fiona Ross, Prof.
and Dr. Hyunguk Ryu, Dr.
Mamoun Sakkal, Zachary
Quinn Scheuren, Manvel
Shmavonyan, Graham Shaw,
Keith Tam, Jovica Veljović,
Danila Vorobiev, and Taro
Yamamoto.

Type Directors Club Presidents

Frank Powers, 1946, 1947
Milton Zudeck, 1948
Alfred Dickman, 1949
Joseph Weiler, 1950
James Secrest, 1951, 1952,
1953
Gustave Saelens, 1954, 1955
Arthur Lee, 1956, 1957
Martin Connell, 1958
James Secrest, 1959, 1960
Frank Powers, 1961, 1962
Milton Zudeck, 1963, 1964
Gene Ettenberg, 1965, 1966
Edward Gottschall, 1967, 1968
Saadyah Maximon, 1969
Louis Lepis, 1970, 1971
Gerard O'Neill, 1972, 1973
Zoltan Kiss, 1974, 1975
Roy Zucca, 1976, 1977
William Streever, 1978, 1979
Bonnie Hazelton, 1980, 1981
Jack George Tauss, 1982, 1983
Klaus F. Schmidt, 1984, 1985
John Luke, 1986, 1987
Jack Odette, 1988, 1989
Ed Benguiat, 1990, 1991
Allan Haley, 1992, 1993
B. Martin Pedersen, 1994, 1995
Mara Kurtz, 1996, 1997
Mark Solsburg, 1998, 1999
Daniel Pelavin, 2000, 2001
James Montalbano, 2002, 2003
Gary Munch, 2004, 2005
Alex W. White, 2006, 2007
Charles Nix, 2008, 2009
Diego Vainesman, 2010, 2011
Graham Clifford, 2012, 2013
Matteo Bologna, 2014, 2015

TDC Medal Recipients

Hermann Zapf, 1967
R. Hunter Middleton, 1968
Frank Powers, 1971
Dr. Robert Leslie, 1972
Edward Rondthaler, 1975
Arnold Bank, 1979
Georg Trump, 1982
Paul Standard, 1983
Herb Lubalin, 1984
(posthumously)
Paul Rand, 1984
Aaron Burns, 1985
Bradbury Thompson, 1986
Adrian Frutiger, 1987
Freeman Craw, 1988
Ed Benguiat, 1989
Gene Federico, 1991
Lou Dorfsman, 1995
Matthew Carter, 1997
Rolling Stone magazine, 1997
Colin Brignall, 2000
Günter Gerhard Lange, 2000
Martin Solomon, 2003
Paula Scher, 2006
Mike Parker, 2011
Erik Spiekermann, 2011
Gerrit Noordzij, 2013
David Berlow, 2014
Louise Fili, 2015

Special Citations to TDC Members

Edward Gottschall, 1955
Freeman Craw, 1968
James Secrest, 1974
Olaf Leu, 1984, 1990
William Streever, 1984
Klaus F. Schmidt, 1985
John Luke, 1987
Jack Odette, 1989

2016 TDC Scholarship Recipients

Gabriela Carnabuci,
Parsons The New School
for Design

Liang Dai and Siling Zhao,
School of Visual Arts•

•(SVA has selected two
students who will share
the $1,000)

Brian Parisi
Pratt Institute

Yachun Peng
Cornish College of the Arts

Maciek Połczyński
Polish Japanese Academy
of Information

Man-Ping Wu
Fashion Institute of Technology

Andrea Villanueva
The Cooper Union School
of Art

TDC Beatrice Warde Scholarship

Ania Wieluńska
Academy of Fine Arts
in Warsaw

2016 Student Award Winners

Student Best in Show ($1,000)
Elisa Foster, Los Angeles
California State University,
Long Beach, California

Second Place ($500)
Carmel Gatchalian, New York
School of Visual Arts,
New York•

Third Place ($300)
Brian Lemus,• Betsy Mei Chun
Lin, Henry Nuhn, Kristen
Sorace, Zak Tebbal,
Olivia Wilson, and Anthony
Zukofsky, New York
School of Visual Arts,
New York•

International Liaison Chairpersons

CHINA
Liu Zhao
China Central Academy
of Fine Arts
Beijing
Liuzhao_cafa@qq.com

ENGLAND
John Bateson
Bateson Studio
5 Astrop Mews
London W6 7HR
john@batesonstudio.com

FRANCE
Bastien Hermand
ECV, École Communication
Visuelle
1, rue du Dahomey
75011 PARIS
b.hermand@ecv.fr

GERMANY
Bertram Schmidt-Friderichs
Verlag Hermann Schmidt
Mainz
GmbH & Co.
Gonsenheimer Strasse 56
55126 Mainz
bsf@typografie.de

JAPAN
Zempaku Suzuki
Japan Typography Association
Sanukin Bldg., 5th Floor
1-7-10 Nihonbashi-honcho
Chuo-ku, Tokyo 104-0041
office@typo.or.jp

MEXICO
Prof. Felix Beltran
Apartado de Correos
M 10733 Mexico 06000
felixbeltran@infinitum.com.mx

POLAND
Ewa Satalecka
Polish Japanese Academy of
Information
Warsaw
ewasatalecla@pjwstk.edu.pl

RUSSIA
Maxim Zhukov
3636 Greystone Avenue
Apt. 4C
Bronx, NY 10463-2059
Zhukov@verizon.net

SOUTH KOREA
Samwon Paper Gallery
papergallery@naver.com

SOUTH AMERICA
Diego Vainesman
181 East 93 Street, Apt. 4E
New York, NY 10128
diego@40N47design.com

SPAIN
Christian Giribets
Bau, Escola Superior de
Disseny
Pujades 118
08005 Barcelona
christian@baued.es

TAIWAN
Ken Tsui Lee
National Taiwan University of
Science and Technology
No.43, Keelung Rd., Sec.4,
Da'an Dist.,
Taipei City 10607, Taiwan
(R.O.C.)
leekentsui@gmail.com

VIETNAM
Richard Moore
21 Bond Street
New York, NY 10012
RichardM@RmooreA.com

TYPE DIRECTORS CLUB
347 West 36 Street
Suite 603
New York, NY 10018
212-633-8943
FAX: 212-633-8944
E-mail: director@tdc.org
www.tdc.org

TDC Membership

kHyal™ 2010
David Adams 2016
Jillan Adel 2015
Hannah Ahn 2014lc
Bridget Akellian 2015lc
Seth Akkerman 2008
Marta Cerda Alimbau 2015
Renee Alleyn 2014
Jackson Alves 2016
Lisa Amoroso 2015
Heinz Anderhalden 2015
Gail Anderson 2011
Jack Anderson 1996
Lück Andreas 2006
Ana Andreeva 2016s
Christopher Andreola 2003
Cemile Armas 2015lc
Flavio Arnizant de Zorzi 2013s
Batikan Aslan 2014s
Bob Aufuldish 2006
Yomar Augusto 2013

Luisa Baeta 2015
Linus Luka Bahun 2014s
Dave Bailey 2015
Peter Bain 1986
Sanjit Bakshi 2016
Andreu Balius 2016
Rachel Balma 2014s
Mary Banas 2015
Lindsay Barnett 2015
Jesus Barrientos 2013
Rebecca Bartola 2015s
Mark Batty 2003
Autumn Baxter 2012
Silvia Baz 2016
Allan Beaver 2012
Misha Beletsky 2007
Andrew Bellamy 2015
Jeff Bellantoni 2012
Isabel Bellido 2015•••
Felix Beltran 1988•••
Ed Benguiat 1964•••
Kyle Benson 2015
Anna Berkenbusch 1989
Sam Berlow 2009
Jennifer Bernabe 2015s
Ana Gomez Bernaus 2014
John D. Berry 1996
Peter Bertolami 1969•••
Michael Bierut 2010
Klaus Bietz 1993
Abe Bingham 2015
Henrik Birkvig 1996
Heribert Birnbach 2007
Debra Bishop 2008
R. P. Bissland 2004
Marion Bizet 2016
Roger Black 1980
Thierry Blancpain 2014
Elyanna Blaser 2015s
Marc Blaustein 2001
Susan Block 1989•••
Halvor Bodin 2012
Matteo Bologna 2003
Alexander Bomok 2015
Scott Boms 2012
Denise Bosler 2012
Maury Botton 2008
Chris Bowden 2010
John Breakey 2006
Orin Brecht 2013
Greg Breeding 2016
Melinda Breen 2016
Jax Brill 2016s
Ed Brodsky 1980•••
Craig Brown 2004
Emily Brown 2015s
Poul Allan Bruun 2014
Paul Buckley 2007
Ryan Bugden 2015s
Michael Bundscherer 2007s
Anthony Buza 2013

Christopher Cacho 2015
Claudia Campbell 2004
Ronn Campisi 1988
Kevin Cantrell 2015
Wilson Capellan 2007
David Caplan 2012
Nicole Caputo 2014
Marco Aurelio Cardenas 2014
Paul Carlos 2008
Gabriela Carnabuci 2016s
Frederic Carpenter 2015
Scott Carslake 2001
Michael Carsten 2008
Matthew Carter 1988•••
Rob Carter 2012
Jessica Cassettari 2015
James Castanzo 2008
Mariana Castellanos 2016
Ken Cato 1988
Jackson Cavanaugh 2010
Francesco Cavelli 2012
Eduard Cehovin 2003
Jamie Chang 2016s
Farid Chaouki 2014
Karen Charatan 2010
Christian Charles 2015lc
Frank Chavanon 2014
Len Cheeseman 1993•••
Abby Chen 2016
Alex Chen 2015s
Yue Chen 2011
David Cheung Jr. 1998
Sherlene Chew 2014lc
Patricia Childers 2013
Taylor Childers 2013s
Todd Childers 2011
HanJu Chou 2015lc
Francis Chouquet 2015
Sean Christensen 2014
Yo-Chen Chu 2015lc
Jessica Lauren Chung 2015
Stanley Church 1997
Scott Citron 2007
John Clark 2014
Jamie Clarke 2015
Rob Clarke 2015
Graham Clifford 1998
Marc Clormann 2014
Doug Clouse 2009
Christopher Colak 2014s
Ed Colker 1983•••
Nancy Sharon Collins 2006
John Connolly 2015
Cherise Conrick 2009
Jenn Contois 2015
Nick Cooke 2001
Ricardo Cordoba 2009
Kathleen Corgan 2015s
Owen Corrigan 2016
Madeleine Corson 1996
Lynette Cortez 2015
James Craig 2004
Sarah Craig 2014lc
Lauren Crampsie 2016
Freeman (Jerry) Craw 1947•
Michael Crawford 2015s
Kathleen Creighton 2008
Travis Cribb 2016s
Andreas Croonenbroeck 2006
Dave Crossland 2016
Ray Cruz 1999
Jon Cuervo 2015
John Curry 2009
Rick Cusick 1989
Ken Cutts 2011

Liang Dai 2016s
Luiza Dale 2016
Susan Darbyshire 1987
Simon Daubermann 2015
Jo Davison 2007
Josanne De Natale 1986
Roberto de Vicq de Cumptich 2005
Meaghan Dee 2014
Kai Dellmann 2016s
Liz DeLuna 2005

Richard R. Dendy 2000
Mark Denton 2001
Ben Denzer 2015
James DeVries 2005
Cara Di Edwardo 2009
Tony Di Spigna 2010
Fernando Diaz 2016
Daniel Dickson 2015
Andrew Diemer 2015s
Chank Diesel 2005
Claude Dieterich A. 1984•••
Kirsten Dietz 2000
Rachel Digerness 2011
Joseph DiGioia 1999
Skyler Dobin 2015
Tomo Doko 2015
Joseph Dombroski 2014
Cody Donahue 2015lc
Chelsea Donaldson 2016
Hannah Donovan 2015
Danielle Donville 2016s
Anna Dorfman 2015
Megan Doty 2014lc
Zhihua Duan 2015s
Christopher Dubber 1985•••
Joseph P. Duffy III 2003
Denis Dulude 2004
Christopher Dunn 2010
Maguelone Dunoyer 2016lc
Ariel Duong 2016
Angie Durbin 2016
Alexandra Dusky 2013s
Mark Duszkiewicz 2015
Simon Dwelly 1998

Lexi Earle 2014lc
Anthony Elder 2011
Nicholas Eldridge 2009
Jesse Ellington 2016s
Garry Emery 1993
Marc Engenhart 2006
Erika Enlund 2014s
Juan Espinal 2016
Joseph Michael Essex 1978•••
Knut Ettling 2007
Florence Everett 1989•••
Jesse Ewing 2011

Korissa Faiman 2009
John Fairley 2014
Hannes Famira 2015
David Farey 1993•••
Lily Feinberg 2014
Krizia Fernando 2015
Matt Ferranto 2004
Louise Fili 2004
Anne Fink 2013
Kristine Fitzgerald 1990
Linda Florio 2009
Louise Fortin 2007
Dirk Fowler 2003
Carol Freed 1987•••
Phil Luciano Frezzo 2013s
Ryan Pescatore Frisk 2004
Miranda Fuller 2015
Andrew Fullerton 2015
Leigh Furby 2015
Dirk Fütterer 2008
Mohamed Gaber 2015
Evan Gaffney 2009
Louis Gagnon 2002
Pam Galvani 2014s
Felipe Garcia 2015
Christof Gassner 1990
David Gatti 1981•••
Michael Christian Gaudet 2015
Carrie Gee 2015
David Genco 2016
Porter Gillespie 2015
Ted Gim 2015s
Pepe Gimeno 2001
Laura Giraudo 2013
Lou Glassheim 1947•
Howard Glener 1977•••
Kimberly Glyder 2015
Mario Godbout 2002
Abby Goldstein 2010
Deborah Gonet 2005

Paul Gonzalez 2014
Megan Goodenough 2016
Jesper Goransson 2015
Eber Gordon 2010
Baruch Gorkin 2015
Jonathan Gouthier 2009
Mark Gowing 2015
Diana Graham 1984
Pamela Green 2010
Shanna Greenberg 2016
Joan Greenfield 2006
Benjamin Greengrass 2016
Jessica Griscti 2014s
Jon Grizzle 2012
Amelia Grohman 2014
Frank-Joachim Grossmann 2016
Jordan Grove 2014s
Katarzna Gruda 2009
Ben Ross Davis Gruendler 2016lc
Naoise Guerin 2015
Maria Giuliani 2014
Artur Marek Gulbicki 2011
Marina Gulova 2015s
Nora Gummert-Hauser 2005
Raymond Guzman 2015
Peter Gyllan 1997

Kimberly Ha 2015
Andy Hadel 2010
Annette Haefelinger 2013
Elizabeth Haldeman 2002
Alex Haldi 2015
Matisse Hales 2016lc
Allan Haley 1978
Debra Hall 1996
Jenny Halpern 2015
Carrie Hamilton 2015
Damian Hamilton 2015
Lisa Hamm 2015
Dawn Hancock 2003
Graham Hanson 2016
Egil Haraldsen 2000
Lauren Harms 2015
Jillian Harris 2012
Knut Hartmann 1985•••
Luke Hayman 2006
David Hazan 2015s
Bonnie Hazelton 1975•••
Amy Hecht 2001
Jonas Hecksher 2012
Eric Heiman 2002
Molly Hein 2015
Karl Heine 2010
Elizabeth Heinzen 2013
Anja Patricia Helm 2008
Cristobal Henestrosa 2010
Oliver Henn 2009
Luis Herrera 2014lc
Bernadette Herrera 2016
Chris Herringer 2016
Klaus Hesse 1995
Jeff Hester 2015
Joshua Hester 2015
Jason Heuer 2011
Fons M. Hickmann 1996
Lee Jacob Hilado 2015s
Bill Hilson 2007
Kit Hinrichs 2002
Jessica Hische 2010
Reid Hitt 2015
Amic Garfield Ho 2014
Sissy Emmons Hobizal 2012
Fritz Hofrichter 1980•••
Alyce Hoggan 1987
Richard Holberg 2012
Alex Holt-Coban 2015
Karen Horton 2015
Kevin Horvath 1987
Debra Morton Hoyt 2016
Christian Hruschka 2005
Karen Huang 2012
John Hudson 2004
Aimee Hughes 2008
Keith C. Humphrey 2008
Johanna Huss 2015lc

Ginelle Hustrulid 2014
Grant Hutchinson 2011
Kira Hwang 2016

Luca Ionescu 2016
Paula Ip 2015s
Yuko Ishizaki 2009
Alexander Isley 2012
Borna Izadpanah 2016

Donald Jackson 1978••
Alex Jacque 2014s
Torsten Jahnke 2002
Ankita Jain 2015s
David Jalbert-Gagnier 2015
Mark Jamra 1999
Moon Jang 2015
Etienne Jardel 2006
Alin Camara Jardim 2011
Patra Jongjitirat 2014lc
Alison Joseph 2014s
Allen Joseph 2014
Giovanni Jubert 2004

Edward Kahler 2010
Rachel Kalagher 2015
John Kallio 1996
Nour Kanafani 2015
Boril Karaivanov 2014
Ian Keliher 2015lc
Paula Kelly 2010
Joyce Ketterer 2016
Helen Keyes 2011
Ben Kiel 2014
Satohiro Kikutake 2002
Hayerim Kim 2015lc
Yoni Kim 2015
Rick King 1993
Sean King 2007
Dmitriy Kirsanov 2013
Amanda Klein 2011
Arne Alexander Klett 2005
Ros Knopov 2016
Judy Ko 2015
Akira Kobayashi 1999
Boris Kochan 2002
Masayoshi Kodaira 2002
Mashu Kokawa 2015s
Markus Koll 2011
Scott-Martin Kosofsky 2015
Thomas Kowallik 2010
Dmitry Krasny 2009
Markus Kraus 1997
Stephanie Kreber 2001
Ingo Krepinsky 2013
Bernhard J. Kress 1963•••
Gregor Krisztian 2005
Stefan Krömer 2013
Jan Kruse 2006
Henrik Kubel 2010
John Kudos 2010
Christian Kunnert 1997
Jessica Kuronen 2015lc
Julia Kushnirsky 2015
Dominik Kyeck 2002

Gerry L'Orange 1991•••
Belen La Rivera 2015s
Ginger LaBella 2013
Raymond F. Laccetti 1987•••
Karolina Lach 2016
Nicole Lafave 2012
Brian LaRossa 2011
Gillian Lau 2015s
Amanda Lawrence 2006
Binna Lee 2015s
Edmund Lee 2016lc
Hyela Lee 2016s
YunJung Lee 2014s
Pum Lefebure 2006
GG LeMere 2015
Simon Lemmerer 2016
David Lemon 1995
Brian Lemus 2015
Gerry Leonidas 2007
Reginald LeSane 2015s
Mat Letellier 2010
Kristin Leu 2014

Olaf Leu 1966•••
Jean-Baptiste Levée 2014
Aaron Levin 2015
Edward Levine 2011
Kent Lew 2016
Chenjun Li 2015lc
Iris Li 2015s
Lotus Lien 2015lc
Morgan Light 2016s
Rebecca Lim 2015
Maxine Lin 2013s
Yijun Lin 2015s
Armin Lindauer 2007
Sven Lindhorst-Emme 2015
Shuang Han Ling 2015lc
Domenic Lippa 2004
Jason Little 2014
Wally Littman 1960•••
Richard Ljoenes 2014
Sascha Lobe 2007
Ralf Lobeck 2007
Giona Lodigiani 2016
Sharyn Belkin Locke 2014
Uwe Loesch 1996
Oliver Lohrengel 2004
Amy Lombardi 2013
Dillon Looney 2016lc
Sabrina Lopez 2016
Chercy Lott 2008
Frank Lottermann 2016
Hsin Yin Low 2014s
Christopher Lozos 2005
Wenjie Lu 2016
Luke Lucas 2012
Matthew Luckhurst 2015
Claire Lukacs 2014
Gregg Lukasiewicz 1990
Ken Lunde 2011
Anica Lydenberg 2016

Bruno Maag 2013
Callum MacGregor 2009
Stephen MacKley 2015
Danusch Mahmoudi 2001
Hendrika Makilyn 2015
Avril Makula 2010
Daniel Mangosing 2016s
Eduardo Manso 2016
Joe Marianek 2016
Erik Marinovich 2014
Mary Marnell 2016
Bobby C. Martin Jr. 2011
Alvin Martinez 2014
Frank Martinez 2013
Michael Marwit 2015
Shigeru Masaki 2006
Jakob Maser 2006
Jim Massey 2015
Scott Matz 2011
Ted Mauseth 2001
Andreas Maxbauer 1995
Judith Mayer 2015
Susan Mayer 2015
Cheryl McBride 2009
Louisa McCabe 2014
Mark McCormick 2010
Alistair McCready 2016s
Rod McDonald 1995
Seth McDuffie 2015s
Elizabeth McKinnell 2014
David McLeod 2014
Kelly McMurray 2015
Marc A. Meadows 1996
Pablo Medina 2016
Uwe Melichar 2000
Jon Melton 2014
Adrien Menard 2016
Shenhui Meng 2014s
Abbott Miller 2010
John Milligan 1978•••
Debbie Millman 2012
Michael Miranda 1984
Kelsey Mitchell 2015lc
Ulrike Monch 2015lc
Sakol Mongkolkasetarin 1995
James Montalbano 1993
Aoife Mooney 2016

Richard Earl Moore 1982
Wael Morcos 2013
Richard Wade Morgan 2014
Minoru Morita 1975●●●
Jimmy Moss 2015
Lars Müller 1997
Joachim Müller-Lancé 1995
Gary Munch 1997
Taiki Murayama 2015
Camille Murphy 2013
Kara Murphy 2006
Nicholas Musolino 2015
Jerry King Musser 1988
Mumtaz Mustafa 2015lc
Louis A. Musto 1965●●●

Patricia Sanchez Navarro 2015lc
Ralph Navarro 2013
Jamie Neely 2013
Erik Nelson 2016
Eduardo Nemeth 2011
Titus Nemeth 2010
Helmut Ness 1999
Ulli Neutzling 2009
Christina Newhard 2016
Robert Newman 2015
Joe Newton 2009
Michelle Ng 2016
Vincent Ng 2004
Yoko Nire 2014s
Charles Nix 2000
Stephen Nixon 2015
Hyun-Jung Noh 2010
Dirk Nolte 2012
Gertrud Nolte 2001s
Heidi North 2013
Alexa Nosal 1987●●●
Thomas Notarangelo 2010
Yves Nottebrock 2011
Beth Novitsky 2013
Jan Olof Nygren 2014

Gemma O'Brien 2014
Mark O'Donnell 2015
James O'Loughlin 2015
Tomo Ogino 2012
Felipe Oliveira 2015s
Marissa Olson 2015s
Diana Olszewski 2015s
Ivan Ontra 2013
Santiago Orozco 2015
Robert Overholtzer 1994●●●
Amanda Ozga 2016s

Michael Pacey 2001
Juan Carlos Pagan 2015
Mackenzie Palma 2015lc
Amy Papaelias 2008
Niral Parekh 2015
Brian Parisi 2016s
Sari Park 2014s
Jim Parkinson 1994
Karen Parry 2008
Michael Parson 2016
Donald Partyka 2009
Mauro Pastore 2006
Neil Patel 2011
Gudrun Pawelke 1996
Alan Peckolick 2007
Yachun Peng 2016s
Andre Pennycooke 2008
Lilly Pereira 2016
Sonia Persad 2013
Giorgio Pesce 2008
Xavier Petromelis 2015lc
Max Phillips 2000
Stefano Picco 2010
Clive Piercy 1996
Massimo Pitis 2012
Leon Lukas Plum 205lc
Siri Poarangan 2015
J.H.M. Pohlen 2006
Maciej Polczynski 2016s
Albert-Jan Pool 2000
William Porch 2015
Jean François Porchez 2013
Carolyn Porter 2015

Michael Prisco 2015s
James Propp 1997
Caroline A. Provine 2015s
Regina Puno 2015
Kiran Puri 2013s
Maggie Putnam 2015

Alan Qualtrough 2014s
Vitor Quelhas 2011lc
Nicholas Qyll 2003s

Ionut Radulescu 2015
Jochen Raedeker 2000
Jesse Ragan 2009
Erwin Raith 1967●●●
Jason Ramirez 2016
Steven Rank 2011
Patti Ratchford 2012
Kyle Reed 2016
Astrid Lewis Reedy 2015
Andrea Reeves 2015
Isabella Anne Reinhofer 2015s
James Reyman 2005
Dan Rhatigan 2013
Douglas Riccardi 2010
Helge Dirk Rieder 2003
Michael Riley 2016
Oliver Rios 2012
Phillip Ritzenberg 1997
Jon Robbins 2016
Zackery Robbins 2016
Chad Roberts 2001
Thomas Rockwell 2014
Niurka Rodriguez 2015s
Jeff Rogers 2012
Stuart Rogers 2010
Salvador Romero 1993●●●
Kurt Roscoe 1993
Amy Rosenfeld 2016
Peter Rossetti 2015
Cynthia Roth 2015
Nancy Harris Rouemy 2007
Erkki Ruuhinen 1986●●●
Carol-Anne Ryce-Paul 2001
Michael Rylander 1993

Ida Saeterdal 2015
Aaron Sage 2014s
Mamoun Sakkal 2004
Richard Salcer 2014
Karla Saldana 2015
Christy Saldana 2016
Ilja Sallacz 1999
Ina Saltz 1996
Ksenya Samarskaya 2014
Pedro Sanches 2015lc
Rodrigo Sanchez 1996
Nathan Savage 2001
Nina Scerbo 2006
Hanno Schabacker 2008
Anja-D Schacht-Kremsler 2012
H.D. Schellnack 2009
Paula Scher 2010
Robbin Schiff 2013
Hermann J. Schlieper 1987●●●
Catherine Leigh Schmidt 2015lc
Hermann Schmidt 1983●●●
Klaus Schmidt 1959●●●
Bertram Schmidt-Friderichs 1989
Allison Schmitz 2015s
Thomas Schmitz 2009
Elmar Schnaare 2011
Guido Schneider 2003
Werner Schneider 1987
Wanja Schnurpel 2015
Markus Schroeppel 2003
Eileen Hedy Schultz 1985
Eckehart Schumacher-Gebler 1985●●●
Robert Schumann 2007
Peter Scott 2002
Tre Seals 2015s
Neil Secretario 2016
Nicolette Seeback 2015lc
Alessandro Segalini 2015
Brian Seidel 2016s

Jonathan Selikoff 2014
Johnny Selman 2016
Charlene Sequeira 2016s
Christopher Sergio 2011
Thomas Serres 2004
Michelle Shain 2012
Jackie Shao 2015
Mohammad Sharaf 2014s
Paul Shaw 1987
Russell Shaw 2015
Benjamin Shaykin 2014
Nick Sherman 2009
Thomas Sherman 2016
David Shields 2007
Jeemin Shim 2010
Christie Shin 2015
Ming Yu Shin 2015s
Philip Shore Jr. 1992●●●
David Short 2014
Shirin Shourcheh 2015s
Bernardo Siaotong 2016s
Carla Siegel 2015
Etta Siegel 2014
Nigel Sielegar 2016
Maria Sieradzki 2016lc
Maria Silva 2016lc
Scott Simmons 1994
Mark Simonson 2012
Dominque Singer 2012
Anjana Singhwi 2015
Elizabeth Carey Smith 2010
Matthew Smith 2015
Ralph Smith 2016
Tina Smith 2016
Melissa So 2016
David Solomon 2015
Jan Solpera 1985●●●
Patrick Marc Sommer 2012
Brian Sooy 1998
William Sorrentino 2015
Erik Spiekermann 1988
Maximilano Sproviero 2012
Will Staehle 2016
Brandon Stammen 2015
Rolf Staudt 1984●●●
Gwendolyn Steele 2015
Carissa Stein 2014s
Maurann Stein 2015s
Olaf Stein 1996
Charles Stewart 1992
Roland Stieger 2009
Michael Stinson 2014
Clifford Stoltze 2003
Sumner Stone 2011
Tracy Stora 2015
Nina Stössinger 2015
DJ Stout 2010
Anastasia Strizhenova 2016
Ilene Strizver 1988
Hansjorg Stulle 1987●●●
Molly Stump 2015
Micah Stupak 2015
Shikha Subramanian 2015lc
Neil Summerour 2008
Stacey Sundar 2015
Derek Sussner 2005
Zempaku Suzuki 1992
Don Swanson 2007
Caroline Swartz 2015
Paul Sych 2009
Lila Symons 2010
Helen Sywalski 2015lc

Yukichi Takada 1995
Yoshimaru Takahashi 1996
Katsumi Tamura 2003
Jef Tan 2011
Trisha Wen Yuan Tan 2011
Matthew Tapia 2012
Abdullah Tasci 2014
Jack Tauss 1975●●●
Pat Taylor 1985●●●
Shaun Taylor 2015
Anthony J. Teano 1962●●●
Marcel Teine 2003
Simona Ternblom 2016
Jnas Thessen 2015lc

Eric Thoelke 2010
Jason Tiernan 2014
Eric Tilley 1995
James Tocco 2014
Alexander Tochilovsky 2010
Laura Tolkow 1996
Justin Towart 2014s
Andrea Trabucco-Campos 2016s
Hieu Tran 2015s
Tricia Treacy 2014
Jakob Trollbäck 2004
Klaus Trommer 2012
Niklaus Troxler 2000
Francesca Truman 2016lc
Elpitha Tsoutsounakis 2016
Ling Tsui 2011
Minao Tsukada 2000
Nina Tsur 2016s
Manfred Tuerk 2000
Natascha Tümpel 2002
François Turcotte 1999
Gabriella Turrisi 2015s
Michael Tutino 2016
Anne Twomey 2005

Andreas Uebele 2002

Diego Vainesman 1991
Scott Valins 2009
Patrick Seymour Vallée 1999
Arlo Vance 2014
Jeffrey Vanlerberghe 2005
Robert Vargas 2015
Rozina Vavetsi 2011
Inigo Vazquez 2016
Meryl Vedros 2010s
Andrea Villanueva 2014s
Juan Villanueva 2013s
Adrian Vincent 2016s
Patricia Vining 2015
Danila Vorobiev 2013
Angela Voulangas 2009

Frank Wagner 1994
Oliver Wagner 2001
Allan R. Wahler 1998
Jurek Wajdowicz 1980●●●
Sergio Waksman 1996
Garth Walker 1992
Adam Wanamaker 2015lc
Craig Ward 2011
Tiffany Wardle 2013
Katsunori Watanabe 2001
Chris Watson 2015
James Wawrzewski 2016
Graham Weber 2016s
Harald Weber 1999
Claus F. Weidmueller 1997
Kim Weiner 2015lc
Terrance Weinzierl 2014
Craig Welsh 2010
Adam Wester 2015
Shawn Weston 2001
Alex W. White 1993
Anna Widdowson 2015s
Christopher Wiehl 2003
Ania Wielunska 2016s
Michael Wiemeyer 2013
Richard Wilde 1993
James Williams 1988●●●
Luke Williams 2015
Steve Williams 2005
Grant Windridge 2000
Conny J. Winter 1985●●●
KC Witherell 2014
Delve Withrington 1997
David Wolske 2012
Jason Wong 2015
Fred Woodward 1995
Man-Ping Wu 2016s

Sixing Xu 2015s
Wendy Xu 2011

Hui Chen Ou Yang 2016s
Susan Yang 2015
Izgi Yapici 2015s
Batrek Yassa 2015lc

Henry Sene Yee 2006
Tanya Yeremeyeva 2016
Jieun Yoon 2016s
Bumhan Yu 2013
Chen Yu 2015s
Ev Yu 2016s
Garson Yu 2005
Norika Yuasa 2015

Bibi Zafirah Hanfa Badil Zaman 2016
David Zauhar 2001
Roxana Zegan 2015
Chufeng Zhang 2016s
Haoqian Zhang 2014s
Siling Zhao 2016s
Maxim Zhukov 1996●●●
Marie Zipprich 2015lc
Roy Zucca 1969●●●

Corporate Members
Adobe TypeKit 2014
Agency Access 2015
Berard Associates 2015
École de Visuelle Communications 2011
ESPN The Magazine 2016
Grand Central Publishing 2005
Pentagram Design, New York 2014
School of Visual Arts, New York 2007

● Charter member
●● Honorary member
●●● Life members Student member (uppercase)
lc Lowercase student member
a Associate member

Membership as of May 9, 2016

Type Index

General Index